Power, Value, and Conviction

William Schweiker

POWER, VALUE, AND CONVICTION
THEOLOGICAL ETHICS IN THE POSTMODERN AGE

The Pilgrim Press

Cleveland, Ohio

The Pilgrim Press, Cleveland, Ohio 44115
© 1998 by William Schweiker

"One World, Many Moralities," from *Criterion* 32, no. 2 (1993): 12–21. Reprinted by permission of the University of Chicago Divinity School. • "Power and the Agency of God," from *Theology Today* 52, no. 2 (1995): 204–24. Reprinted by permission. • "Understanding Moral Meanings: On Philosophical Hermeneutics and Theological Ethics," in *Christian Ethics: Problems and Prospects*, ed. Lisa Sowle Cahill and James F. Childress (Cleveland: The Pilgrim Press, 1996). Reprinted by permission of The Pilgrim Press. • "Radical Interpretation and Moral Responsibility," from *The Journal of Religion* 73, no. 4 (1993): 613–37, published by the University of Chicago Press. © 1993 by The University of Chicago. All rights reserved. Reprinted by permission. • "The Drama of Interpretation and the Philosophy of Religions." Reprinted from *Discourse and Practice* by Frank Reynolds and David Tracy. State University of New York Press, © 1992. • "Divine Command Ethics and the Otherness of God," in *The Otherness of God*, ed. Orrin F. Summerell (Charlottesville: University Press of Virginia, 1998). Reprinted with permission of the University Press of Virginia. • "The Sovereignty of God's Goodness," in *Iris Murdoch and the Search for Human Goodness*, ed. Maria Antonaccio and William Schweiker (Chicago: University of Chicago Press, 1996). © 1996 by The University of Chicago. All rights reserved. Reprinted by permission.

Biblical quotations, except where otherwise noted, are from the New Revised Standard Version of the Bible, © 1989 by the Division of Christian Education of the National Council of the Churches of Christ in the U.S.A., and are used by permission

Published 1998. All rights reserved

Printed in the United States of America on acid-free paper

03   02   01   00   99   98   5   4   3   2   1

Library of Congress Cataloging-in-Publication Data

Schweiker, William.
    Power, value, and conviction : theological ethics in the postmodern age /
William Schweiker.
        p.   cm.
    Includes bibliographical references and index.
    ISBN 0-8298-1290-3 (alk. paper). — ISBN 0-8298-1297-0 (pbk. : alk. paper)
    1. Christian ethics.   I. Title.
BJ1251.S295   1998
241—dc21   98-36259
                                                                              CIP

for

MOM and **DAD**, **KATHY** and **CLAIRE**

Contents

Acknowledgments

This book is the result of several years of thought and work. I acknowledge the occasion of the original writing of each chapter in the notes. I now want to thank people who have so deeply informed my thought.

My friends and colleagues are many. I thank some of them: Per Anderson, Maria Antonaccio, Edward Arrington, Dennis Bailey, Harlan Beckley, Don Browning, Len Caquelin, Kelton Cobb, Kristine Culp, Lois Daly, Jean Bethke Elshtain, Franklin I. Gamwell, Langdon Gilkey, James M. Gustafson, Thomas Hay, David E. Klemm, Robin Lovin, Terence Martin, Richard Miller, Douglas Ottati, Frank Reynolds, Susan Schreiner, Kathryn Tanner, David Wadner, Michael Welker, Charles Wilson, and many others.

My research assistants Heidi Gehman, Kent Reames, and Darlene Weaver each provided help, as did my secretary, Ms. Marsha Peeler. I also benefited from the comments of students, especially the members of my dissertation group. I thank Linda Clum, Sharon Hunter-Smith, Charles Mathewes, Paul Nielson, Kent Reames, Eric Bain-Selbo, James J. Thompson, Kerry Tupper, John Wall, and Darlene Weaver.

I am also indebted to my neighbors Mike, Dawn, and Laura Kokaska. These kind folk have been willing to watch my house, feed my cat, and collect my mail during the many professional trips I have had to make. Their good graces always remind me how dependent scholars are on the support of others. That support was also extended to me by Wallace Alston and the Center of Theological Inquiry at Princeton, where I put the finishing touches on this book. I owe the Center, its staff, and the scholars a deep debt of thanks.

ACKNOWLEDGMENTS

I dedicate this book to my parents and sisters. Parents are our first teachers about how to live. Mom taught me the importance of passion for moral matters; Dad showed me the joy and demand of inquiry and the willingness to question with the belief that answers are findable. Now in their waning years, they are teaching me not only how to live, but also, and importantly, how to face the end of life. My sisters have also been my teachers. Kathy Barnhill with her wit, determination, and clarity of conviction has taught me to strive for what I hold to be true. Claire M. Schweiker has shown me that nothing is so important as the struggle to define one's own life. To Mom, Dad, Kathy, and Claire I give my thanks and my love.

Finally, there is my son, Paul. While these chapters were being written, he was growing into a marvel of a nine-year-old and teaching me about the vitality of heart and imagination. He is, quite simply, my joy.

Introduction

Grave moral challenges face contemporary human beings and their communities. These challenges range from questions about genetic engineering to the threat of ethnic and international conflict. The list of problems seems endless. Nations, cultures, and religious communities are morally and politically divided. There are those who insist that traditional modes of thought cannot meet the challenges of the age. Old ways no longer suffice. The ethicist needs to develop new forms of moral thinking. There are also traditionalists who believe that the task is to mine traditions for moral wisdom. One must reclaim the past and not seek novel moral visions. We seem caught between advocates of novelty and champions of tradition. Meanwhile the problems mount, and a deep skepticism about the capacity to meet life's challenges creeps into every facet of personal and social existence.

This book advances a theological ethics that accounts for both tradition and novelty. The Christian faith holds surprising resources for human existence, but this tradition demands creative reinterpretation for each and every age. The resource most important for our time centers on the complex connection between power and value expressed in Christian convictions about God, Christ, and human life. These beliefs resonate deeply in experience, because we are creatures who desire, esteem, seek, and praise power. Yet the radical claim of Christian faith is that power is not our ultimate good; it must be made perfect, it must be transformed, in order to respect and to enhance the gift of life. Even this radical claim resonates in experience. We love mercy, not tyranny; we seek justice and not oppression; in our best moments we know in all humility that might alone does not make right. To be sure, the resonance of Christian conviction in our age is partly attributable to the historical fact that this civilization has been decisively shaped by the biblical religions. But one can also give good arguments, rooted in the texture of life, for these beliefs about power and value. With arguments we hope to limit the glorification of power while affirming the good of human freedom and our capacity to create cultures and to shape our world and our lives.

The approach to theological ethics presented in this book draws on the resources of the Christian tradition not only to speak to Christians, but also to articulate and to reflect on our lives as moral beings. It assumes that there is an intelligible structure and dynamic to human life and, further, that Christian discourse is an indispensable way of grasping its meaning. Christians should not see themselves as "resident aliens" struggling to preserve their identity amid a fallen and hostile world. We ought not to abandon the world for the security of the "Christian tribe." There is, of course, hostility enough in this world. But engagement and not retreat is the real possibility and demand of faith. The Christian task, I insist, is to struggle to form new worlds, to change lives, to bind up the weak and the suffering, to aid the work of justice, to give voice to the hope that surrounds life, and thus in all things to engage in the great and enduring task of civilization. This task is why Protestantism, from Luther and Calvin through Wesley to our own day, has been profoundly concerned and active in the founding of schools, universities, and hospitals and in advancing the causes of learning and social justice in all domains of life. It is time to reclaim this profound legacy of Christian cultural commitment.

Because of this orientation, my work has focused on matters of culture and not only on the church. I have been developing a theological ethics of culture. This requires engaging thinkers and currents of thought beyond the walls of the church in an attempt to show the meaning and truth of Christian commitments for our time. And it further means seeing that a central fact of life in our age is that we increasingly move between worlds. We exist in diverse social roles, in societies with divergent religious communities, on a planet with vastly different cultures. What is more, the need to navigate this complexity is not something to bemoan; it is, I believe, a genuine human good. It fosters a wider perspective, a more capacious form of consciousness, about the adventure of life. But to affirm this as a *human* good is itself to take a moral stand. Put in historical terms, I identify with a line of thinkers, spanning the ages, dedicated to the enterprise of what used to be called Christian humanism. This position has been and will always be highly contested. Antihumanists of various stripes, Christian and otherwise, chide it for being naive, overly zealous for bettering this world, and anthropocentric. Secular humanists, old and new, believe anyone a fool who insists on religious matters in morals. They cannot imagine the reach and worth of life exceeding the human grasp. Nevertheless, I remain firmly convinced of the possibility and importance of "Christian moral philosophy."[1] The purpose of this introduction is to explain the main outlines of this approach to theological ethics and culture.

THE HUMAN EDGE OF THINKING

Ethics is the human edge of thinking. It aims to answer the basic dilemmas of life. Moral reflection seeks to permeate existence with thought and to make our thinking come alive. Any coherent ethics, I contend, entails five dimensions of reflection.[2] Thinking about the moral life requires that we (1) provide interpretations of moral situations; (2) specify the values and norms that ought to orient personal and social life; (3) clarify the demands of practical reasoning about moral questions; (4) develop and defend some picture of human existence in relation to self, others, and God; and finally (5) provide arguments for the truth of the moral vision. Ethics, then, has interpretive, normative, practical, fundamental, and meta-ethical dimensions. The theologian will, furthermore, draw on a variety of sources (scripture, tradition, philosophical discourse, etc.) as well as interpretive theories (e.g., social theories, text criticism) in presenting a view of the moral life. This book is, then, a diagnosis of the postmodern age that also presents a specific approach to thinking about the moral life.

In what follows, I am exploring culture from a standpoint of theological ethics. What does this mean? While now suffering from neglect, theological reflection on culture has been an important strand of Christian thinking during the twentieth century. The Protestant theologian Paul Tillich, for example, understood culture as the *form* of religion; religion, by which he meant that which concerns us ultimately, was the *substance* of culture.[3] This meant that one could look at the diverse spheres of culture—art, literature, mass movements, psychological trends, moral beliefs—and try to grasp the religious substance of that culture. Further, these domains of culture were all expressions of what Tillich called the human spirit. The exploration of culture was a means of attaining self-knowledge by way of decoding the manifestations of spirit in distinctive cultural forms. While there are points of similarity between my argument and Tillich's work, there are also deep differences. Clarity about these points will help to indicate the direction of the present volume.

First, Tillich thought that the basic human question arose out of what he called the experience of "ontological shock"—that is, the unsettling experience of wonderment over why there is anything at all and not nothing. Without denying the importance of such matters, I think that we never confront life simply in terms of Hamlet's question—whether to be or not to be. The most pressing and basic question of life is the question of the goodness of existence.[4] That is, it is the connection between being and value, existence and goodness, that matters most to us. Is life good? Is it good to be, or better to die? How do we account for innocent suffering? Will all of our hopes fail us? Do animals and the earth have moral value? What makes a life a good life? Why do the wicked seem to flourish? Taking these questions, and others like them, seriously entails the belief that morality is not simply a "sphere" of culture, but is also a clue to how people construe their world and the very point of life. And because of this, I speak of moral spaces and moral worlds and not simply of culture. More pointedly, I try to show that the root question of our age turns on the equation of value with power. At least in Western cultures, we live in a time when the deepest assumption is that human beings must make meaning and create value because life is devoid of worth without our action. So when human power fails—say, to relieve suffering—what then is the value of continuing to exist? It is this "axiology of power," this valuation of power, that I try to explore and contest from a theological perspective.

Second, if human life is set on edge by questions about existence and worth, our planet will be home to as many "moral worlds" as there are moral belief systems. Tillich held that every sphere of culture manifests *the* human spirit. This meant that there is a spiritual continuum throughout culture; in spite of obvious diversity, at root there is unity to the human project. This argument is now difficult, if not impossible, to sustain. We can no longer hold that every culture is at root a manifestation of the same human spirit, or even that all of the spheres of culture can be decoded in order to understand the working of spirit. Questions of diversity and pluralism strike at the root of human life itself; they must be addressed without the a priori assumption that a human "unity" undergirds all civilization. One of the gains of the postmodern age is the insistence that all claims to human commonality recognize, respect, and enhance real differences. This is meant to protect us from the "tyranny of the same" and also from false abstractions about the real stuff of life. And it is one reason why I begin with problems of pluralism and diversity and seek to compare, not simply decode, moral worldviews. More pointedly, my approach means that we should see ourselves as travelers and interpreters of diverse moral worlds rather than trying to catch *the* human spirit through the spheres of one culture. This does not necessarily entail radical moral relativism or demand that diversity as such is inherently good; it means, rather, that the continuities in human life and among cultures are intertwined with dimensions of existence that foster and preserve diversity.

Taking these two points together—that is, a concern for moral diversity and a belief that basic questions are about value *and* being—one can understand what I mean by "moral ontology." Tillich and other twentieth-century theologians of culture insisted on the priority of questions of "being." Ontology, or discourse about "being," was therefore fundamental to all other modes of thought. Recent so-called deconstructionist theology denies the priority of the question of "being" and thus heralds the death of ontology. But in each case, the question of being or nonbeing seems to be of central concern. I reflect theologically on the cultural situation attuned to the fact that, at root, human "worlds" are shaped and constituted by convictions about what is worthy of human striving. As Charles Taylor has helpfully put it, we exist in a moral space. This space confronts us with questions about how to orient our lives and also provides a background of distinctions of worth that persons use to guide their lives.[5] As I explain in chapter 2, a moral ontology, as I develop it, seeks to examine the space of life, the moral world we inhabit, in order to judge the values and norms used to orient lives in a world. To undertake such an examination theologically signals that we are also concerned with the meaning and truth of Christian convictions for understanding and assessing moral worlds and thereby giving guidance for life. More pointedly, my purpose is to show how a moral vision rooted in Christian faith is an answer to the current threat of the disintegration of life. The core of this threat is found, again, in the equation of power and value. There is a deep fear and skepticism within the postmodern situation. This is an attitude contrary to the claims of Christian faith. This faith is permeated by gratitude, reverence, and joy for the mystery of existence. It articulates a sense of the reality of goodness. In this respect, theological ethics uncovers, criticizes, and seeks to transform the convictions of an age about what is good and right.

This is, then, a work in theological ethics and cultural analysis. I try to read cultural developments from the perspective of theological ethics, and therefore I also present an account of the dimensions of ethics. Yet I am not only exploring our age; I also provide an interpretation of Christian faith. Influenced by the Wesleyan strand of Protestant Christianity, I see several convictions as central to Christian existence. I want to note these convictions at the outset because they inform the book as a whole. Taken together, they signal my hope to avoid some of the abstraction of previous theologies of culture—such as, say, speaking of God as "Being Itself"—by attending to the complex and polysemic ways of speaking found in the biblical traditions and the Christian community. The task is then to show the illuminative power these forms of thinking have for current life and action.

The first conviction informing this book is that faith has to do with life. Doctrine is in the service of living well. Matters of faith are about our fundamental attitudes or dispositions toward life; faith is an identity-conferring commitment. The connection between faith and life means that theological ethics responds Christianly to the basic moral question of how we should live. It is this question, and not simply matters of duty or virtue, that is the heart of moral reflection. Furthermore, the connection between doctrine and life requires that I seek in each chapter to clarify the moral meaning of some Christian claim. This will be true of beliefs about God, Christ, sin, and redemption, and of ideas about the future and creation. What do these distinctively Christian beliefs mean morally? How can and ought they inform how we live? Christian faith is a way of life. Theological ethics, if nothing else, explores this way of life in order to clarify its meaning and truth.

Second, the challenge of the moral life is to become better. Grace and responsibility are intimately related.[6] Happiness and holiness, as Wesley would say, are primordially bound together in the idea of perfection. A conception of perfection, or moral betterment, is inescapable no matter what critics might think. And what critics there are! If any one term casts fear and provokes anger in the hearts of contemporary Western people, it is "perfection." It seems to suggest that we are to be complete, lacking in nothing, without any flaws in our lives. But this is not what Wesley meant by "Christian perfection." He granted human fallibility. The perfection one can and should seek is a "wholeness" in life through active love of God, others, and oneself. In terms of this book, "moral integrity" is my restatement of perfection as the aim of life. The reason why we need the idea of perfection in ethics is simple enough. One cannot imagine commending a way of life built on the premise that people ought to become morally worse, become less loving, less just, less truthful. We cannot escape the idea of progress in goodness.

Third, progress in life is not simply a personal matter; it is also a social one. Morally and religiously serious persons are interested in transforming the world, making it better. To use traditional Methodist terms, sanctification and social holiness are essential to Christian existence. This means that reflection on moral matters is intrinsically linked to social and cultural analysis, critique, and reconstruction. Not only does this back the enterprise of a theological ethics of culture, it also means that one must uncover the distortions and injustices of a society as well as seek to advance social transformation. Again, thinking is in the service of living well, becoming morally better, and furthering social well-being.

This brings us to a fourth basic conviction. Becoming morally better is in large part a matter of seeing more deeply and more clearly the world, ourselves, others, and God. Drawing on Hebrews 11, Wesley developed what has been called an account of perceptible inspiration in his notion of faith. Faith is the evidence of things unseen as well as a salvific relation of trust in and loyalty to God in Jesus Christ. The connection between conviction and moral perception is basic to the argument of this book. It is one reason why hermeneutics is so important for theological ethics. What I call "radical interpretation" is a contemporary restatement of the claim that a basic problem in human life is one of perception, how we see the world and others. The moral life is about knowing and loving the real—especially real other people and the living God.

Given the connection between perception and conviction with respect to knowing and loving the real, a fifth feature of this position comes to the fore. The Christian tradition insists that persons have undefinable worth. Becoming better persons and reforming our social life have as their norm the integrity of particular forms of life. Our age is one in which the reality of the individual is threatened by global systems. As I argue later, these systems threaten to subsume persons into furthering networks of power/meaning. In this situation, Christians are challenged to stand for the worth of persons and, indeed, of all life. The imperative of responsibility, then, as I formulate it, is this: respect and enhance the integrity of life before God. I take this to be a contemporary restatement of the Methodist insistence on perfect love. It is also why, as far as I can see, Christians must once again endorse a humanistic strand in their faith.

The final conviction of this book is perhaps the most controversial. The proper object of faith and theological reflection is God and God alone. Christians do not believe in the Bible, the church, or religious experience; Christians believe in the deity witnessed to by scripture, the God of the church, the divine known in faithful experience. The theocentric focus of my argument is not meant to deny the importance of Christ and the Holy Spirit in the life of Christian faith. On the contrary, it is meant to show that what Christians believe about Christ and the Spirit are necessarily claims about the divine. What is more, the chief problem of our age is the threat to the integrity of life by forces of destruction and disintegration. But Christianly understood, the integrity of life is found in God and God alone; this warrants the kind of theocentrism developed in the book. And it also means that I seek to uncover the forces of disintegration operative in the postmodern age as nothing less than rival gods to the living God of Christian faith.

Of course, some will find odd, if not contradictory, my insistence on a theocentric imperative of responsibility and a form of Christian humanism. Have we not been told that all forms of humanism are anthropocentric and secularistic in outlook? Must we not glorify God alone? Here is a failure to understand the task of theological ethics. A central claim of Christian faith is that human life is demeaned unless seen in relation to God, and, further, whatever we can and want to say about God morally must be said in relation to matters human. It is necessary to reclaim the insight that knowledge of God and knowledge of self are related. But that insight simply is the mediation of theocentrism and humanism in Christian conviction. My principal concern, then, is with showing the moral cogency of faith in God in a technological, postmodern age that threatens personal, social, and planetary life with disintegration. In order to do so, I draw on the richly symbolic and conceptual resources of the Christian tradition and seek to unlock their illuminative capacity for today.[7]

What I argue is found in the New Testament in 1 John 4:20: "Those who say, 'I love God,' and hate their brothers or sisters, are liars; for those who do not love a brother or sister whom they have seen, cannot love God whom they have not seen." The struggle of this life is to see others in their unique worth and dignity and to see the divine. Religious claims, even beliefs about God, are subject to moral evaluation. This was the insight of the Hebrew prophets, and Jesus; it was also the witness of the New Testament.

MATTERS OF REALISM

The reader will quickly note how centrally the question of moral realism factors in every chapter of this book. In the context of theological ethics in the United States, realism is often associated with Reinhold Niebuhr's Christian realism and, for others, with Paul Tillich's insistence on self-transcending realism.[8] There is, as noted, some affinity between the theological ethics outlined in this book and the work of these theologians. Yet my concern with realism arose for somewhat different reasons than those of either thinker.

The modern/postmodern world is one in which the human capacity to respond to, shape, and influence reality—that is, human power—is believed to be the origin of value. The central task of life is to increase human power, since it is the root of all other goods. In depicting our age in this way, I agree with thinkers who see the widespread loss of a sense of the sheer goodness of being as the deepest fact of the modern age, a loss that post-modernity both struggles against and perpetuates.[9] It is not the awareness of "ontological shock" that grips our day; it is, if I may coin a term, the experience of "axiological surprise." Seemingly against all odds, there is the amazing sense of the worth of life that will not fall into an abyss of power. The face of a child, a wondrous moonlit night, outrage at injustice, the last, lingering touch of a dying parent, and a word of forgiveness all surprise us with the sense that to be is good, that life is to be respected and enhanced. These are experiences of the source of responsibility; they are an awareness, despite all distortion, that reality is in fact God's good and gracious creation. Immanuel Kant could argue two centuries ago that these two things fill the mind with wonder: the starry heavens above and the moral law within. Christians and Jews throughout the ages have insisted that goodness is real because it is rooted in God's life and governance of the world.

These confessions about the depth of goodness now seem lost, or at least in grave danger of being lost, even among believers. Despite the high-sounding rhetoric of moral concern and spirituality, we live out a "practical atheism." We too easily deny the reality of goodness and look to the works of human power to give our lives meaning and purpose. Some champion erotic power, others herald strategies of self-creation, many work for political power, and we hear of spiritualities of empowerment, and so, amid the din of voices, one can hardly miss the age-old quest of the all too human will-to-power. Given the noise of this chatter, it is vitally important to reclaim and to rearticulate experiences of intrinsic worth, values not reducible to our power. The Christian conviction is that goodness is rooted in God and, further, that God is a power whose identity is constituted by a relation to the worth of finite reality. Faith in God entails a moral transvaluation of power. The integrity of life and not power is morally central in the Christian moral vision. These connections among power, moral norms, and the integrity of life focus ethics on the problem of moral realism.

The question I have asked myself often over the last years is why anti-realism—that is, the theory that moral values are human inventions and thus social constructions—has such a grip on our moral imaginations. The reason is that by insisting on moral value as a construction, we maximize human freedom; human freedom is not constrained morally by the real. There is an obvious truth to this claim. For example, simply because heterosexual intercourse is oriented to procreation does not mean that every sexual act ought to be. Sexual freedom comes in no small measure once we see that how we value sexuality exceeds a simple report about nature. The liberation of women from patriarchal structures, the development of birth control, and a more healthy understanding of sexuality all rest on this in-sight. Yet there is also a paradox in this development. If one is not careful, the proper insight that moral value is not *reducible* to "the natural" can lead to the claim that it *is* reducible to our powers of social construction. And this is the claim of antirealists in ethics. These theories make human power morally central.

So, one reason why antirealism has a grip on our moral imaginations is that it helps to advance the cause of freedom by distinguishing between claims about what is and claims about what ought to be. This is called the *is/ought* problem in ethics; I explore it later in the book. But there is really more at stake morally in antirealism than simply clarity about the kinds of claims we are making. Perhaps the deepest characteristic of the twentieth century is the experience of and resistance to tyrannies. Most of these tyran-nies, such as sexism, racism, and fascism, try to establish their validity by ap-peals to the nature of things: patriarchy makes claims about the nature of men and women; racism rests on beliefs about the nature of race; fascism de-humanized Jews and heralded the triumph of the Aryan. Tyranny has clothed itself in realism.

Sadly, the same can be said for much of Christian morals. Some the-ologians under German National Socialism drew on the so-called orders of creation to legitimize oppressive political and familial structures. Traditional arguments about natural law ethics have been used by Roman Catholic moralists to stifle dissent and to reassert traditional social and personal rela-tions. Conservative thinkers, especially in the United States, insisting on the centrality of God's commands for the moral life, have too often found a happy confluence between what God wills and the status quo in all its racial, gender, and economic injustice. Here, too, the voice of antirealism in ethics is important. When feminist theorists show the social construction of gen-der, when African American theologians and ethicists chart the develop-ment of racism, then tyrannous appeals to "the real" are unmasked. The em-peror has no clothes! Antirealism in ethics has been in the service of liberation.

My argument is in utter agreement with the moral passion of antireal-ism. To speak of *hermeneutical* realism, as I do, is to acknowledge the in-escapable fact of human meaning-making in an account of morals. Insofar as this is the case, we can change the values we have lived by under the de-mand of the integrity of life. We can struggle to become morally better; we can overthrow tyrannous beliefs and forms of life. But why then insist on hermeneutical *realism*? There are several reasons for such insistence. The first reason arises from an ambiguity in the critique of realism. Classical moral realism held that there was an intelligible moral order written into nature and the human mind. The task of the moral life was to conform to that order. For reasons I chart later, this argument is now difficult to sustain. Yet, while we must acknowledge this fact, we need not grant the antirealist claim that moral values are solely human inventions. Indeed, to grant this proposition is to picture human existence as transpiring in a morally neutral universe and so to insist that human beings must make their way in the world heroically or tragically through the creation of values.

The difficulty with such a picture of human life is that it fails to recognize how moral values and disvalues denote a *relation* between moral agents and their world—a relation, I suggest, characterized by integrity or disintegration. The ambiguity of the antirealist position is that while accenting freedom it also threatens to isolate human beings from their surrounding world. Insofar as it does so, antirealist arguments too easily endorse a purely instrumental relation to the world, seeing the world only in terms of its utility for us. This is why, as I show in various places in this book, the technological age bent on subjugating life to networks of meaning/power is deeply antirealistic in its moral outlook.

This ambiguity in how antirealistic ethics pictures human existence exposes the root problem in such positions. Since human life supposedly transpires in a morally vacant universe, we have the task of making values, creating meaning. This is why, we might imagine, the image of the artist is so dominant in contemporary self-understanding. We like to think of ourselves as makers of meaning engaged in acts of self-creation. And insofar as this is the case, power becomes the central value, the value on which all other goods depend. The irony is that in its very concern for the expansion of human freedom, antirealist ethics too easily makes us slaves to the unending quest for power. The problem for ethics, accordingly, is to outline a moral vision that endorses the centrality of freedom in human existence without making power morally basic. This is the problem that hermeneutical realism and responsibility ethics try mightily to address.

My response to the antirealist challenge is admittedly complex. I try to show that in the very experience of being an agent, in the sense of exercising freedom, what is revealed within consciousness is an intrinsic connection between power and value such that human power is validated as a real good but is not endorsed as the root of all value. We do have moments of "axiological surprise" linked to our own capacities for action. Further, this fact about moral consciousness is the connection between knowledge of God and knowledge of self. To grasp the connection of power/value in your consciousness of being an agent is nothing less than an inarticulate sense of the divine. This is why Christian discourse resonates in our lives. By drawing on that discourse, we can see that in our freedom we are empowered by a higher source, enlivened by an other, related to God. One can, in fact, articulate experiences of worth not reducible to the machineries of power and domination.

This brings us to the distinctly theological dimension of my encounter with antirealism in ethics. Christian theologians must endorse the quest for genuine freedom as a basic component of the moral life. Liberation in all of its dimensions is a great moral and spiritual theme of Christian faith. However, we must resist the idea that humans simply create values because this claim alienates life from the created order and makes power morally basic. Christian faith is necessarily realistic in its moral outlook. The source and ground of moral values is not social convention, human creativity, or personal preference. The source and ground of value is God. God is not a human invention, even though our ways of thinking and talking about the divine are imaginative constructs. Once we see this point, it becomes imperative that the theological ethicist get clear in regard to the moral meaning of Christian discourse about God.

My claim, surprisingly enough, is that the symbol or name "God" designates in the Christian imagination ultimate reality as self-transforming power in which what is other than God (namely, finite existence) is valued in its fragility and finitude. This is the ethical meaning of the basic Christian confession that "God is love." But it is a meaning we catch only by exploring the variety of experiences and forms of speaking about the divine through diverse texts, communities, and traditions. It is from the perspective of the reality of God inspiring such faith that the theologian examines the world and human life. And this shifts the meaning of moral realism. The reality that is morally basic is not the nature system or human nature (however these are understood) but, rather, the divine reality. Once we understand the meaning of faith in the living God, moral realism cannot rightly warrant oppressive and tyrannous orders. This form of moral realism ignites a passion for freedom and the integrity of life.

One final matter about realism remains to be noted. I have argued that the motivation behind antirealism in ethics is to challenge all forms of tyranny that appeal to "nature" as their warrant. But I have also been suggesting that antirealism too easily makes power morally basic. If this is at all correct, it is not surprising that the dominant form of realism in current ethics is political realism. By political realism is meant an account of political existence that avoids sentimentality about human interests and purposes; it expects human beings to act out of self-interest even to the point of conflict. Political realists insist that in the arena of politics power must contend with power. Granting the obvious insight of these claims, it is equally clear, at least to me, that a theological ethics must push the question of realism deeper and further. For what is at stake is not only the character of political existence, but the divine and thus the human good. How then should we speak ethically about this good?

The supreme ethical good is *moral integrity*. By this term I mean rightly relating the complexity of natural, social, and reflective goods through a commitment to respect and enhance life before God. This does not deny the reality of conflict and tragedy in life, but quite the contrary. No finite life can achieve the unity of values in time, but my position provides a means of addressing this fact of finite existence; existence is to be integrated through a commitment to respect and enhance life *before God*. The integrity of life, and not the unity of human spirit, is basic to theological ethical reflection. And the coherence or integrity we can hope for in life is nothing less than a wholeness grasped in faith and faith alone in and through diverse realms of goods. This faith is an identity-conferring commitment; it shapes life, self-understanding, and communities.

My argument about integrity will be contested by thinkers, often antihumanists, who insist that once we reject belief in *the* human spirit we cannot reasonably speak of a "coherent self." Their argument, briefly put, is that, given the diversity of roles people inhabit, the conscious and unconscious forces operative in life, the manifold forms of discourse we use, the social construction of gender, and the swirl of relations that constitute our complex lives, the postmodern self is fragmented and multiple. Any attempt to lead an integrated, humane life from this perspective is illusory or tyrannous: it either denies the multiplicity in the self or attempts to impose a false unity on existence. On my reading, this is one more instance, like the conflict between theocentrism and humanism, of the inability to think dialectically about the moral life. Fragmentation and false unity are not the only options we face. We can also explore and then depict how being a person means having a sense of self as an integral complexity. We can show, as I try to do, that there are multiple values that permeate existence, and yet see how the moral life for individual people is always a struggle rightly to integrate these values in relation to others, the world, and the divine. As far as I can tell, the current celebration of the fragmentary self is a false option; it cannot be lived by any real human being. Human beings seek coherence in their lives and relations. Ethics should help in this adventure by specifying right and good forms of coherent living. And this is what I mean to show by the idea of moral integrity.

What I trust has become clear is that the question of moral realism touches on normative issues in ethics but also on the interpretive dimension of ethics because it concerns how one sees and understands the world and moral matters. Further, the question of realism sparks reflection in the fundamental dimension of ethics, because what is at stake, finally, is the meaning of our being agents, the coherence of our lives, and also the being of God. So too, this issue is deeply practical and raises meta-ethical questions about how to establish the truth of a moral outlook. The focus on moral realism, then, draws us into every dimension of moral reflection in a most decisive way. Fashioning a theological ethics that can be realistic and at the same time account for the insights and passion of antirealism has required development of the idea of hermeneutical realism. Whether or not this moral theory stands is a matter of its ability to answer basic questions in ethics more adequately than forms of antirealism in ethics can answer them.

IMAGE, CONCEPT, AND THEORY

Alongside these ideas about hermeneutical realism, moral integrity, the dimensions of ethics, and moral worlds, another feature of this book is my insistence that theological ethics include hermeneutical reflection. Hermeneutics, as I explain, provides an account of meaning and human understanding. The basic claim is that human beings are interpreters of meanings, and these meanings are presented through, but not reducible to, images, concepts, and theories embedded in cultural worlds. Theological ethics, accordingly, must operate at all of these levels of reflection in order to explore cultures and to understand and direct human lives. By including hermeneutics, theological ethics seeks to show that the question of how we ought to live, the root question of morals, is basic to human understanding. Hermeneutics helps in the task of moral ontology.

Happily, theologians and moral philosophers no longer believe that moral maturity is simply a matter of knowing moral ideas and how to use them. There is a new sensitivity to the places of narrative, symbol, and metaphor—that is, "images"—in the moral life. It is also obviously important for the theologian to examine the images of the Christian tradition and of a culture in terms of how they inform life. In this book, I am especially concerned with images of human existence and the divine in various cultures. For instance, I argue that the symbol "God" in Christian faith is a specific way of thinking about the relation of power and value—a way with radical moral implications. In order to interpret such images of the divine, one must grasp the inner workings of Christian faith, its logic of symbols, if you will, and also how these images fund moral understanding. I also seek to explore the main "images" of the postmodern age, such as ideas about persons as moral artists or the future as an empty space.

However, images are not all that we need to think about the moral and religious life. If anything characterizes current work in Christian ethics it is a misunderstanding of this point. We are told, for instance, that narrative alone is sufficient for moral thinking or that the stock of Christian symbols (most of them patriarchal in nature) can be read and dismissed as nothing but the products of the (patriarchal, Western) imagination. The assumption is that moral thinking can get along solely with making and breaking images. This is an assumption I strongly contest. Coherent ethical reflection also requires the use and analysis of concepts, concepts such as "good," "love," "virtue," "responsibility," and the like. We even need to explore the conceptual character of theological discourse.

A concept is simply a general idea used to organize experience by specifying the essential features of something. When I contend that "God" specifies for Christians the divine reality as ultimate power limiting itself in order to respect and enhance finite existence, I am providing conceptual analysis of the symbol. To use another example, I propose the idea of radical interpretation as the means for understanding conscience as a practice of moral knowing and self-transformation. In doing so, I am presenting a concept meant to pull out the essential features of a particular dynamic of human life. The importance of insisting on this point about concepts is that we are not left only with "images" and disputes about them. We have to decode or interpret symbols, metaphors, and narratives, and this requires forming useful concepts. In this respect, I simply reject the all too pervasive belief that somehow we can never get beyond the images—symbols, narratives—of our traditions or those we form on the basis of experience. This belief allows the ethicist to dismiss other positions as nothing more than the projections of someone's experience. But, in fact, we use concepts all the time in our moral and religious lives. Theological ethics must interpret and also formulate coherent and clear concepts for moral reflection.

Insofar as we want to understand the *meaning* of our moral existence, theological ethics must examine images and concepts. But this is not all. I also contend that we need a theory of the moral life. This is a very unfashionable claim. There is currently a pervasive assumption that such reflection is impossible, unnecessary, and maybe even dangerous. Some thinkers, usually theologians, contend that if we try to develop a moral theory, we will submit the uniqueness of the Christian witness to general ideas of moral goodness and thus be unfaithful to the particularity of Jesus Christ. Others, usually philosophers, contend that the moralist's job is simply to clarify our moral concepts and/or answer specific moral questions. Still others, both theologians and philosophers, believe that life is so complex, moral communities so different, and world views so divergent that the attempt to develop a coherent moral theory is an illusion and dangerous. It is thought to deny the distinctiveness of people's moral lives.

I grant these criticisms of much systematic theological ethics. Yet I reject the conclusion that we can and must somehow forgo the attempt to develop ways of thinking coherently about moral, religious, and cultural life. The theory developed in this book is a construal of the nature of moral existence. It is intended to guide reflection on the complexity of life without thereby asserting that the richness and travail of life is ever a matter of a "system." The possibility and need for this kind of reflection arise, as I have already said, out of the simple fact that we all exist in a space of questions about how to live. One avoids reductionism in ethics by seeing that we have to adopt multiple perspectives on the moral life. One avoids cognitive incoherence by seeing how these perspectives mutually entail each other. And this is what my claim above about the dimensions of ethics was meant to show. Theological ethics, on my account, presents a multidimensional theory of the moral life by charting dialectically the connections among the dimensions of ethics.[10] Such a theory is necessary for making sense of images and concepts, since we need to see how our manifold images and various concepts are related. It helps us to interpret culture from the perspective of theological ethics. It is also important for the moral life: we seek to live coherent rather than chaotic lives.

A hermeneutical approach in theological ethics moves on a variety of levels of reflection, ranging from the examination of symbols, narratives, and metaphors through the exploration and formation of concepts to, at its widest compass, the development of a theory of morality and culture. Obviously not all of this can be undertaken in any exhaustive way in one book. Yet these matters are present in each of the chapters of this book— all in the service of answering the question of how we should live before God. No doubt this makes some demands on the reader, but this is as it should be. Moral reflection is self-involving. It requires our participation, because what we are talking and thinking about is our lives and how we should live them with integrity.

A MATTER OF STYLE

This volume reflects work, done over the last few years, that traffics among reflection on culture, matters in moral theory, and theological concerns.

Several of the chapters have appeared in other books and in scholarly journals (although each has been revised for the present volume), which means that there is some repetition among the chapters, and yet a coherent argument is made throughout the course of the book. Part 1 tries to make sense of what the postmodern age means morally and theologically, and also to isolate the form of skepticism that too often colors contemporary life. Part 2 turns more directly to matters of moral theory. I present an approach to ethics that centers on responsibility, hermeneutical realism, and the good of moral integrity. Part 3 concludes the volume by moving the discussion to the moral significance of God's power as conceived in Christian thought. By examining options in ethics on this topic, I address debates about the connection between religion and morals. In the chapters to come, I examine the ideas of many of the best thinkers in the field of theological ethics in order to develop a complex theological, ethical, and cultural argument encompassing a variety of topics and problems that are central to contemporary human existence, but my basic concern is simply to present a viable and exciting approach to moral living.

Christian faith is about a love and knowledge of the world and other people that do not leave us unchanged. A life without love lacks vitality and the thirst for righteousness, delight, and affection. Life wrapped in ignorance, unmindful of the effects of human action or naive about the best means needed to attain valued ends, betrays human dignity. The enterprise of moral reflection is to aid knowledge and cultivate love in the service of respecting and enhancing the integrity of life. This book presents an account of theological ethics dedicated to that task.

PART 1   MORALITY AND POSTMODERNISM

T he purpose of part 1 is to provide an overview of our moral situation and then to introduce elements of a theological ethical response to it. I am not primarily interested in the ongoing debate about how to "define" postmodernity and its relation to "modernism." I seek to understand the moral meaning of our situation. On my reading, this situation is characterized by the interweaving of several facts. First, there is a deep and pervasive sense of the moral and cultural diversity on this planet even while people struggle for a global moral outlook. The question of diversity, and thus the problem of the meaning of moral values, is examined in the first chapter of the book. Second, our situation is characterized by the increase of human power to the extent that we can alter our environment and even our own species. This increase of power previously unknown in human history makes responsibility central in ethics. It challenges many traditional claims about the nature and status of moral value. I address these matters in chapter 2 by contrasting the contemporary outlook with a biblical and Christian construal of the world.

The final characteristic of our situation links the first two and serves to shape contemporary consciousness. We live in an age of information technology. The fact that we can now create media systems that link the world increases human power, confronts us with the diversity of peoples on the planet, and also encodes consciousness and those diverse cultures within a global context. Chapter 3 turns to these issues and their relation to moral skepticism. It also begins to fashion a response to the postmodern situation. Part 1 moves from what is most obvious about the postmodern condition (diversity), through an analysis of its underlying equation of power and value, and finally to the connection between goodness and contemporary consciousness. In this way the three chapters form a circle: they begin with and return to the postmodern age by traversing distinctly Christian claims about God and reality.

Part 1 accomplishes some other things important for the book as a whole. First, I engage in dialectical thinking throughout the book. Dialectics designates a form of thinking that addresses questions by engaging divergent positions while striving for an account that can answer more deeply and comprehensively the question at hand. Yet this "answer" will always be tentative, will always be open to question, and is never able to capture the whole of reality and truth in one system of thought. Dialectical thinking, as I take it, is a tribute to the finitude of human understanding: despite our longing, we never attain God's perspective on the world. We are limited creatures hoping to apprehend the meaning and value of our lives and our world. This means, as I said in the introduction, that the book is an invitation to thought.

Second, part 1 introduces a pattern of theological ethical reflection seen also in parts 2 and 3. I begin with an account of our situation (chap. 1), turn to a discussion of the meaning of God's being and power (chap. 2), and then explain what this means for the reality of the good (chap. 3). This pattern is nothing other than a dialectical engagement with the question of the relations among power, value, and reality. It is repeated in the other parts of the book. Thus, part 1 provides an overview of our situation, introduces a way of thinking ethically, and begins to outline a distinctive description of the moral life from the perspective of Christian faith. In this way, the following three chapters initiate the inquiry of the book as a whole.

1

One World, Many Moralities

As we face the twenty-first century, people around the world are becoming increasingly aware of the great diversity of their cultural, religious, and moral beliefs.[1] We witnessed the clash between Christians and Muslims in Bosnia and the horror of the rape camps. Most of us, all of us, have grave difficulties in comprehending how these things could happen. This problem of understanding the moral outlooks of others is not abstract and distant. It takes very personal forms. During the war in Bosnia, I met a young Serbian man on a flight from Germany to the United States. He was saddened by the fact that he could not be with his people and fighting for their cause. He could not understand my reaction to the events in his homeland. I found his convictions simply unbelievable. Experience and history aptly testify to the fact that moral diversity all too often breeds conflict. However, we are also aware, at least in our better moments, of the ways in which many cultures and peoples—Native Americans, African Americans, and Christians in the former Soviet Union, to name just a few—are now able to escape forms of repression and assert the dignity of their traditions. Moral diversity characterizes human life on this planet. This diversity can foster hatred and conflict or a recognition of the dignity of cultural traditions.

The fact of moral diversity and the ways it permeates our lives is not the whole story. It is also the case that, for technological, political, economic, environmental, and social reasons, these diverse cultures and societies are increasingly interdependent. We now have the technological capacity to alter the genetic structure of species, including human life, and thus alter the future of life on earth. The genetic revolution will have worldwide impact we can scarcely imagine. As the Christian ethicist Paul Ramsey once noted, we face a situation in which "human beings" who come after us might not be genetically like us.[2] Likewise, the interdependence of the global economic system means that no country's market is free from the influence of the economies of other nations. Military conflicts, such as the Persian Gulf War, if they are to gain international sanctions in order to succeed and if they are not to spill over into widespread armed conflict, require some measure of cooperation among states and even world opinion. Finally, we are also witnessing a worldwide concern for human rights and genuine freedom.[3] From the most basic levels of life through economic and political matters to widespread beliefs about human rights, our world is increasingly interdependent. The question is, what is the moral implication of growing global interdependence?

We live in one world, "a global village," as it is often put. But this global village is composed of radically different cultures and systems of belief. We live in one world of many moralities. What is important to note about this is not the brute fact of moral diversity; human life has always been diverse. Rather, the moral situation in which we live is best characterized as one caught between traditional forms of belief and life rooted in ancient cultural, ethnic, and religious traditions, and the increasing interdependence of the world brought about by the radical extension of human power in our time. In the face of the development of human capacities to alter life and the environment, it appears to many ethicists, political theorists, and social critics that traditional moral beliefs, ways of thinking, and forms of faith are simply unable to deal with our moral problems. Yet the fact is that these are the resources we have to work with in our moral thinking. Our moral thinking and indeed our lives are caught between traditional values and the search for new answers. This is the reality of the postmodern age.

In this situation, how are we to think about the moral life? This question is the focus of the book. In this chapter, I want to address a more limited but still pressing question: can we make valid moral judgments across cultural lines? That is, based on our own beliefs, realizing that these beliefs are, in some respects, relative to our time and culture, can we say that something is wrong in another society or in another subculture within our own multicultural society? We must be very clear about what is being asked. The question is not whether we do in fact make such judgments. Obviously we do. People have almost instinctual moral reactions to events around them and in their own lives. For instance, we read about some crime, and we make a judgment about guilt and innocence. Yet if we are honest, we know that we often make these judgments based on scanty knowledge, prejudice, and even self-interest. We do make judgments across cultural lines: this is simply a fact of life.[4] The real question, then, is whether or not we can give good *reasons* for our reactions and thus make valid ethical judgments. This is not a question of interest only to theologians, philosophers, and social critics. What is at stake is how we decide about valid norms and values for leading our lives.

A DIAGNOSIS OF OUR MORAL SITUATION

By focusing on the problem of moral judgment, my concern in this chapter is to provide an initial diagnosis of the postmodern age. In chapter 2, I will explore in more detail the question of postmodernism with respect to biblical beliefs about power and value. In chapter 3, I will further nuance this account by uncovering the moral skepticism of the information age. Throughout these three chapters, we will be exploring the mentality of our time, especially the connection between pluralism and power as the defining facts of the postmodern world. My task, then, is to deepen our understanding of our moral situation and thus ourselves.

What do I mean by a diagnosis? By this term I mean an interpretation of our situation aimed at uncovering problems and possible ways of dealing with or treating them. The medical analogy of a diagnosis is stretched, of course. It is not at all clear that we are facing moral illness, although many critics believe we are. We are also facing moral possibilities and even moral vitality, as, for instance, in the worldwide struggle for human rights. What the term "diagnosis" is meant to convey is that ethical reflection is concerned with understanding ourselves and our world in order to meet the problems we face. Ethics aims to help guide the lives of human beings insofar as we have some control over our conduct and exert some power in the world and thus make things happen. And this means that we need some understanding of ourselves and the situations in which we live.

As noted, our world is composed of diverse cultures and societies that hold different sets of beliefs, values, and standards about how individuals and communities *ought* to live. We can clarify this point by noting that imperatives and rules for action are expressed in a society's conventional beliefs about what determines right and wrong conduct—that is, in a society's *ethos* and *mores*. The mores of a society or culture are its binding customs about how to live, its rules of conduct. In this respect no human community and no human life is without a moral framework; to be human and to live in community with others requires some rules about how to live and act and how to relate with others. Obviously, mores can differ between communities and also develop through time. Simply reflect for a moment on how the family has been understood in Western society.[5] The norms that technological societies hold about the family are different from those of previous ages. The so-called nuclear family is not only endangered in our situation, it might even be seen as irrelevant. Obviously there are different customs regarding family life, not only within any single society but among cultures as well.

However, it is also the case that the mores of a community are not necessarily truly *moral*. The twentieth century has witnessed too many examples of this fact. The Nazis had a moral code, a set of beliefs about how to live, but none of us would think that this code was genuinely moral in character. As feminist thinkers have shown us, too often the moral code of Christian faith has actually endorsed unjust and cruel attitudes about women. In this situation, one must critique and revise the tradition.[6] When one calls into question conventional mores, one is engaged in ethical reflection. In ethics, one explores what defines genuine moral action—that is, the idea of "morality" itself.

A "morality" is what backs valid norms, imperatives, and rules that a society or culture holds about how to live. A morality is a table of values. It is a scheme about what ought to be done and what kinds of persons we should be, based on convictions about what is valuable in and for human life. For instance, a heroic culture values honor and valor; ancient nomadic cultures, as we know from the Bible, sought land and relied on distinct sets of rules and moral codes. In each case, rules are deemed morally binding and certain traits of character are called virtuous, as opposed to vicious, because they embody the deeper values of the culture. When we grasp this point, we realize that the diversity of mores in the world is not really the problem. People have always lived with different rules of conduct. The problem is that there are diverse standards of what defines genuinely moral behavior and what is valuable, and thus divergent ideas about which set of mores properly reflects that standard. Insofar as there are different *moralities*, how are we to make judgments across cultural lines?

What we need to explore is not simply the diverse sets of mores in our world, but the different conceptions of the standard for a good life and right conduct—that is, different *moralities*. We are asking an *ethical*, as opposed to a purely sociological, question. It is a question about the conventional beliefs about how to live and about the meaning and truth of those beliefs in situations where there is no agreement concerning moral standards.[7] This diagnosis of our situation centers on the problem of how to determine a standard for judging diverse mores or conventional moral beliefs in an increasingly interdependent world. In this chapter our focus is on the problem of diversity; in chapters 2 and 3 we will extend this discussion by exploring the centrality of power in the postmodern moral outlook.

THE PROBLEM OF PLURALISM

The first step in providing a diagnosis of our situation is to clarify what is meant by moral pluralism. This clarification is needed because the moral theories we will note below and explore throughout this book are responses to pluralism. Yet in one respect, the problem of pluralism is quite unremarkable.[8] If pluralism is assumed to be synonymous with "plurality," then it is simply the case that there has always been a diversity of moral outlooks. Our planet is the home of many moral worlds. Beliefs about human sexuality and kinship, ideas about the moral standing of persons outside of one's own community, systems of punishment and retribution, and basic ideals of the human good simply differ among cultures.

Until relatively recently, the diverse value systems, or moralities, existed in relative isolation from each other. When cultures did meet, the encounters were too often characterized by violence simply because neither culture could acknowledge the moral standing of the other. Only with modern colonial expansion and developments in international relations, transportation, technology, communication, and economic and environmental interdependence has the fact of plurality raised profound questions for ethics. In fact, as long as it was assumed that Western cultures, values, and beliefs represented the apex of human development, even the awareness of other systems of moral belief did not challenge moral inquiry.[9] The problem now is the diversity of traditions on our planet and even in the same geographic space.

The term "pluralism" actually means more than simply the recognition of the diversity of moral outlooks. More strictly speaking, it is the view that affirms that diversity is a good thing and, moreover, insists that this affirmation ought to be constitutive of one's moral outlook.[10] Pluralism so defined is a moral outlook. Yet, because it is a moral stance and not simply a description of moral diversity, pluralism raises a profound problem for ethics.

Moral beliefs are the condition for our thinking, speaking, and acting together. Without some shared values and convictions about how to interact with others, a basic commitment to criteria of judgment, and some consensus about how to adjudicate disputes, human interaction would be difficult if not impossible to sustain. The problem posed by pluralism is the possibility that moral outlooks are simply incommensurable—that there are no shared grounds for understanding others. By "incommensurability" ethicists mean that one cannot perfectly translate a set of moral beliefs into another moral language, develop a neutral moral language, or specify a common morality such that a viable comparison and testing of different sets of moral beliefs can take place.[11] If the moral beliefs are in fact incommensurable, and yet such beliefs are the condition for our thinking, acting, and speaking together, then we would have no way of understanding those who hold moral beliefs and outlooks different from our own. It would be impossible to make moral judgments about the beliefs and actions of persons and communities that hold different moral outlooks.

For example, we might believe morally abhorrent the traditional Inuit, or Eskimo, custom of abandoning the aged and feeble due to the burdens they place on their communities. But this judgment is properly a reflection of our own moral outlook and not justly applied to that culture, if and only if the argument about the incommensurability of moral beliefs is right. That is to say, if the argument about incommensurability is correct, then we simply do not understand what is actually going on in another culture and thus cannot formulate valid judgments about it. We lack the cognitive grounds for making truthful moral judgments. All that we can do, therefore, is to try to understand and to tolerate the moral outlooks and actions of others.

At one level, the awareness of radically divergent moral outlooks bespeaks the value of tolerance deeply ingrained in modern, liberal democracies. It might also save us from types of moral imperialism found in the colonial past of the West. As Mary Midgley has noted, it "is indeed almost incredible with what naive over-confidence Europeans have often crashed in to change the customs of the countries they invaded."[12] But the problem for ethics remains. Is it possible to make moral judgments across cultural boundaries? This question becomes more pressing in the face of rape camps, death squads, and religiously sanctioned terrorism than in the case of traditional Inuit customs. If we cannot make judgments about others, can we hope for a viable future on this planet?

Again, what is at issue is not the fact that we do make such judgments. Rape is always wrong. The question is an ethical one: can we give public, compelling reasons for our judgments or do those judgments simply reflect our present values? This is the problem that diversity poses for ethics. And it brings us to the ethical positions I want to outline here and explore in more detail throughout the remainder of this book.

REALISM AND ANTIREALISM

Let us start with moral realism.[13] This is the claim, or any theory used to make the claim, that moral judgments can be true or false because valid moral norms are rooted in the nature of reality or the nature of human existence. For most of Western history, ethics has been realistic in this sense of the word. People have believed that there is a moral order to reality and that the good life is about living in conformity with that order. Moral beliefs have entailed claims about the way things are in reality.

Examples of moral realism abound in the ancient world. The Greek philosopher Aristotle argued that all human beings seek happiness and that the happiness we ought to seek is rooted in the fact of the kind of beings we are. We are rational and social creatures, so we should seek friendship and also the perfection of our rational capabilities. Stoic philosophers argued that there is a natural moral law written into the structure of reality. Human beings can know this law through the use of reason, and the purpose of this law is to guide our actions. Christian theologians insisted that God has inscribed the moral law on the conscience. Conscience is a guide in human life, because it grasps the distinction between good and evil, even if, they noted, we can err about particular moral cases and judgments. In part 3 of this book, we will explore forms of moral realism that have influenced Christian moral thinking, especially divine command ethics and kinds of Platonic ethics. The point now is that in spite of the diversity of moral outlooks in the world, moral realism holds that there is actually one true moral order—say, the command of God—and that we can discern this order. Moral diversity is a fact, but it is not a problem because there is a discernible moral order in the world. For the moral realist, some moral outlooks are simply wrong.

Traditional moral realism rested on claims that have been rejected by the modern Western world. First, moral realism was often based on the belief that the moral order is established by God. If we question the existence of God, this moral order seems vacuous. As Dostoyevsky put it, if God does not exist, then everything is permissible. This is an overstatement, no doubt, but it expresses a judgment that is widely held in secular societies. Despite the rhetoric of faith, in fact most advanced Western cultures are practically atheistic in their moral outlook. It is also the case that liberal democracies insist on the separation of church and state and this is taken to mean that moral principles have to be grounded on something other than the revealed will of God.[14] Thus, for a variety of reasons, traditional realism and the beliefs it entailed are challenged.

Second, traditional realist arguments seemed to require that one believe that the nature of reality is itself moral in character. The connection between nature and value was God. As Bertrand Russell put this in his famous essay "A Free Man's Worship," "Thus, man created God, all-powerful and all-good, the mystic unity of what is and what should be."[15] But in fact there is no simple harmony between nature and value, between what is the case and what ought to be the case. The good die young. The universe seems ignorant of our hopes. It is deaf to our cries of outrage at injustice. What is and what ought to be often conflict, at least from a human perspective. Furthermore, the advances of modern science and technology have thrown convictions about a moral order in the universe into question. As many thinkers put it, modern people see the world as disenchanted; the natural order is value-neutral.[16] We do not assume that you can find out from looking at the natural world or the natural tendencies of human life how we ought to live. Indeed, we discover freedom in our capacities to escape these natural tendencies—say, for instance, through birth control. It is the combination of these factors—that is, the modern criticism of religious belief as the grounding of morality and also our scientific view of the world—that has backed moral relativism. Later we will see how this worldview makes power morally basic in the postmodern world.

What do we mean by moral antirealism, or, as I also call it, constructivism in ethics? It is not the implausible claim that everything is permissible. That outlook is simple nihilism. Rather, moral constructivism contends that moral principles and values (say, human rights) are valid only for the cultures in which they are found. Values are not ontologically real as moral realism claims. Ethics is about inventing right and wrong, as J. L. Mackie puts it.[17] The truth of moral principles is determined with respect to the beliefs about the world and human life represented in different cultural, or religious, traditions. This kind of relativism does not deny that moral beliefs can be validated or shown to be true. However, the validity of those beliefs and the practices of validation are relative to the culture in which they are found. Antirealism in this form leaves open the question of whether or not fruitful comparisons between moral traditions can take place, even as it insists that demonstrating the truth of any moral claim will always be community- or tradition-specific.

Thus, if we find the Eskimo practice of abandoning the aged morally wrong, we do so simply because our moral sensibilities have been formed in a certain way. And there is no way in which we might test our own beliefs other than on their own terms; we cannot discover from a non–tradition-specific point of view how those beliefs match or fail to match the world. This means that one cannot make judgments about the truth of the moral principles of another culture outside of the terms of that culture. At best one can express one's own preferences or adhere to one's own social mores. In religious circles, this means, as the theologian Stanley Hauerwas argues, that the Christian task is simply to be faithful Christians; it is not to try to find common moral ground with those who hold other beliefs.[18] Christians cannot argue with others about moral values and beliefs; Christians must simply witness to others in the hope that they will convert and see the truth of Christian conviction.

Most contemporary Americans and Western Christians hold to some form of moral constructivism although they often talk as realists. We believe that certain moral principles are in fact valid, true—such as human rights. Yet on reflection we grant that the truth of those principles is in fact relative to our culture and our faith traditions. We make judgments about other cultures and our own, but we sense that behind our judgments are simply our cultural biases, our prejudices, our values. The current obsession with "political correctness" in American society grows out of the uneasiness this awareness fosters. Yet there is an insight here, too. Antirealism in ethics is sparked by a concern for human freedom; it insists that the values we live by must be our own and that our lives are open to change and improvement. But recall: the question we want to ask is an ethical one. Ought "antirealism" guide our moral self-understanding and our judgments? I want to turn to this question now. And I suggest that what we ought to adopt in moral thinking is not relativism but a form of an ethics of responsibility.[19]

ON RESPONSIBILITY

The linchpin of moral constructivism is the conviction that there are really no universally shared human values or norms for behavior and so all of our judgments reflect our cultural tradition. This conclusion is reached because of the fact of moral diversity, criticisms of any religious grounding of morality, and also the loss of a sense that nature has a moral structure or purpose. But is it really the case that there are no shared human moral values or norms? Is it the case that our examination of the basic features of human life provides no guidance for how we ought to live?

Here we must note an important fact. All human life, every known culture, entails beliefs and values about several interrelated dimensions of human existence.[20] The fact that cultures have different beliefs about these dimensions of life does not negate the fact that all people and communities share them. Furthermore, all cultures provide norms and rules for how to act in order to respect and to enhance these dimensions of life. If a culture does not *respect* and *enhance* these dimensions of life, we have reason to judge it morally wrong because the very necessities of life are denied. At least that is what I will be arguing throughout this book.

What are these dimensions of life? They all center on human needs and the goods these needs implicitly entail. First, human beings have needs that arise out of the fact that we are bodily creatures. There is a need for bodily integrity, a need for the regulation and respect of sexual activity, and also the pressing need for adequate food and shelter. Admittedly, cultures understand these needs, and regulate the means of fulfilling them, differently. But there is little doubt that these are actual human needs and that they entail certain goods, what ethicists call premoral goods. Second, all human beings have needs rooted in the social character of life. There is the need for stable social environments and thus some rule of law or order, the need for basic systems of justice in economic and political affairs, and also, although it is not often noticed, the need for the mechanism of social tradition and memory, and thus education. This second level of human needs is specified within social codes of conduct for the interaction of individuals and also the transmission of cultural forms.

Third, all human beings have needs rooted in the fact that we ask about the *meaning* of our lives as creatures and of our social existence. Here we have the needs of culture itself: the need to provide systems of meaning to deal with human aspiration and also human suffering and failure, the need to ask about the truth of cultural beliefs, and, ultimately, the need to explore the meaning of the value of existence itself that is often, but not always, expressed in religious traditions. Here, too, there are distinctive goods, not premoral or social goods but what we might call reflective goods. These goods inhere in the fact that human beings ask about the meaning of their lives. A society's mores are responses to all of these basic human needs by formulating rules for respecting and enhancing the goods these various and diverse needs entail. An ethics of responsibility means that we must respond to others with respect to these basic human needs *and* to the ways in which these needs and goods are understood and valued in different cultures. And if one acts on this claim, then a fourth, unique kind of human good comes into being—the good of moral integrity. In other words, living morally helps to bring into being a new form of life, a new reality of our personhood, designated as moral integrity. By this I mean that one's life is integrated, drawn together and made whole, with respect to a specific moral project. The project is that of respecting and enhancing the integrity of life.

Does this account of responsibility ethics entail constructivism? It does to the extent that we recognize that cultures manifest different responses to basic human needs. Does this mean realism in ethics? It does to the extent that we are concerned with basic human *needs* and not with the way of life a culture believes its members *ought* to pursue. In other words, a responsibility ethics can grant some of the insights of realism and antireal- ism without agreeing fully with either moral outlook. It does so by insisting that there are certain features of life that place constraints on human action and what is choiceworthy, and that human communities respond creatively to those constraints by fashioning diverse forms of life. Those limits are rooted in basic human needs and the goods they entail; human creativity is seen in the ways of life fashioned to respect and enhance the integrity of life. Given this, an ethics of responsibility insists that we must creatively re- spond to new and novel situations with respect to these needs and goods.

Does this enable us to make moral judgments about other cultures? It does insofar as a culture's mores deny and destroy these basic human needs. Is this an imperialism of our own values? It is not, because these needs seem to be shared by all human beings, and, what is more, this requires that we judge and criticize our own culture when it backs policies that destroy these basic needs and goods. Progress in moral understanding is the process of realizing just how basic these needs are and then seeking to develop policies, institutions, and ways of life that respect and enhance the goods they entail. To respect and en- hance the integrity of life—this is the imperative of responsibility.

Now why should we think about the moral life in these terms? For two reasons. First, the diversity of our world is a fact, and, if I am right, there is a human need to participate in the transmission and creation of cultural forms. Pluralism in this sense is a human good. Any ethics for our time must grant this form of the human good. Second, the vast developments in tech- nology, communication, and international relations also mean that human power is radically increased and therefore there is the need for some princi- ples regarding how we ought to exercise that power. The imperative of re- sponsibility I have just formulated is to help in that regard because it entails the claim that in the exercise of power we must respect and enhance the in- tegrity of life. There are constraints on what we ought to do no matter how much we think we can do. In other words, we need an ethics of responsi- bility because our moral situation is one caught between tradition and nov- elty, between the plurality of moral traditions in our world that still inform our thinking and the demands of future life on this planet. An ethics of re- sponsibility is the means for thinking and acting morally in this situation.

Why ought we respect and enhance the integrity of life? Let me con- clude this chapter on that note. It returns us to claims I made at the outset of these pages. It also signals the distinctly theological and religious direc- tion of the inquiry of the following chapters.

WHY BE RESPONSIBLE?

The question is, really, why be moral at all? There are two answers to this question in our current context. These answers might in fact lead to the same conclusions about practical matters, but these answers reflect very different attitudes toward life. First, we might come to see that if we do not respect and enhance the integrity of life on this planet, we simply will not have a viable future. The threats of global conflict and ecological disaster can, and indeed must, motivate us to act responsibly. The reason for responsible action is born out of fear and self-interest.

Second, we might also see that what we are ultimately responding to in our moral lives is not only the integrity of life, but also some reality, the divine, endowing life with value and in relation to which the integrity of the whole of life is found. In this light, responsible action is born from gratitude and even reverence for the fact of existence in its fragile goodness. In the Christian and Jewish traditions, gratitude and reverence are the proper responses to the goodness of creation expressed in commitments to justice and mercy. By respecting and enhancing the integrity of life that we do see, we are responding in gratitude and reverence to the God whom we do not see (see 1 John 4:20). Accordingly, a Christian must reformulate the imperative of responsibility in order to capture the full force of the moral life: respect and enhance the integrity of life *before God*.

Why be responsible? This is a question about what binds human beings to the project of the moral life. In our situation we see different answers to this question. These answers reflect the deepest attitudes individuals and communities hold about life and also the perils and possibilities we face. What I have argued in this chapter is then quite simple. In our pluralistic world, we are not as bereft of guidance for moral reasoning as we often think. We can take our clues from some basic human needs and from how our traditions have understood and valued the goods they entail. We can make moral judgments across cultural lines with respect to these basic needs and goods. At the same time, we confront the demand to understand what is required of us and the communities to which we belong in order to respect and actively enhance the integrity of all life. This moral response to our situation requires courage and creativity in our personal and political lives. And I conclude by noting that the courage and creativity demanded of us in our age cannot finally be sustained by attitudes of fear and self-interest. It can be sustained only, I judge, through gratitude for and reverence toward the goodness of existence. Recognizing this point brings us to the theological horizon of moral inquiry.

2

Power and the
Agency of God

In an age of technological power and radical moral diversity among peoples and cultures, it is not surprising that theologians and moral philosophers are exploring the complex relation between beliefs about the world and specifically moral norms and values.[1] How a culture or community conceives of the values and norms that ought to direct human conduct is intimately related to beliefs about the world in which human beings act and suffer. Stated differently, at the root of all cultures and communities is some construal of the moral space in which human life takes place and how persons and communities are to live in that space. The context of this book is the search in a postmodern age for an ethics capable of directing human power in the project of respecting and enhancing the integrity of life.

In this chapter I continue my account of postmodernity by comparing the contemporary moral outlook with the biblical construal of the world—a construal that, I argue, pivots on the idea of the agency of God. What can a biblically informed moral ontology contribute to moral reflection in the present time? This is the specific question I seek to answer in the following pages, and in so doing I hope to make some small contribution to the larger agenda facing ethics.

ON THE IDEA OF A MORAL ONTOLOGY

I intend to compare dominant features of the biblical construal of reality and the moral outlook of post-theistic, technological societies.[2] This form of reflection presupposes that it is possible to compare moral beliefs across time and culture based on an important, but modest, claim about the nature of human existence. As Charles Taylor has recently argued, human beings exist in a moral space of life constituted by questions about how to live.[3] What is more, we orient ourselves in life with respect to some implicit or explicit idea of the good. The place of human existence is always a space defined by questions about how to live and commitments to what is and ought to be valued in human life. The commitments and values that individuals and communities hold, no matter how divergent and different, provide a framework within which questions about how to live are assessed, criticized, revised, and, finally, answered. Without such commitments and our interactions with others, it is not clear that we would have any sense of who we are. This seems to be true of all human existence. The great diversity of moral outlooks on this planet negates neither this modest, formal claim about human life nor, as we saw in the previous chapter, the presence of values rooted in human needs.

Given these facts about human beings, we can isolate features of a moral ontology—that is, features of critical reflection on the moral space of life aimed at providing direction for how to live. First, a moral ontology presents a picture of the moral space of life. In other words, it provides a generalized description of how a community or society understands the domain of human life. This feature of a moral ontology is, properly speaking, an act of metaphysical reflection. The purpose is to provide an account of reality and the places of human beings and moral values in that reality.[4] In this respect, any culture will be characterized by some implicit or explicit metaphysical beliefs. In what follows, I intend to focus on the connection among agency, power, and value in beliefs about reality found in technological societies and the biblical texts.

Second, a moral ontology is also the analysis of the basic structure of the moral space of life. The concern here is not to develop a generalized "picture" of reality, but to analyze what is presupposed in moral existence as its basic elements. This is, strictly speaking, the work of ontological analysis. The basic elements of the moral space of life, I contend, are (1) human beings as self-interpreting, social agents; (2) patterns of interaction between people and their world(s), including different modes of being in the world(s); and (3) the mediation of self-understanding, and thus the identities of individuals and communities, by values and norms. The fact that these elements are basic can be seen by noting that cultures always picture human agents in some world, we always act and exist "somewhere," and we exist and act *in* that place with respect to values, symbolic resources, and norms that guide our lives. A moral ontology provides an analysis of these basic elements of the moral space of life aimed at understanding the meaning of our existence as agents.

These two basic features of a moral ontology, what we might call the acts of *articulation* and *analysis,* mutually entail each other. How one pictures reality must meet the test of analysis; examining basic elements of existence is always in the service of deepening our insight into the reality of our lives and our world.[5] Third, then, these features of a moral ontology relate to normative, *prescriptive* claims—that is, claims about how we *ought* to live. Accordingly, the three features of moral ontological inquiry I have isolated (articulation, analysis, prescription) guide the argument of this chapter in order to compare the moral outlooks of the technological world and the biblical texts. The crucial point of comparison is the place of power in a moral ontology—the relations, as it were, among agency, power, and value in finite existence. I want to show that power is basic to the moral ontology of a technological age, whereas a biblical construal of the moral space of life centers on the transvaluation of power. This biblical outlook becomes crystallized around the center of faith, the reality of God.

The implicit moral ontology of postmodern societies is one in which human agents exert power through action in an otherwise value-neutral, materialistically conceived universe and, thereby, constitute the value of their world. This is, at one level, hardly a novel insight. But what has not been explored is how basic the connections among agency, power, and value are to the contemporary understanding of reality and human existence. As we will see, contemporary societies dominated by technical rationality operate with two overlapping principles for understanding the moral space of life: (1) that the human agent, or a community of agents, is sovereign in the creation of value through the exercise of power, and (2) that value is not ontologically basic for understanding reality, because reality is the scene for the human creation of value. The conjunction of these two principles means that the technological world is one in which the maximization of power is the primary good of life. Power does not serve a value beyond itself, because it is believed to be the source of value.

If the argument above is at all correct, the moral ontology of contemporary Western societies has no norm for evaluating the moral rightness of creation versus destruction or preferring viable future life over present interests as long as in any particular action or policy—even a destructive one—power is maximized. And given this, it is hardly surprising that postmodern societies are dominated by economic conceptions of value; strongly individualistic ideas of the self; the constant threat of meaninglessness and alienation from the value-creating centers of culture; unending conflict over access to social, political, cultural, and economic power; and increasing violence and the glorification of destruction. This domination is possible because the value and meaning of human life are thought to rest in the exercise of such forms of power.

The current view of the world and human life is at odds with the biblical construal of reality. Admittedly, it is difficult, if not impossible, to speak of *the* biblical view of reality given the immense variety of biblical strands of thought. To account for some of this diversity I will explore cultic, prophetic, and legal discourse with respect to the question of the direction of human power. Each of these forms of discourse helps to circulate within a society a construal of reality that centers on the agency of God and thereby structures or forms the moral self-understanding of that society. In other words, these divergent forms of discourse are deployed to enable a community to understand itself through a theological vision of the world. The agency-power-value connection remains basic in biblical thought, but it is, in principle, internally transvalued.

The distinctiveness of a biblically informed moral ontology is that to identify ultimate reality as an agent (for example, "God")—that is, to specify the inner meaning of ultimate power as an identity-bearing actor—is to assert a value that transcends natural, social, and political power, namely, the value of a commitment to respect and enhance identifiable agents and the conditions necessary for ongoing action. That is to say, the name "God," and its polymorphic expression in divergent forms of discourse and symbolism, expresses the transvaluation of power; the name "God" specifies power as the *origin* of value but, importantly, does not instigate it as the sole *content* of value.[6] This is, for instance, the moral significance of God as creator; it is also the meaning of the Christian claim that God is love. Love and creation are instances of power in which power generates value. That is, power (creation, love) bestows value on another, but power alone does not define value. What is basic to understanding the moral space of life from a theological perspective is, then, not a materialistic account of reality or of human capacities for creative action, but the transformation of power in which power binds its identity to the worth of finite existence.

From this perspective, one sees the world neither as a web of interdependent processes nor as so many historical monuments to human civilization and barbarism. Rather, the world is seen as a field of action composed of diverse struggles to transform relations of power for the sake of respecting and enhancing the integrity of life. Identifying or naming ultimate power "God" entails a construal of the world, or a moral ontology, and a set of moral commitments that necessarily focus on the transvaluation of power. This is so because in understanding the world in which one lives any affirmation of and fidelity to an agent—for example, faith in "God"—entails a commitment to the well-being of agents and the necessary conditions for action—that is, the natural, social, political, economic, cultural, and interpersonal conditions necessary for agents to act. Social and political institutions as well as interpersonal relations and moral aspirations are judged to be right or wrong in relation to the demand that the integrity of historical agents be respected and enhanced.

My contention, then, is that, in spite of their diversity, the biblical texts assert that the question "Who is acting?" is basic in a construal of the world, in a moral ontology. The first questions to be asked about the meaning of reality are not about the structures and dynamics of natural processes. They are, rather, questions about who is acting, who is responsible, and what is going on. Although this line of thinking has often been used to explain and even justify human suffering and misfortune through ideas of retribution, punishment, divine intervention, and so on, something else is actually at stake. What is at stake is how individuals (or communities) understand the moral space in which they exist and thus how they ought to live.

My argument centers, then, on the *moral* and *hermeneutical* import of claims about divine agency. This means two things. First, I am not trying to denote a literal, individual acting being, as in traditional theism, with purposes, intentions, and acts of will who is (or is not) causally responsible for bringing about events in the world. Neither am I making an argument for God as the inclusive individual, as some process theologians do, or, for that matter, exploring how the biblical narrative renders an agent, as many so-called narrative theologians argue.[7] Rather, I am exploring how the construal of ultimate power as an agent constitutes an individual's or a community's understanding of the meaning of life in the world, how it entails *in nuce* a moral ontology. Stated differently, I am concerned with the practical status of theological discourse with respect to the moral life rather than offering a theoretical argument about God in God's self. Questions about the *aseity* of God are simply beyond the scope of the present inquiry.[8]

Second, I also want to show that, from the perspective of theological ethics, claims about the divine are needed in ethics in order to affirm the value of existence as such. These claims are validated insofar as they help articulate and analyze what must be affirmed in order to hold the moral commitments that already define who we are as well as the commitments we must adopt in order to have a viable future. In this respect it is proper to say, borrowing from Paul Ricoeur, that, in theological ethics, we invent in order to discover. We construe the world theologically in order to discover our own most basic moral affirmations; this is the point of hermeneutical realism. An affirmation of the right of finite life to exist and make a claim against ultimate power, rather than valorization of finite existence in terms of power, is at the heart of a theological ethical worldview and interpretation of the moral life. This affirmation endorses a project of actively seeking to transform oppressive and destructive structures and relations.

With these matters in mind, I want now to expand the diagnosis of our contemporary context as presented in chapter 1, since it is the *Sitz im Leben* of theological ethical reflection. Following this I will explore resources within biblical texts and ancient ethics in order to advance the claims made in the preceding paragraphs. This chapter concludes with directions for constructive theological ethical reflection, which will return us, by way of an engagement with traditional and contemporary modes of thought, to our current situation.

AGENTS, WORLDS, AND MEANING

Several factors in our current world situation are of special importance for theological ethics. The first is the moral outlook of post-theistic societies. These are societies in which there is the widespread loss of any sense that fundamental norms and values concerning human well-being and justice are consistent with or dependent on beliefs about God. A post-theistic society is one in which, practically speaking, beliefs about God do not motivate or empower people to live by the norms and values they hold. Individuals and communities are motivated by moral or purely prudential considerations, and religious claims are interpreted in their light. These are societies in which the context of human action, the "world," is not understood by appeal to God—that is, to creation, providence, or judgment. A post-theistic society holds that nature is not to be understood as creation and thus as dependent on a transcendent source of value; the dignity of human life is not dependent on the human reflecting the divine as the imago Dei. It is also a society in which the meaning of social and historical existence is not to be grasped by appeal to divine providence. This means that human beings, or human collectives, are seen as the sole agents in reality. Again, in these societies the theistic conceptual framework within which the moral life has been understood by most, if not all, Western thought is simply no longer integral to the actual, practical beliefs by which human beings live.

The second factor confronting contemporary ethics is the radical extension of human power through technology. This power alters our understanding of reality as much as it confronts us with new and different degrees of responsibility. Some thinkers see this change in human action ontologically, as a change in our understanding of reality itself.[9] For instance, we can now change the genetic structure of future generations and thus alter the human species. We can also alter the environment to the point that it cannot sustain life as we presently know it. What then is our moral relation to those in the future? The manifold questions that surround technological innovation have led some thinkers to claim that previous moral and religious beliefs are simply unable to answer our ethical questions because of the interpretation of action and view of reality they entail.

This brings us to the third factor confronting current ethics. John B. Thompson is correct that contemporary societies are increasingly dominated by mass communication and the circulation of symbolic forms.[10] In this situation, as Thompson notes, meaning is in the service of power—that is, in the service of forms of domination. Given this, we must consider the "circulation of symbolic forms," such as legal, political, and economic discourse, if we are to understand questions of human agency and thereby respond to the plight of the oppressed and the struggle for liberation. We must do this because moral knowledge is bound to the forms of discourse, the symbols and narratives that are found in a society. As I have noted above, a basic element of a moral ontology is the belief and discourse about values that mediate self-understanding and a construal of the world. The symbolic forms important for this chapter are beliefs about "agents" and the "world."

I am suggesting, then, that in order to forward an adequate interpretation of our situation we must address the question of agency with respect to claims about reality and the symbolic forms that circulate in a society and in its legitimate structures of power. We can thus deepen our interpretation of the contemporary situation first by exploring the relation between accounts of moral agency and worldviews and then by turning to the question of the circulation of symbolic discourse. That is, we can now analyze in greater detail the elements of the moral ontology of technological, post-theistic societies.

It is not difficult to grasp the conceptual relation between some construal of reality and beliefs about the nature of agents. By definition, an agent always acts in some situation and at some time. We are always acting somewhere. The situation in which an agent or community acts can sustain or impede human action. Political and economic situations of poverty and oppression, for instance, radically impede the opportunities for persons to act. In this respect, every human action—and thus all human suffering as well—attests to the relation between an agent or community of agents and the world in which the agent or agents act. Given this, a view of reality is at least implicitly entailed in beliefs about moral agents—that is, in some construal of the spatial and temporal situation of life and action. Of course, there can be widely divergent ways of construing the world. For instance, apocalyptic language pictures reality differently than does the machine of a deistic conception of reality; contempt for the world warrants different patterns of life than an affirmation of worldly existence. These different ways of picturing the world bear on human action, either enhancing or impeding it. Similarly, there are different ways of being *in* the world (however that world is pictured). Being in the world as an agent can be characterized by hope, fear, struggle, compassion, courage, and what have you. But in each case this is different from being in the world as an object (for example, a tool) or as simple chemical processes. Agents (however understood) always act in some world (however understood) in terms of different *modes* of being *in* that world, modes that, for agents, always have an evaluative character. That is, contempt, courage, fear, faith, and other beliefs, attitudes, and feelings characterize the lives of agents and express evaluations of the world(s) in which the agents live.

Given this, any comprehensive construal of the situation of life, or a moral ontology, is dependent on symbolic forms. Since we have no perception of the "whole," the totality of what is the context of existence and action can be conceived of and spoken about only through symbolic or metaphorical means. Indeed, even to speak of the "world" as the place of human action is to use a symbolic discourse open to a variety of interpretations.[11] For example, is the world "fallen," as in traditional Christian belief? Is it an expression of the creative grace of God? Is the world a complex of natural and social processes? In this light, a crucial feature of technological societies is that they picture human agents as acting in a value-neutral time and space. The modern world, as scholars note, is disenchanted. The "whole" in which human beings act is pictured as a complex interacting matrix of natural processes. Moral values and norms are not written into the fabric of the world; they are human creations to serve specific needs and purposes, often the needs and purposes of the powerful.

The defining characteristic of the modern Western moral outlook is that it pivots on the metaphysical proposition that humans are the only agents in the world. Value is dependent for its existence on the power of human beings to act and create their world; the greater the power of human beings, the more they can and will endow their world with value. Because of this, all worldviews, and the values they endorse, are necessarily seen as nothing but human constructs that serve human purposes. And the first imperative of such an outlook is to acquire power in order to create value. In this anthropocentric worldview, the value of human purposes is written onto a value-neutral time and space. Beliefs about the world must be explained in terms of their social, psychological, or political utility for human beings.

The relation between human agents and the value-neutral environment in which we are condemned to create value has been given expression in two seemingly competing positions. First, work in the natural and biological sciences as well as evolutionary forms of thought in other disciplines have attempted to explore the appearance or *emergence* of human agents from natural reality. Human beings are to be understood as a subset of a comprehensive history of the natural world. In their capacity to act in the world, human beings are the leading edge of the material universe—the emergence of freedom in reality. As Gordon Kaufman has put it, a biohistorical view of the human being is one that accounts for "the biological grounding of human existence in the web of life on planet Earth and the many different sorts of historical developments of humankind in and through the growth, over thousands of generations, of the varied sociocultural patterns of life around the planet."[12] Second, this account of the emergence of human freedom amid a value-neutral background exists alongside modes of thought that begin with our experience of being agents. Because we exert force on the world in such a way that we have some self-conscious apprehension of ourselves as agents, it is possible to construct a plausible interpretation of reality from this fact. Forms of idealism and existentialism attempted just such an enterprise. Jean-Paul Sartre, for instance, insisted that "man being condemned to be free carries the weight of the whole world on his shoulders; he is responsible for the world and for himself as a way of being."[13] From this perspective, the reality of the acting subject is the condition of the possibility of making claims about the meaning and value of reality. In an act of freedom, the agent transcends the natural conditions of life to constitute her or his own identity and to create value. *Self-transcendence*, rather than emergence, is the character of the relation between human beings and their natural and social environment.

The usual assessment of modernity by theologians sees materialist and existentialist arguments as radically opposed and thus posing different challenges to Christian faith. Theologians then take up the challenge of "religion and science" or matters of "faith and meaning." But these trends in modern thought are, in fact, interlocking features of one comprehensive moral ontology that characterizes the distinctiveness of human beings by the power to create value within a value-neutral universe. In spite of differ-

ences, "transcendence" and "emergence" articulate and analyze human beings *in* the world in terms of human power as the origin and end of value. It
is also important to grasp that each of these positions conceives of the future as the "space" onto which the value of freedom must be projected and
in which it must be realized. Freedom must emerge into an open future from
natural processes; in the act of choice, the self stands out, transcending itself into a future it creates. Thus, not only is natural reality understood in
value-neutral terms, but the future, as the crucial condition for human freedom, is also conceived as empty and waiting for the work of human power
to fill it with value. This is, I judge, what defines these modes of thought as
thoroughly modern in character.[14]

Each of these positions is necessarily post-theistic. On the grounds of
a materialistic theory of reality, claims about God or the agency of God are
rendered meaningless and void in any account of the world. Appeals to God
do not "explain" anything except, perhaps, the psychological needs of those
who continue to believe in God. One does not need the concept of God to
understand the structure and dynamics of natural processes. The idea of
God is metaphysically void; it has no descriptive force in understanding the
world. Conversely, from an existentialist reading, human freedom is not
genuine if it is dependent on a power other than self—e.g., on the divine.
Theological claims seem to violate the conditions necessary to grasp the
meaning of our being in the world—that is, that we are free, self-constitut-
ing agents—and so do not aid in analyzing the structure of life. Theistic
claims can then be decoded as symbolic expressions of our freedom whereby
we act *as if* our moral duties are from God, as Immanuel Kant said. More
likely, religious beliefs, as Friedrich Nietzsche insisted, feed a slavish mentality destructive of real human vitality and flourishing—that is, the exercise of human power.

Let me summarize the argument of this chapter thus far. First, I have
argued that the current criticism of traditional theistic ethics centers in part
on the moral ontology those moral beliefs entailed. Second, I have further
shown that a post-theistic social milieu backs that criticism given basic suppositions about the relation (emergence; transcendence) between human
beings as agents and the spatial-temporal nature of reality. Yet, however that
relation is understood (emergence or transcendence), the origin and content
of value are understood in terms of power. Thus, third, I have argued that the
moral ontology that backs postmodern societies is one in which reality is understood in value-neutral and materialistic terms while the distinctiveness of
human existence is our capacity to exercise power (freedom) in the creation
of values—values specified through law, art, morality, economics, and the

like—in an open future. What is basic to this moral ontology insofar as it concerns the values we ought to seek is then power itself. Only through access to power do agents or communities of agents endow their world with meaning; only through the exercise of power, the capacity to change the world for human purposes, is the distinctiveness of human life to be found. The technological age, as I show in the next chapter, is merely the working out and institutionalization of this moral ontology.

Thus far I have been exploring in some detail the moral ontology implicit in postmodern technological societies. I wish now to compare this ontology with the moral outlook of biblical texts. Put as a question, if it is one of the central claims of biblical thought that God "acts" in some fashion, and if mythic modes of interpreting the world think in agential terms about deities, how, if at all, are we to make sense of biblical claims once we grant, as I think we must, the contemporary criticisms of agential accounts of the world? In order to address this question we must now explore strands in biblical thought and also developments in the history of ethics. This is a necessary step on the way back to the contemporary situation.

BIBLICAL THOUGHT AND THE HISTORY OF ETHICS

In order to link our discussion of biblical thought with the contemporary moral outlook, we can consider a text that centers on the exercise of power in the creation of value. That text is the story of the Tower of Babel.

> Now the whole earth had one language and the same words. And as they migrated from the east they came upon a plain in the land of Shinar and settled there. And they said to one another, "Come, let us make bricks and burn them thoroughly." And they had brick for stone, and bitumen for mortar. Then they said, "Come, let us build ourselves a city, and a tower with its top in the heavens, and let us make a name for ourselves; otherwise we shall be scattered abroad upon the face of the whole earth." The Lord came down to see the city and the tower, which mortals had built. And the Lord said, "Look, they are one people, and they have all one language; and this is only the beginning of what they will do; nothing that they propose to do will now be impossible for them. Come, let us go down, and confuse their language there, so that they will not understand one another's speech." So the Lord scattered them abroad from there over the face of all the earth, and they left off building the city. Therefore it was called Babel, because there the Lord confused

the language of all the earth; and from there the Lord scattered them abroad over the face of all the earth. (Genesis 11:1–9 NRSV)

This well-known narrative is often seen by scholars as an etiological explanation of the origins of different nations and languages. It also is the climax of the prehistory of humanity introducing the age of the patriarchs. The subtlety of the narrative is that the motive for the building of the tower

> lies within the realm of human possibility, namely a combination of their energies on the one hand, and on the other the winning of fame, i.e., a naïve desire to be great. [And this further means that] God's eye already sees the end of the road upon which mankind entered with this deed, the possibility and temptation which such a massing of forces holds. A humanity that can think only of its own confederation is at liberty for anything, i.e., for every extravagance.[15]

The city of Babel arises as a sign of self-reliance, the work of civilization, while the tower is a testimony to their fame. God acts punitively, but also preventively, by confusing tongues and scattering peoples. The text inscribes divine action as setting limits on human possibilities with respect to the *future* viability of civilization, or, to put it differently, setting limits on the unification of power as the precondition of building a civilization with respect to future possibilities and intentions. There is no question about the centrality of power to value; the question is whether or not there are limits on future expressions of human power other than its exercise.

Several of the features of this narrative stand out for the purpose of our present inquiry. First, the narrative focuses attention on the power of humans to create culture through technical capacities to build, centralize political organization, and produce material conditions for civilized life. This power is linked, second, to motives—the drive to be great, to make a name for themselves—as the unifying forces of a civilization ("they are one people," the text says). The fundamental motive is the exercise of power in order to accomplish values that seem dependent on that power—the values of unified political existence, the goods of civilization (the city), and the establishment of cultural greatness (the tower). Third, this motive stands out against the backdrop of the fear of chaos and social anarchy ("otherwise we shall be scattered abroad"). Thus the problem of social unity—and, with it, peace and stability—is linked in the text to the exercise of power in building a civilization. Yet, fourth, the actions of people do not take place within a value-neutral space and time, nor are human goods defined only through the exercise of human power. Rather, God "came down" to "see the city and the tower." Human civilization, and thus the exercise of power in the creation of distinctly human values, transpires within a context defined by the action and vision of God. God's punitive action has the effect of overturning the supposition that *solely* through human power is the unity and greatness, and thus the coherence and peace, of a civilization to be found. The narrative intensifies the alienation of the human from God (Gen. 3:22–24) and from other humans (Gen. 4:1–16) by portraying the alienation of all society from God and from other peoples. The answer to this alienation must be a reconciliation between peoples and the divine, and even between society and the divine.

The problem of what grounds the unity and greatness of human civilization as well as the limits on human power is answered within the narrative once the link between the prehistory and the age of the patriarchs is seen (Gen. 12ff.). While the "mortals" try to make a name for themselves, Abraham, who will be the father of many nations, is named by God.[16] Likewise, the nation of Israel will be one nation, a holy people, defined by its relation to the transcendent source of existence amid the dispersion of peoples resulting from the drive of human power in the creation of civilization. The text does not entail a denigration of human capacities for action or demean the significance of the creation of culture, the great task of civilization that befalls the human species. The text suggests that the fundamental problematic of human civilization is how to make right contact with power(s) other than the human in and through the exercise of power. What is at issue is the charting of the inner limits of human possibilities in the creation of a viable social world. This is the case because, we might say, outside of contact with this other power, with the divine, the value of human existence becomes dependent solely on the mechanisms of human power with all the dangers that such dependence entails. The basic human problem is not that of exercising power in the creation of civilization, but, rather, fidelity to a power that grounds and limits human power—the divine. This is a problem that is endlessly examined throughout the biblical texts.

The parallel between Genesis 11 and our contemporary moral worldview is perhaps too obvious to elaborate. Of more immediate importance is the need to examine the moral ontology implicit in the text. As we have seen, the question of human agency is unavoidably bound to how a culture, or an individual, understands the nature of reality, to the worldview of that culture or individual. If we take this text as emblematic, it is a safe generalization to say that for the ancient world human beings are not the only agents active in the world. That is to say, in a mythic construal of reality, human beings encounter other powers—whether conceived as deities or not—that act on and in human existence, often determining human destiny. The context of human action—the very structure of reality—and human action itself are understood as intimately bound to the question of other operative forces or agencies. As Walter Wink has noted, within the modern materialistic conception of the world we "do not have categories for thinking of such Powers as real yet unsubstantial, as actual spirits having no existence apart from their concretions in the world of things."[17] How are we then to make sense of these ancient texts? Is it enough to say that we must demythologize them? Are there resources in these ancient modes of thought for considering the meaning of human freedom in the world?

In classical thought, the operative power(s) other than the human might be understood through the idea of "fate," the actions of the gods, demons, the furies, or the divine lordship. But in each case, reality cannot be totally explained through a model of natural causation and the uniformity of natural processes even as human action itself cannot be understood simply with reference to human creative capacities. One sees this, for instance, in the biblical context through the idea of election and also the charismatic power of the prophets. God speaks through the prophet. God and the prophet act, each is accountable, in one and the same action. More graphically put, nonhuman powers take possession of persons directing their actions (see the betrayal of Judas in John's Gospel). And even St. Paul can state that it is not he but Christ in him that is crucial to the life of faith. We might speak of these as examples of the phenomenon of dual agency. Clearly it is not, as critics argue, simply an example of heteronomy; that is, the prophet's or demoniac's action is not simply defined and motivated by some external authority. Yet it is also not an act of brute autonomy. Rather, we have something like what Paul Tillich and others called "theonomy."[18] The point, I take it, is that human responsibility is not believed to be violated when it is asserted that a power or powers other than the human are operative in human action.

Interestingly, there is a conflict between naturalistic and non-naturalistic construals of reality in Greek and Roman thought that is different from such conflicts in the biblical texts. Pre-Socratic thinkers questioned the validity of mythic and agential, especially retributive, visions of reality out of a concern for giving a naturalistic explanation of the universe. Even Socrates, in the attempt to bring philosophy down to earth, is concerned with grasping the distinctive character of human action and the principle for right action (see *Euthyphro*). His claim that knowledge is virtue means that the operative power (*arete*) of excellent human action is knowledge. While scholars such as Donald Wiebe disagree, this shift to understanding human agency in its own distinctive light is shared with Socrates by Plato and Aristotle.[19] However, this does not deny the fact that in Greek and Roman thought the character of human action is not understandable outside of its relation to nonhuman powers or reality. Moral action entails some right relation to these other powers. The Epicureans, for instance, related ethics to their physics, even though they held the gods to be unconcerned with human flourishing. The Stoics, in arguing that virtue is happiness, insisted that one must live according to nature, a nature permeated by *logos*. In spite of the grave differences between these moral systems, there was a shared assumption about the fact that the moral life strikes at the very core of reality. The debates in ethics, accordingly, were at bottom debates about the nature of reality.

Seen in this light, the moral problem for biblical thought is how to discern or judge which powers *ought* to be operative in human life and then how human beings or communities *can make right contact* with them, be morally empowered by them, in and through the exercise of power by human agents. We can see the social means for answering this problem practically by isolating diverse forms of biblical discourse and practice. First, in cultic practice, contact with divine power is established through the ritual act. Cultic activity reenacts in time and space the fundamental structure of reality (whether cosmogonic or historical, or both) and thereby stabilizes the present social order. And it valorizes the ritual object not simply through the exercise of human power but in relation to the divine. Next, in prophetic discourse, contact with the source of empowerment is attained through moral action, by seeking justice, through loving mercy, and by walking in humility with God (Mic. 6:8). The community is charged with understanding itself, with interpreting its existence, with respect to norms and values that are to be endorsed in all actions. The appropriate worship of God, and thus contact with the source of empowerment, is transformed beyond previous cultic and sacrificial means to include matters of justice and mercy. In short, a construal of reality and its ritual reenactment in cultic practice and an account of just and merciful social relations are symbolically mediated by prophetic discourse.

There is then a concern in cultic and prophetic discourse with making contact in action with power(s) other than the human. This is further elaborated in legal discourse. Through the structure of law—what came to be called by Christian theologians the moral, civil, and ceremonial law— there is increasing differentiation of types of actions and norms for conduct with respect to the ongoing life of the community. This organization of life takes place against the backdrop of the cultic need to reenact the structure of reality and the prophetic claim about the values that should inform and guide self-understanding and action. This is why the manifold forms of action mediated by legal discourse are seen as basic to the formation of human identity. We might go so far as to say that a community's identity, its "name" (to recall the text from Genesis 11), is enacted and constituted through a host of types of action and their legal mediation. These types of action are in the service of power and contact with power(s) other than the human— that is, the power of the divine rule, covenant fidelity, the eschatological presence of the divine, as well as the exercise of human power.

My concern here is not to trace the development of divergent strands of biblical thought and discourse, a task which is, quite frankly, beyond my scholarly abilities. Yet it is also not to enter more deeply into ancient ethics, although these are matters more within my expertise. The point to grasp is that in much of ancient ethics, and certainly in all Christian theological ethics, the most basic moral problem was how the agent or community was to relate to some source of power that was other than itself and yet empowered the self or community to act. In Christian thought, this "source" was conceived in agential and personal terms ("God"), and this provided the grounds for a construal of reality, an understanding of the origin and status of moral norms, and also proper moral motivation. This source of value was, furthermore, depicted in polymorphic forms of discourse that then served to structure the identities of individuals and the community. This form of moral identity entailed the endorsement of beliefs about reality which asserted that the context of human action is not value-neutral. And it also implied a commitment to respect and enhance the conditions necessary for human action. In my judgment, these beliefs and commitments are the hermeneutical point of biblical and Christian agential construals of reality.

Much of modern ethics, as we have seen, has tried to show how the self acts out of its own freedom, and this has made power central to an account of the human. This has meant the attempt to reduce an analysis of the moral space of life to a theory of the emergence of freedom from matter, or, conversely, to existentialist theories of the transcendence of freedom over matter. In this light, the moral ontology found in the biblical texts is surprisingly complex. It does not reduce the moral space of life to the interaction between autonomous agents seeking power and value-neutral matter understood simply in terms of either emergence or transcendence. Rather, human beings act in a moral space defined not solely by their own power; action is mediated by forms of discourse and practices that reinforce the moral order (cultic action); human freedom is directed to the ends of justice and mercy (prophetic discourse); and the social system is differentiated into interacting domains of activity (legal discourse). Most importantly, human power is not definitive of value even if diverse forms of power are the origin of value. Human power is exercised for good or ill within a horizon of value symbolized through the divine and mediated by different forms of discourse. Surprisingly, the biblical texts taken in their diverse strata seem truer to the complexity of the moral space of life than do the forms of conceptual and axiological reductionism characteristic of modern philosophy and theology.

The great danger of biblical and Christian thought is when contact with this other power becomes the warrant for the establishment of a "Christian civilization" that shifts the question of value back to the domain of human power now sanctioned by what ostensively are divine commands. Such developments, which, we must note, mark the whole of Western history, violate the best insights of the moral ontology articulated through the complex forms of discourse seen in the biblical texts. And this is why theological ethics must articulate, critique, and revise prevailing discourses and patterns of action both within and outside the religious community. Mindful of the real and present danger of biblical thought, the orienting question of this book returns: what, if anything, might theological ethics contribute to contemporary thought?

THE TRANSVALUATION OF POWER

I have been arguing that we must explore the biblical texts in search of symbolic resources capable of transforming our perceptions of power and thus endorsing a moral commitment to respect and enhance the integrity of life. In light of our discussion, the most important resource seems to be found in the dialectical relation between cultic and prophetic modes of discourse for conceiving how persons and communities make contact with the source of value. Cultic practice, as we have seen, reenacts the order of reality and, when mediated by the name "God," asserts that value is not dependent solely on human activity. In terms of the basic elements of a moral ontology, cultic actions enact a "world" in which the exercise of power, the cultic act, actually transvalues power through the symbol "God." However, while cultic action can stabilize the community or culture, it does not necessarily specify principles for moral action *in* the actual social—as opposed to the ritualized and symbolic—world. Prophetic discourse provides those principles for existence *in* the social world (justice, mercy, humility), which are then to structure the self-understanding of persons and communities. As a basic element of a moral ontology, prophetic discourse provides beliefs about the meaning of our existence as self-interpreting agents. Prophetic discourse circulates in a society to test, transform, and radically interpret social mechanisms and relations operative in that society. It endorses the demands for mercy and justice within a commitment to an inclusive moral community depicted as the reign of God. Thus, prophetic discourse works to transform the ritualized "world" of cult in terms of the demands of justice and mercy even as it seeks to apprehend the work of social justice as a "cultic" means for contact with the divine.

Cultic and prophetic discourse express two elements of the biblical moral ontology (that is, world enactment and moral agency). They provide a view of reality (cult) and human, social agents (prophetic discourse) which are then further mediated by legal discourse aimed at social interaction and, thus, the exercise of power. When the complex relations among these practices and forms of discourse are severed, there is a degeneration into brute moralism, self-legitimating sacrificial mechanisms, and barren legalism. This degeneration takes place when a discourse and practice for enacting a symbolic world (cult) are severed from a discourse uniquely concerned with moral norms for human action (prophetic) and the means for structuring social interaction (legal). In this case, power fills a void as the basic value. The fact that this possibility is examined in the biblical texts themselves—such as in the case of the Tower of Babel—is a testimony to the fragility of this moral ontology and its capacities to shape and direct human life.

Thus, I have examined the moral ontology of a technological age and have shown how it centers on power as the origin and content of value. With this we have seen how depictions of our being in the world in terms of emergence and self-transcendence specify the spatial-temporal conditions of life as value-neutral. I have also explored the moral ontology of the biblical texts in order to clarify (1) symbolic means and forms of practice for transvaluing power, but also (2) how this moral outlook too can devolve into a reduction of value to power. Given these results of our inquiry, how might a thorough understanding of the contemporary moral outlook and the complex relation between the modes of action and discourse that circulate in the biblical texts help address contemporary theological ethical questions? What has our work in comparative moral ontology shown?

A central moral and religious problem in contemporary life is the degree to which the possibility of viable life on earth in the future entails imperatives for action. This means that moral character and conduct must now be defined through the imperative that persons and communities understand themselves as agents who respect and enhance the conditions necessary for the continuation and flourishing of life. Further, the world we are *in* must now be conceived in terms of the *temporal* arena or horizon of life—that is, the possibility of future life on earth. In the light of our inquiry, we can say that technological societies are characterized by a form of "cultic" action—that is, ritual acts aimed at enacting a "world"—in which the future is defined in terms of efficiency based solely on the exercise of human power. Possibilities for life are to be sacrificed for the sake of present empowerment and control. It is hardly surprising, then, that the future, as the horizon on which we project a construal of the world in which to act, must be seen in value-neutral terms in post-theistic societies. To speak of the moral standing of the future is nonsensical within the context of purely technical rationality and the moral ontology it entails. Technological action does not reenact a moral order or redirect the exercise of human moral action under norms to protect the powerless.

Criticizing the technical rationality that characterizes post-theistic social life does not entail a romantic longing to return to a supposed pretechnological state. Such a state has never and will never exist. It is axiomatic of human existence that we are technological beings. This can be seen in the text from Genesis 11. Human beings face the great task of civilization and the exercise of technological power because of the fact that we are instinct-poor. The point I am making, then, is that the technological outlook must be criticized and limited by the circulation of another form of discourse in the social order—specifically, prophetic discourse.

What does this mean? It means that from a prophetic stance the future is not conceived in value-neutral terms but with respect to the symbol of the reign of God. This symbol, which, we must see, defines an evaluation of the world with respect to the affirmation of reality by an agent, potentially reconstitutes an understanding of time and history as the context for human action. That is, prophetic discourse charts the limits of human possibilities and powers in terms of the annunciation of a just and merciful future condition (the reign of God) placing a claim on the present for its realization. This ethical-religious outlook asserts that human integrity is determined by an orientation toward that inclusive community characterized by justice and mercy rather than with respect to sources of immediate empowerment that negate possibilities for real future life. And this stance further means that human agents make contact with the source of empowerment, and thus the divine, by dedicating themselves to respecting and enhancing the integrity of life. In other words, prophetic discourse functions to constitute communities that seek to reenact this claim as basic to their own identity, because this symbolism helps us to specify why finite existence matters on grounds other than its utility to power, namely in terms of a future condition of justice and mercy. This articulates a root affirmation of finite being as good in its very finitude, an affirmation basic to the moral viability of post-theistic culture itself.

What I am arguing is that in a post-theistic context we must understand biblical, agential construals of the divine and reality in hermeneutical and practical terms. We can explore how that discourse circulates in Israelite, biblical society to reconstitute the self-understanding of individuals and communities in their construal of the world and also to guide action. The importance of the biblical texts is that, through prophetic discourse, cultic practices are reconstituted as the means for contact with the source of empowerment. This reconstitution has the effect of morally transforming power in the social order because it endorses an inclusive moral community characterized by justice and mercy as that which persons and communities can and ought to respect and seek in all their actions. This is the case because to identify ultimate power as an agent (God) is to assert a value that exceeds power—namely, the value of a commitment to respect and enhance identifiable agents and the conditions necessary for ongoing action. And this follows because, as we have seen, to specify any agent is also to affirm some construal of the world. The insight of biblical discourse is to identify or name ultimate power in such a way that the affirmation of the value of finite being (the world and future finite life) is entailed in that identification, and, given this, fidelity to God requires a commitment to respect and enhance the integrity of life. To interpret one's own life or the life of a community from this perspective has the effect, I am suggesting, of transforming assessments of power, both personal and social, and thus the origin and content of value. And it is a small—yet crucial—step to the realization that this specifies the empowerment of the powerless to be active, identifiable agents in history as a basic moral and political requirement. Only in this way can we make sense of the right of life to exist on this planet in the future, a claim that must surely be binding on all of us.

The validity of this theological perspective for ethics must be demonstrated hermeneutically and practically, or through dialectic, which amounts to the same thing. That is to say, this perspective must demonstrate its capacity to isolate and answer problems found in rival ethical theories of how we should understand human existence and the world with respect to guiding action. In this chapter, I have attempted this dialectical demonstration along two lines. First, I have tried to show that the contemporary moral ontology constricts our moral outlook with respect to the demand that future life ought to exist by focusing on the maximization of power. This constriction of our moral outlook manifests itself, I believe, in the indifference to these matters in current technological societies, even though an open future is seen as the basic human freedom. In the next chapter we will uncover the moral skepticism of the current outlook. Second, I have also tried to show how a moral ontology centered on power alone cannot specify whether or not there are limits on the exercise of power and thus is unable to provide the means of distinguishing morally between creative and destructive expressions of power. Because power serves nothing beyond itself—because it is, as I have put it, the origin and sole content of value—all that matters is the maximization of power. In this respect, the perspective of theological ethics outlined in this chapter provides resources for articulating an imperative for present action, critically assessing current modes of thought, and also specifying a revised understanding of Christian faith. The question that necessarily remains open is the extent to which this ethical-religious outlook can actually empower human life.

CONCLUSION

In this chapter I have tried to practice a mode of theological ethical reflection that can at one and the same time engage the biblical texts as well as debates in contemporary thought and society. Yet the questions that surround our ideas and beliefs about the meaning and significance of human agency are not merely academic. They touch on the most basic matters of human life. The responsibility placed on theological ethics in an age of human power is to bring its resources to bear on these basic matters in order to provide some guidance for considering how we should live.

3

Moral Skepticism and the Postmodern Age

There is little doubt that we are in the midst of a global, technological revolution affecting all aspects of life.[1] We must think morally and theologically about these developments. As Mary Midgley has recently noted, "Our sense of value-contrasts is needed for the very possibility of our perceiving anything else."[2] What I want to show in this chapter is that technology, paradigmatically seen in current information technologies, can shape our sense of value-contrasts and thereby contribute to the spread of moral skepticism in the postmodern age. In this way, the chapter deepens the account of postmodernism and moral theory undertaken in the previous chapters.

Central to my diagnosis of our situation is the connection between how we picture the human and the reality of moral goodness. The problem for ethics is to foster our capacity to perceive goodness.[3] Without the sense or perception that the integrity of life is intrinsically good and is to be respected and enhanced, all the moral appeals in the world will not help us. It is this sense of moral responsibility that is threatened in our age with the continuing spread of technical rationality and moral skepticism. The reasons for this threat are subtle and complex. I will address some of them later in this chapter. But the main point is that technology is fundamentally a way of knowing and valuing that can too easily corrode our capacity to apprehend the goodness of existence. The theological ethics I will advocate is a response to this corrosion. In terms of moral theory, it is called "hermeneutical realism." I hope to show the importance of taking this stand in ethics. The theory will be developed further in subsequent chapters of this book. For now, I want to clarify how a hermeneutic stance in theological ethics makes sense of beliefs about human existence implicit in current culture and Christian faith.

I will begin by deepening our understanding of the postmodern situation beyond the discussion of the previous chapters. Second, I am going to explore moral skepticism and its relation to information technology. At the outset, an important point must be grasped. I have no interest in demeaning the importance of technology in our lives, or to suggest that somehow we must rid ourselves of these devices. The computer age is here to stay, thankfully. My point is a more basic one. We must attend to the ways in which our perception of life is shaped by images, words, symbols, and narratives—or, more comprehensively, by language itself. I am exploring information technology, or cyberspace, as a kind of "language" and analyzing its impact on moral consciousness. Only in this way can we grasp the full moral import of this technology. Given this, in the final parts of the chapter I will show what theological ethics has to say about moral skepticism. In doing so I will contrast hermeneutical realism with internal realism found in narrative theological ethics and the kind of critical realism seen in so-called metaphorical theology and ethics.

THE TRIUMPH OF SYSTEMS AND THE THREAT TO LIFE

One essential fact seems clear about the postmodern age: the *integrity of life* is mightily threatened.[4] Our age is marked by a conflict between impersonal and seemingly uncontrollable matrices of power/information and the basic interests of the concrete individual. We all worry about what personal life will mean when the Human Genome Project enables us to contemplate the refashioning of our species. Every day, hundreds of square miles of rain forest are destroyed, species are becoming extinct at an alarming rate, and global pollution continues unabated as 78 million tons of carbon dioxide is released into the atmosphere on a daily basis. The sheer demand of human consumption threatens the integrity of the ecosystem. In effect, political, economic, and technological systems seem to undercut the interests of people and also threaten our planet. The possibility is that humans and natural resources will be encoded in systems that exist solely in and for themselves.

What is lost in the triumph of rationalized systems is the sense that all of life exists within a preexistent horizon of value and the belief that this finds a testimony in each and every human heart. Long ago, this sensibility about value and being was captured in Western cultures through beliefs about creation, the idea that human beings are created in the image of God, and also claims about moral conscience. These religious convictions asserted the intrinsic worth of human beings and pictured life within a surrounding space of value. As we have seen in previous chapters, this traditional form of moral realism is now lost to us. In our time, personal and natural existence is increasingly situated, valued, and directed not in creation, but within the sociolinguistic machineries of meaning and power we have invented yet seem increasingly unable to control.

The postmodern information age signals a fundamental shift in self-understanding and our experience of reality. It does so because it alters how we see, perceive, and understand the world and human existence. As Václav Havel puts it, "As soon as man began considering himself the source of the highest meaning in the world and the measure of everything, the world began to lose its human dimension, and man began to lose control of it."[5] The challenge of our day is to struggle against the forces that fragment life and suppress the quest for integrity or that falsely unify human existence by wrongly subsuming people into impersonal forces. The hunger for some kind of connection to a value beyond human systems of power cannot be denied. It is seen in the various forms of spirituality that are reasserting themselves around the globe, in traditional faith, fundamentalist revivals, and also in New Age movements.

The religious and moral questions of the postmodern age are these: how might we respect and enhance the integrity of life, and how ought we to resist forces of disintegration? It seems that global technology can actually work to affirm integrity. It unifies life and provides new avenues for human wholeness. Although cyberspace is impersonal and wholly a human construction, it nevertheless is a realm of free personal expression. Information technology has certainly accelerated our sense of living in a global village. The debates about privacy and access to information are nothing less than attempts to protect the personal. Yet, while this is true, everything depends on what *connection* we make between what transpires in cyberspace and how we live in the other spaces of our lives.

An example will help make this point. I recently heard of an eighty-year-old woman in a nursing home who is a seductive young man on the Internet. Technology grants her a new form of existence through the encoding of her thoughts and desires and transmits them to others who dwell in that information system. This woman exists in at least two distinct moral worlds, one electronic and one in a care facility. Contrasting sets of values define her life: the values of sociality and seduction in an electronic existence she creates, and other values that are not created by her but demand recognition, such as the value of life in its passing. This woman's experience manifests a deeper cultural fact. Contemporary humans, especially in the West, have an uncanny ability to compartmentalize their lives, to live in multiple worlds. We move quickly among different experiences, contexts, and value schemes. I jump on a plane in Chicago having made arrangements for the care of my son and his schooling. I land a few hours later in Washington to give a lecture about technology and moral theology. I check my voice mail to hear if any friends have called. Father, scholar, friend; Chicago, Washington, Ameritech. Who am I? Where am I? This situation leads some to speak of the postmodern self as fragmented, dispersed through a multiplicity of roles, values, purposes, and meaning systems. But this view of the self, I suggest, is just part of the wider threat to the integrity of life found in our time.

The question of how to respect and enhance the integrity of life in a technological, postmodern age comes to mean how we *ought* to integrate our lives as we traverse worlds—worlds of culture, cyberspace, and the everyday relations of life. And we need to realize that these "worlds" have diverse value schemes: some values we fabricate; others testify to the roots of worth in finite existence. There is a picture of human life implicit in this fact of postmodern existence. Like the Greek god Hermes, who was the messenger from Zeus to mortals, we are beings who traverse worlds bearing messages. To be human is to be an interpreter of worlds and values. We are adventurous, hermeneutical beings through and through; understanding is our mode of being in the world. This is a basic fact about human beings central to what I am calling hermeneutical realism in theological ethics.

How ought we to respect and enhance the integrity of life? This is *the* moral and religious question of our time. I want now to address just one aspect of this question that defines our situation—an aspect that concerns beliefs about value and value-contrasts basic to the rest of our perception of life. And in order to do so, we need to pick up general trends of twentieth-century thought powerfully seen in information technology. This will also deepen the discussion of pluralism and moral theory in chapter 1.

VALUE AND THE SOCIAL CONSTRUCTION OF REALITY

Contemporary philosophy and social sciences have been dominated by two basic themes: the turn to language, and the insistence on the social construction of reality.[6] The basic claim is that the whole domain of practices, cultural activities, and meaning systems that constitute social life are nothing but human inventions. Culture is a process of symbolic world-construction; human beings are culture-creating beings. This is the dominant post-Kantian view of culture and human existence. It is found in virtually all disciplines: anthropology, sociology, history of religions, philosophy of science, and, of course, ethics. If we are honest, it is what we all believe. And it makes the human power to create cultures and civilization basic to our existence.

The principal way we create meaningful worlds is through language. From Friedrich Schleiermacher in the nineteenth century to current post-structuralist philosophers such as Jacques Derrida, language has been seen as a system of signs productive of meaning and also the medium of human conversation. In the acts of speaking and writing, we utilize a system, a linguistic code, for the distinctive enterprise of communication, an enterprise with its own rules and purposes. In this sense, meaning is always produced or created *internal* to a system. Linguistic systems are also reflexive: they refer back upon themselves in the generation of meaning even while making it possible for us to talk to each other about something else. Consider a simple example. I tell you that the windswept clouds dotting the sky fill me with joy. Hopefully, you will understand what I mean: language is a medium of communication. And yet in this very act of communication, language reflects back upon itself. We both know, implicitly at least, that the words "windswept," "clouds," and "joy" are not the realities they designate, but are simply words within the system of the English language. In another language, we would have to use different words, and in doing so we might reach a different sense and understanding of a cloudy day. Every language is thus a reflexive, human invention. Words are arbitrary with respect to nonlinguistic reality while also determined by the specific linguistic code. This is why a German can say *Baum* and I can say *tree* and we can both be right about the leafy object before us, and also say something meaningful to those who speak our tongues. At root, this fact about language seems to designate the arbitrariness of human meaning; we live within schemes that we create but that are groundless, without depth.

On the face of it, the claim that reality, at least any "reality" we find meaningful, is a social, linguistic construction is obviously right. Current information technology is a powerful instance of this belief in social construction. Indeed, cyberspace is a linguistically constructed domain of meanings encoded and transmitted electronically. This implies, as the feminist philosopher Donna Haraway has noted, that information technology is bent on "the translation of the world into a problem of coding, a search for a common language in which all resistance to instrumental control disappears and all heterogeneity can be submitted to disassembly, reassembly, investment and exchange."[7] Just as in any language, there is, we might say, an *economy* of meaning in cyberspace that converts the world into a system of encoded signs. Natural speech is encoded digitally; images are disassembled and then reassembled electronically; the imaginary is produced as virtual reality. This economy of encoding poses moral issues. One issue is about the means of resisting the forms of control that a totalized system of meaning represents. Another issue is how we ought to acknowledge genuine diversity, real otherness, in a unified, encoded system.

However, these moral concerns rest on deeper issues about value-contrasts. Every economy of meaning—including a language—is not only about encoded messages. A system of encoding is also a system of values; it entails, in the terms I used in chapter 1, a morality or moral worldview. Two kinds of value-contrasts are always at work: (1) the contrast between what is valuable and what is not valuable and (2) a ranking of values wherein things with value are ordered in relation to each other. (For example, current American culture values economic power more than rhetorical skill, a truth our presidential campaigns aptly show.) These two kinds of value-contrasts are present in everything we think and imagine. We are always engaged in judging some things better and higher and more worthy than other things. In fact, conflict over what to value and how highly to value it is the fuel of human strife. The social construction of reality is then not only a matter of the encoding of meanings: it also entails the belief that value-contrasts are defined by the capacity of a social system to encode a standard of worth and importance, a standard of value. And it asserts that values go no deeper, have no greater status, than the languages we use to construct some social sphere of meaning. In this light, information technology is a symbol of our cultural situation. To interpret the demand this symbol places on moral reflection is to clarify exactly what is meant by moral value.

Ethicists have long noted that what is unique about "moral" value, as distinct from other human values, is that it is regularly placed at the top of a culture's or a person's scale of values. A moral claim seems to override other values in dignity and importance. It is sovereign over other ideas and values. We think it more important, for instance, to protect human dignity than to debate the relative merits of various kinds of art. We do not morally blame people for having poor taste; we do blame them if their actions demean and destroy life. Put more technically, moral value is unconditional—that is, its claim on us is not limited or conditioned by other considerations. And, further, moral value is noninstrumental. We sense that we ought not to use something having moral value merely as a means or instrument to some other end.

In the history of Western ethics, two basic options have been taken on this point about what has unconditional, noninstrumental value. Understanding these positions is essential if we are to grasp the full moral texture of our situation. First, ancient eudaimonistic ethics such as Aristotle's tried to specify what is intrinsically good, that is, happiness, in terms of human activity; it usually identified this with the soul's virtuous action and contemplation. Modern versions of this focus on activity and its goods are found in Friedrich Nietzsche's celebration of the will to power in the creation of values, and, recently, in the search of Alasdair MacIntyre and others for goods internal to practices.[8] For these positions, what is unconditionally good is some form of *activity*, some exercise of human power. Second, forms of ethics influenced by Jewish and Christian faith see some being, usually God, as the good-in-itself. In the modern, secular position, under the influence of Immanuel Kant, not God but individual persons are morally central. Only persons are intrinsically good, never only means to other ends.[9] In this moral outlook, it is not the exercise of power, even its exercise in virtuous action, that is morally central; what is central are things—persons, God, forms of life—and these are to be respected and enhanced in all actions.

Whether we insist on *activities* or *persons* as intrinsically good, some unconditional, noninstrumental good seems necessary for any livable culture. It is hard to imagine a human world in which everything could be freely used, controlled, demeaned for whatever purpose. Such a world would be hellish, it would be a nightmare. This is true of the postmodern age as well. In fact, the reality of cyberspace is one in which *activity*—the activity of encoding meaning—threatens to subvert the facticity of *persons*. The intrinsic good of this activity is not happiness or persons; it is the encoding itself and thus the power to create meaning. Cyberspace seems to wed Aristotle and Nietzsche: the intrinsic good is the activity of power in encoding meaning.

While this appears to be the case about cyberspace, there is another problem for ethics. Not only must we define moral value, we also need to specify its source or origin. Yet it is not at all clear how to speak about the *source* of moral value. The problem is that moral values do not seem to be anywhere; they seem to have no space other than in our heads and hearts. Look as long as you like at a practice, a person, an animal, or a community; you cannot easily show its moral value. Do we "see" justice; do we "feel" goodness; can we "touch" dignity? To be sure, we might have a sense of justice or desire goodness. But are the objects of these sensibilities (justice, goodness, humanity) real or merely expressions of subjective experiences?

As one can imagine, these are hotly debated issues in ethics. Some thinkers argue that moral value *supervenes* on the nonmoral facticity of a thing, action, or person. Early in the twentieth century, G. E. Moore and his disciples argued that we simply have an intuition of non-natural, moral value. Advocates of human rights, such as Alan Gewirth, argue that human beings as rational agents evoke moral respect. Christian thinkers, both conservative and progressive, make claims about the human as created in the image of God. The ancient Stoics thought that everyone participated in the divine *logos* permeating the universe.[10]

Despite the differences among these moral positions, they are all forms of moral realism. As we know from chapter 1, for the realist, moral claims are not solely expressions of emotions, reports of personal preferences, or even products of social agreement and convention. Moral statements make claims about reality, such as the dignity of persons, independent of our ideas of reality. We *encounter*, not only *make*, values. The "place" of value, we might say, is in the space between our heads and hearts and the reality surrounding us.[11] In this light, it is important to grasp that any genuine Christian theological ethics must be a form of moral realism, for two basic reasons.

First, a theological ethics holds that God—the ultimate good—is not a human invention even if our ways of speaking and thinking about God are human constructs. The good is real because God is God. The religious believer seeks to know or see or discern the divine purposes for life; moral goodness is ultimately not a matter of preference or social convention. Second, theological ethics asserts that the primordial distinction between good and evil, the value-contrast par excellence, is itself a kind of godlike knowledge. This distinction is not a product of the human world; it is the *condition for* a human world. This is why, symbolically, Adam and Eve are confronted by God with a command about the Tree of the Knowledge of Good and Evil. The value-contrast of good and evil precedes our act of world-construction. The world Adam and Eve fashion outside of Eden— that is, the whole domain of human civilization—presupposes knowledge of a contrast they did not invent but rather stole. Thus, in traditional Christian discourse, the source of value, God, and also the knowledge of the most basic value-contrast are thought to be other than simple human inventions.

We have seen that the dominant assumption of contemporary culture is some version of the idea that moral values are social constructs. As I put this before, contemporary culture is riddled with forms of constructivism or antirealism in ethics. Cyberspace is an instance of the social construction of reality. In terms of a theory of value, it embodies the centrality of activity as the intrinsic good, and, specifically, the activity of encoding meaning. This has the effect of making power—the power to create meanings—morally basic. In the process, the worth of persons and the reality of value are placed in jeopardy. Moral values seem to have no standing in reality other than that which flows from our minds and passions. The belief about the lack of a connection between reality and goodness is actually the backbone of moral skepticism. Thus, by moving from the pervasive idea about human reality as a social construction through the question of value and its source, we have finally reached the problem of moral skepticism at the heart of the postmodern age. And we have begun to see it in contrast to theological ethical realism. The next step in our inquiry is to clarify what exactly is meant by moral skepticism. At this level of reflection, we will have reached the deepest suppositions of our time.

THE CLAIMS OF MORAL SKEPTICISM

Moral skepticism is doubting that there can be any valid reasons for holding some values as real and true beyond our wishing, saying, or believing them to be real and true. Put differently, a moral skeptic is an ethical antirealist. As J. L. Mackie has put it, moral values and even moral imperatives "are constituted by our choosing or deciding to think in a certain way."[12] In its hardest form, skepticism is simple subjectivism: values are made by people given contingent desires and social conditions. Moral claims—such as the claim that human beings have intrinsic worth—cannot be true or false because moral values are not real. Moral values are matters of taste. Softer forms of skepticism hold that we can judge the truth or falsehood of moral claims, but only with respect to the forms of discourse and social practices of our community. Soft skeptics, such as the American philosopher Richard Rorty, say something of this order: "We citizens of liberal democracies value personal rights, but there are societies that do not and we can make no judgments about which moral stance is true."[13] For both hard and soft skeptics, there is nothing external to a community or individual actor that grounds criteria for distinguishing between better and worse, or true and false, moral beliefs. Value and value-contrasts are products of our social encoding.

There is something intuitively odd about the antirealist, skeptical argument. All of us have had experiences of things and persons being valuable beyond our thinking them to be valuable. This is especially true of love. My love for my son I do not feel simply because I think of him as lovable. He *evokes* my love. Similarly, we all have a sense in facing moral problems that we are trying to arrive at the right answer and not simply deciding what we prefer to do. We regularly think we can be wrong about moral problems. We do find ourselves in a space of values. Take another example. In erotic love, I am overcome with desire for, care for, and wonder about my beloved; sometimes I am perplexed about what to be and to do. These experiences—love, perplexity, desire—are common to us all. Skepticism and its conceptual expression in antirealism is thus actually a second-order stance wherein we decide to doubt our usual ways of getting on in the world. It supplants our natural wonder and perplexity about life with doubt, and, in this respect, it is a negative remnant of the modern, Cartesian search for the undoubted foundation of all claims. This is what makes current moral antirealism distinctly *postmodern*. But most of the time, we are in fact struck with moral wonder and perplexity and not radical doubt. The real question is why skepticism has such a grip on our moral thinking when it is contrary to our ordinary experience, when it denudes our world of the values that are integral to our daily lives.

The reasons for our skepticism are simple. The pervasive assumption that reality is a social construct makes us believe that whatever values we experience must be inventions simply because we have to speak about them in human terms. And this seems to make good sense, because, as we have seen, it is exceedingly difficult to find moral values written into nature.[14] Further, if morality is a product of social practices, then we are bound only by our inventions. Freedom is a matter of casting off false beliefs—that is, beliefs that do not maximize freedom. This is surely right. Most of the movements of liberation in our age require demonstrations that what was previously believed to be natural—such as women being naturally less capable than men—is not natural at all. And this is an important moral advance. Thus, the centrality of freedom and also the failure to discover value are the deep reasons why skepticism grips our moral lives. And it should be clear, again, that information technology is an instance of this postmodern outlook about values. Cyberspace is a linguistically constructed world in which one is free to engage others, to create a personality and relations, but it is also a world that goes no deeper than the system itself. It is a world that manifests the power of human beings to create meanings regulated by the rules we invent.

I need to be crystal clear about what is being argued. As noted above, I am *not* criticizing technology and recommending a return to some pretechnological human state. While some thinkers advocate this stance, I hardly believe it is possible or wise. If I am right, there is no such pretechnological state. We are cultural animals. The creation of culture demands human labor and its interdependency with tools, with technology. To be a cultural animal is to exist in a world partly of one's making, a world shaped by some form of technology. The problem is not technology per se, and much less the quest for extending the domain of human freedom. What I am saying is that any form of technology can be, but is not necessarily, a vehicle for inscribing a pervasive outlook of moral skepticism into our consciousness. The postmodern age, I am arguing, is one in which technology functions in this way because contemporary technologies are so deeply linked to the general loss of the sense that life transpires against a background of value, a background that surrounds and sustains life. Information technology is an encoding process, an economy of meaning, but what it encodes is a specific moral outlook asserting that moral value is no deeper than our meaning systems. This shift in the meaning of technology blinds us to values rooted in the nature of things. It truncates the moral sense of *encountering* value in experiences of wonder and perplexity, because it augments the sense that we *make* values through acts of encoding.

A technological age is one in which the value-contrasts basic to meaningful life are believed to be rooted in the human power to create meaning. In postmodern cultures, many human beings no longer believe that the value of their existence is tied to an ultimate, transcendent source of good. The cosmic pride of seeing ourselves in the image of God has been destroyed. But with this humbling has come the exaltation of the human to almost Godlike stature through the maximization of power.[15] The world thus loses its human dimension. It is this moral worldview that is of special concern to theological ethics. So our inquiry must go one step further. We need to consider theological ethical responses to skepticism and the will-to-power of our technological age.

OPTIONS IN THEOLOGICAL ETHICS

Moral skepticism as a moral outlook and antirealism in moral theory are clues that we have become strangely inarticulate about the very thing we need in order to have a meaningful world. Theologians have rightly been preoccupied with this problem. Two answers dominate current trends in theological ethics; each is a modification of classical, Christian moral realism. One trend in theological ethics is a form of *internal realism*. This is seen in narrative ethics. It is advanced by thinkers as diverse as Alasdair MacIntyre, Stanley Hauerwas, and other theologians.[16] On this account, moral character is formed through virtues, or skills, needed to tell the kinds of stories that are important for shaping how we see and value the world. The linguistic code of the Christian faith is the means to a distinctive perception of the world. We see the world in a certain way because we know the story of God's action in Christ. We do not *create* these narratives; in a profound sense the story creates us. Further, the truth of these stories cannot be determined apart from the stories and the community that tells them. There is no value-neutral place where we may stand and see the world in order to judge the truth of moral beliefs. The truth of a narrative is the life it informs. The moral purpose of a community, accordingly, is to embody its narratives in such a way as to present to others a distinctive way of life.

In narrative ethics there is no knowledge of value-contrasts independent of socially constructed knowledge. Values are *internal* to the economy of meaning in the narrative that creates a community's worldview and that the community struggles to embody in the world. One cannot ask a narrative ethicist if non-narrative or non-Christian reasons can be given for the truth of those values. The basic value-contrasts, including that of truth and falsehood, are internal to the narrative world. Internal realism, as Hilary Putnam has noted, "is, at bottom, just the insistence that realism is not incompatible with conceptual relativity."[17] Human beings are members of a community and see the world though that community's conceptual scheme. Given this, a narrative ethics, or any form of internal realism, beseeches one to enter the community shaped by its narrative world. This is why, as a form of traditionalism, narrative ethics is often antimodern. Insofar as modern thinkers have sought to reconstruct inherited beliefs and conceptual schemes prompted by methodological doubt, the modern project, so the traditionalist holds, destroys the very condition of possibility for perceiving value. But although narrative ethics and internal realism might offer some security of moral identity in a pluralistic world, it is unclear how one might avoid moral skepticism if our perception is dependent on a conceptual scheme. Doubt the scheme and the perception of moral value evaporates.

The other trend dominating much of theological ethics can be called "metaphorical ethics." It is a form of *critical realism*. In the United States, this trend can be seen among thinkers such as Gordon Kaufman, Sallie McFague, and other ethicians deeply interested in the role of the imagination in morals.[18] The claim, basically a Kantian one, is that our understanding of the real is always critically factored through the human imagination. The theological point is that "God" is a metaphor or image we construct in order to orient human life in the world. As McFague puts this, we can use metaphors of God as Friend or the world as the Body of God to orient our action in an age of ecological crises. This imaginary construct is simply the way we organize reality for moral purposes; its truth is determined by its pragmatic value. In an ecological age, we need to imagine God in new ways that will serve the plight of our planet. We see the challenges we face; we need a set of images or metaphors to aid us morally in this task of coping with the real. "The vocation of theology, thus, like reflection in other religious traditions, seeks to serve the human need to find orientation in the world and in life."[19] Metaphorical theological ethics insists on adventure in moral thinking and thus the demand to reconstruct beliefs and values to serve human purposes. It reflects a stance on the facts of modernity that differs from that of narrative ethics.

This kind of theology rests on two important claims. The first claim is that we can restrict the meaning of Christian belief about God to the *functions* certain ideas have in our moral lives. If an idea of God—say, God as Father—does not seem to serve us well in coping with reality, then we simply change the idea. Ideas about God strike no deeper than our ways of talking. The second claim, ironically, is that in fact "God" is not the most basic idea in theology or Christian faith. Because we judge the truth or falsehood of theological constructs by their pragmatic value, the *moral* distinction between good and bad humanly considered is more basic than claims about God. But where does such a value-contrast come from? Critical realism provides the means of judging imaginative constructs, but only in terms of our coping. If this is so, how does this differ from antirealism in ethics? Although this second trend in theological ethics helps us face squarely both the fact that human reality is a social construction and the need to think about the integrity of creation, it seems to provide little help in thinking about the source and status of the value-contrasts basic to any significant world.

These two ways of undertaking theological ethics manifest divergent ways of being "postmodern." And, ironically, each can reinforce the prevailing skepticism by further inscribing it into consciousness. In spite of their realist intent, they suggest that our sense of value is no deeper than our community's conceptual scheme or the metaphoric constructs we develop to further our purposes. We need another way to address these matters. With that in hand, let me now try to draw this chapter to a close by isolating the possibility of hermeneutical realism in theological ethics. This will enable us to connect previous discussions of the problems of pluralism (chap. 1) and power (chap. 2) with the question of how we are to understand ourselves and our world from the theological point of view. Hermeneutical realism is a response to the fact that we must decide how to interpret the world in order to respect and enhance the integrity of life. In part 2 of this book, I will expand this initial account of hermeneutical realism, and then, in part 3, I intend to link it to Christian convictions about the reality, goodness, and otherness of God.

HERMENEUTICAL REALISM AND THEOLOGICAL ETHICS

I have been making a rather complex argument in this chapter. I began with the religious and moral challenge to the integrity of personal and planetary life. We have seen that this challenge is bound up with the fact that we have the power to create social worlds and to move between these worlds. Cyberspace is a forceful symbol of this outlook, and, what is more, it can function to inscribe skepticism in consciousness. The kind of skepticism found in current thought makes power morally basic in a scale of values and threatens to diminish human dignity because of its focus on the activity of encoding the world.

It is crucial to see that I have also uncovered two pictures of human existence that dominate the technological age: the human as maker of worlds, and the human as traveler between worlds. These pictures are also seen in current moral theologies: metaphorical theology insists on the creative imagination; narrative theologians bid us to travel from the wider cultural world to the world of the Christian story. Yet it is not clear if these moral theologies escape moral skepticism. Given this, we can now grasp the task facing theological ethics: to present an account of human existence faithful to the realism of Christian faith and credible to current self-understanding, but one that combats the skepticism of our age.

First, how do we picture theologically the human as creating and traversing worlds? Surprisingly, Christian discourse holds the key in its depiction of humans created in the image of God. Classically, the imago Dei was believed to reside in a faculty of the human—say, in rationality or will. Now we must think of the imago Dei not in terms of reflecting the divine, but in terms of an *activity*, specifically, imitating God.[20] Human beings are not simply mirrors of God as in traditional religious realism, but, rather, manifest the deepest meaning of their lives by imitating the divine through creative action and moral perception. If we can make sense of this picture of human existence, we also will have drawn the connection between *activity* and *persons* basic to accounts of moral value.

In the Genesis story, God's perception of goodness is bound to the act of creation. "And God saw that it was good," as we have it in scripture. This means that the "goodness of the world is not something quite independent of God's seeing it as good. His seeing it as good, loving it, can be conceived not simply as a response to what it is, but as what makes it such."[21] So, too, we must conceive of the human as a creator and interpreter of worlds; we make and respond to goodness. But we only imitate the divine; we are not God. Human seeing does not make the world in the way that God creates. Better yet, there is always a gap in human meaning-making between our cultural acts and the simple facticity of existence. The deepest error of the information age—or of any age—is to imagine that we are more Godlike than we are. In our time this idolatry takes the form of the celebration of power as the origin of value; it aims at reducing or forgetting the gap between the creation of meaning and the recalcitrance of existence. To recall an earlier example, the electronic seducer ultimately cannot escape the passing of the aged woman. The moral project is the imitatio Dei insofar as we, too, create and perceive value. It is not to play God.

So, the first point is that theological ethics provides a symbolism of the human that makes sense of the current experience of creating and traversing worlds. The symbolic connection between the imago Dei and the imitatio Dei curtails the seduction of power implicit in a technological worldview. And it brings us to the second point. How does this position relate to the problem of a moral perception capable of combating skepticism? In order to answer this question, we need to articulate what is implied in the very act of understanding ourselves as moral beings who create and traverse worlds. Specifically, we must grasp the connection between commitment and perception in moral understanding. I will expand on this point in the next chapter; at this juncture we can simply introduce this theme in our reflection.

Recall that in 1 John 4:20 we read this: "Those who do not love a brother or sister whom they have seen, cannot love God whom they have not seen." In theological thinking, one moves from the seen to the unseen, from our actual world of sensibility, relations, events, and action to an apprehension of a depth and transcendence permeating the seen. This movement, this traversing of modalities of reality, is more a matter of wonder and perplexity than one of doubting; it begins with the complexity of our experience of value and seeks to understand the source of that value. But interestingly, perception of this source, of the divine, is tied to a moral project: the one who has not loved cannot see the unseen. As the work of love increases, so does vision, which then reflexively deepens the capacity to love. The nature of such understanding is why the world's great religions link moral discipline to enlightenment, revelation, or mystical knowing: by love and right conduct one is brought to see what is the case, one perceives the depth of the real. In a reflexive movement, this perception fosters and empowers right conduct. This form of understanding the reality of goodness is an insight, a wonder, a new sensibility about the worth and importance of things.

My second point is then that the structure of moral understanding theologically conceived draws a connection between commitment and perception. It does not assume that somehow we just "see" goodness or the source of moral value, the divine, like other forms of sensibility. So a theological ethics is not surprised that values do not appear to us as other things in the world appear. To put it differently, we all live by some faith, some identity-conferring commitment, and this commitment factors in our perception of the world. The answer to skepticism entails a moral commitment that forms the context for the perception needed to apprehend the depth of value in being. And it is precisely by insisting on the *reflexive* relation of perception and commitment that this position diverges from internal and critical realism. Narratives and metaphors shape but do not determine perception; perception can demand radical revision in our conceptual schemes. Hermeneutical realism, as I call it, focuses on commitments and forms of understanding and not on linguistic forms (narrative) or cognitive acts (imaginative construction). And this means that the connection between perception and commitment is more complex in hermeneutical realism than in these rival forms of theological ethics.

This brings me to the third and final point of the present chapter. Granting that we now have a symbolism of the human as creator and traveler of worlds, granting too that the problem of moral perception is bound to commitments and thus is more complex than antirealism or other forms of theological ethics hold, what is the warrant for this position? Am I not simply saying, like moral skeptics, that value depends on what *we* decide to value, on the shape of our commitments? Am I not really just using the resources of the Christian tradition to decode our own acts of meaning-making? How is this theological ethics a form of *moral realism*?

The answer to this question is simpler than one might imagine. In every act of meaning-making, in every act of traversing worlds, some form of existence—whether fictive or actual—is *affirmed* against its negation. This is so because to act at all is to bring something into being against its possible nonbeing and destruction. The ability to sense the goodness of existence is endemic to the very consciousness of being an agent. As far as I can tell, this is as true in cyberspace as in the rest of our lives. Information technologies actually enhance our sense of agency by maximizing our ability to create and communicate. In other words, implicit within the sense of being an agent is an affirmation of being as good. We interpret religious symbols and narratives to bring this fact to articulation against loss, forgetfulness, and corrosion in other cultural forms, and, thereby, reflexively to further the works of love. The connection between being and value we have sought is thus not dependent on our commitments; our commitments are either faithful to this fact at the root of our consciousness of being agents or in conflict with it. The task of the moral life *realistically* conceived is to conform our lives to the real. Theologically stated, it is to imitate the divine, because God simply is the source of value. This is the inner meaning of the human as created in the image of God. But the fact that we affirm the goodness of being in all our actions does not reduce the risk of the moral life. It does not provide practical, moral certainty amid the wonder, perplexity, and even terror of human existence. It is, much more, the challenge of faith to form an abiding commitment to respect and enhance the integrity of life in the use of power.[22]

The challenge of our time is to form a commitment to the perception of the goodness of finite existence, an existence in which we participate as agents but which does not simply conform to our wishes. Information technology seems to be a challenge to the formation of that commitment. But one might also imagine that it could further our moral insight when used to deepen our sensibilities. This deepening would come with the realization that we can now move between worlds and thus in a profound way map the moral texture of reality. Theological ethics provides resources for that very task. And it frees us from the glorification of power as the origin of value. This freedom, I submit, is absolutely necessary if we are to sustain and dignify human life on earth.

CONCLUSION

In this chapter I have tried to present an account of our age and also a picture of the human vis-à-vis the question of moral value. There is a theological reason for this pattern of argument. The purpose of theological ethics is not to prove that goodness exists. God is God. The purpose of theological ethics is to help us see our lives in the light of the divine and to see how this insight directs and invigorates what we ought to be and to do. For we live in a world forgotten in a technological age, but a world that we must dare to see by committing ourselves to the integrity of life.

PART 2 RESPONSIBILITY AND MORAL THEORY

P
art 2 explores issues in moral theory. The chapters set forth an ethics of responsibility that centers on the problems of understanding others and critical self-examination. Specifically, I develop in chapter 6 an account of comparative ethics and responsibility necessary for our age of moral diversity. The issue of critical self-examination, the purview of conscience, is developed in chapter 5 through the idea of radical interpretation. Here the issue is how we are to transvalue and direct our use of power. Chapters 5 and 6 thus return to the connections between power and moral diversity developed in part 1 of the book. These chapters do so by advancing a distinctive ethics of responsibility.

The imperative of responsibility is this: in all actions and relations respect and enhance the integrity of life before God. This imperative is meant to protect the diversity of values isolated in chapter 1, guide our understanding of others, and also serve in our own critical self-evaluation. However, understanding others (chap. 6) and ourselves (chap. 5) presupposes some account of how we understand our lives and our world morally. Given this, part 2 begins with an account of moral meanings. In chapter 4 I try to show how a hermeneutical approach to theological ethics continues deep strands within the Christian tradition but in ways that meet the challenges of the contemporary world. Taken together, the chapters of part 2 explain what I mean by hermeneutical realism and its relation to an ethics of responsibility.

As was true of part 1 of the book, part 2 also undertakes dialectical reflection on the moral life from a Christian perspective. It does so, furthermore, by following the same pattern as that in part 1. We begin in chapter 4 with problems of understanding the meaning of reality, in this case the reality of moral ideas. This discussion is extended in chapter 5 through an examination of the connection between power and value in our own self-understanding. Finally, in chapter 6 we move the discussion, as I did in chapter 3 at the end of part 1, to the question of the good, specifically, the good of understanding others. Taken as a whole, then, the chapters of part 2 are a dialectical engagement with the question of the relations among reality, power, and value in moral responsibility and human understanding.

Part 2 also engages in theological reflection, in terms of both the nature of human understanding (chaps. 4 and 6) and the connection between power and value (chap. 5). However, the theological dimension of the argument in these chapters is not fully developed or defended. Part 3 will turn directly to theological reflection and so complete the path of reflection begun in the first chapter.

4

Understanding
Moral Meanings

In the previous chapter I undertook to examine the impact of postmodernity on moral consciousness. I tried to show how forms of technology can, but need not, help in spreading moral skepticism by shaping our consciousness of ourselves and our world. The task of this chapter builds on the previous discussion while deepening the analysis. More specifically, the aim of this chapter is to make explicit my case for a hermeneutical approach to moral realism in theological ethics.[1] Hermeneutics claims that human beings are self-interpreting animals, and, further, that human life transpires within a space of meaning and distinctions of worth.[2] We are creatures who seek understanding of ourselves and our world, we are beings endowed with self-consciousness, and what we seek to understand most profoundly is the "meaning" of our lives and our world. Given this, for hermeneutics, understanding, consciousness, and meaning are deeply interrelated phenomena of human existence.

Such claims would seem consistent with the deepest impulses of theological ethics. Christian faith conceives of human life within a reality created, sustained, and redeemed by God that manifests the divine goodness and yet maintains that persons also confront the perplexities and choices of life. This means that creation is a domain of meaning and value, but one in which human beings always face the dilemma of their own existence. We exist in a space of value and must also orient our lives. However, noting the formal similarity between a Christian outlook and hermeneutical reflection is not enough to warrant the use of hermeneutics in theological ethics. A theologian must provide distinctly theological reasons for the use of philosophical resources in moral inquiry. A theological ethics, in other words, begins and ends with claims about God; it does not move from moral theory to postulate beliefs about the deity.

In order to make a case for a hermeneutical turn in theological ethics, the present inquiry progresses through interrelated layers of reflection. I begin with the purpose of current hermeneutics. At issue here are matters broadly epistemological: the relation of self and other in postmodern theories of human understanding and meaning. Next, I turn to a core axiological question in moral theory: how to account for the source of value. We will see that the current dispute over realism in moral theory explored in previous chapters is actually the ethical parallel to the relation of self and other in hermeneutics. Finally, I make the turn to anthropological and theological matters. This step in the argument draws the connection between the question of value and the self/other relation with respect to the surprising return of God-talk within postmodern thought. This progression of thought from meaning through value to anthropological and theological claims is itself the journey of hermeneutical inquiry within theological ethics. In this way, the form of the chapter enacts its own most basic claims.

However, I undertake this inquiry not simply to offer a distinctive "method" for ethics. Something more is at stake in developing hermeneutical realism in theological ethics. I am actually trying to rehabilitate a venerable but now much maligned strand in Christian thought. This mode of reflection, evident in thinkers as diverse as Augustine, Calvin, John Wesley, and many others, holds it important to discover *within* the dynamics of self-consciousness the connection between knowledge of self and knowledge of God. The worth of human life and all creation is irreducible in relation to God, and for this strand of Christian faith there is testimony to this worth and relation in every human heart. This is why our reflection pushes toward the connection between claims about individual persons, or anthropological claims, and discourse about God. Making this connection between our existence as moral creatures and the very being of God necessarily entails realism in ethics, because the good is not reducible to what we make; the moral good is found in our relation to God. But this connection, as hermeneutical inquiry insists, means as well that any apprehension of moral goodness and rightness is factored through our own sensibilities and self-understandings. Developing these claims means that consciousness and its forms as well as the whole domain of culture once again become central in ethics.

This signals that theological ethics is not developed solely from the dictates of the Bible or the commands of God. Theological ethics brings to articulation the fact that we always and already exist in relation to God; it provides a hermeneutic of our relation to the divine as this relation bears on the moral life.

A caveat is in order, however. I do not imagine, nor did previous theologians believe, that we simply *find* this testimony of heart. After Nietzsche, Freud, Marx, and other critics, reflection on self does not reveal an obvious connection to God. Theologically stated, the reality of sin is such that a direct move from the human heart to God is not possible. There is no simple way into and yet through the human to the divine or to anything else, for that matter. We must contend with the social, psychological, and historical forces that shape and distort human life. The difficult task for ethics, therefore, is to draw the connection between the social and linguistic power to make meaning and the source of value that constitutes moral consciousness while also recognizing the distortions that infest human life, language, and society.

Providing an analysis of human meaning-making along with isolating distortions in understanding and culture is the role hermeneutics must play in ethics. Theological reflection transforms hermeneutical inquiry. It presents the radical claim that at the core of moral self-awareness we are enlivened from a higher source, we contend with powers not our own, we owe our existence to something other than ourselves worthy of reverence, awe, trust, and, perhaps, love. But this insight and grace is only apprehended *within* our all too human acts of meaning-making, our struggles as individuals and communities to make cogent sense of the value and tragedy of our lives and our world. The aim of the remainder of this chapter is to defend these claims.

PRACTICAL PHILOSOPHY AND REFLEXIVE THINKING

Over the last two centuries there has been a widespread debate in the West about how to picture the human being. This debate is manifest in art and literature, competing political ideologies, disputes between atheistic and religious existentialists, and, recently, the question of the "postmodern" and the place of tradition in the moral life. The nub of the matter can be put thus: are human beings creators of meaning, or, conversely, do we always struggle to discover the meaning of our lot and life? As seen in other chapters, the stakes in this dispute are high. If we create meaning, then, while we are alone in a morally vacant universe, we at least have the power to fashion a world we desire. We are trapped only by prisons of our own making—prisons called cultures. This is the argument, we now know, of skeptics in ethics. Conversely, if we discover morality, we inhabit a world permeated with value. This world confronts us with difficult and even tragic choices between goods. Yet, we are primordially at home in the world. This is the claim of traditional moral realism. This dispute about human worth burns in contemporary culture; it is a clash about how we exist in a morally meaningful world. Philosophical hermeneutics purports to offer a way beyond this ongoing cultural battle. In order to see this, we need a clearer grasp of hermeneutical inquiry.

In the ancient world, hermeneutics was the art of interpretation, especially the interpretation of written texts. From the Greek god Hermes, the messenger, the interpreter traverses boundaries bearing the meaning of encoded messages. The interpreter carries meanings from one realm (the text) to the world of human life, traversing the ambiguous and wily realm of images—that is, symbols, metaphors, discourses, and narratives. Yet this would in fact seem to be true of all human life and not simply of the act of reading texts. In every act of understanding, we are in some profound way crossing experiential, linguistic, cultural, or psychic boundaries bearing messages. Seeing this point has meant that, over the last two centuries, hermeneutics widened in scope to encompass inquiry into historical and linguistic consciousness and the entire domain of meaning.

There is something of grave importance in the expansion of hermeneutics beyond textual interpretation into a philosophy of understanding and human existence. Contemporary hermeneutics holds, in Paul Ricoeur's words, that we invent in order to discover; we exert creative energy in making meanings so as to apprehend the character of our existence and our world.[3] Human beings make moral, religious, cultural, scientific, and poetic meanings in order to grasp the truth of their world and lives. This picture of human beings as meaning-makers seeking to discover the truth of their existence is the route hermeneutics takes beyond the clash between construing the human as simply creating or merely discovering values.

Hermeneutical inquiry develops its claim about human existence in a distinctive way. In my opinion, it connects insights from classical practical philosophy with those of reflexive thinking found in ancient and modern thought. As a form of reflexive thinking, hermeneutics explicates the truth of consciousness becoming aware of itself; we are *self*-interpreting animals. As a type of practical philosophy, hermeneutics insists that understanding and meaning are bound to action and practice. Yet my insistence on this connection between practical and reflexive philosophy in hermeneutics is a much-disputed point. I must, therefore, clarify it in order to specify the purpose of this form of philosophy.

Human beings exist knowingly in their world. Given this, one can easily distinguish different forms of human knowing. First, empirical knowledge is rooted in our capacity for perception: we sense, (see, hear, feel, taste, smell) "things." I know things by encountering them in a sensible way, such as the scent of newly mown grass outside my window. One validates empirical claims by testing them—that is, by seeing (sensing) what is the case. I stand and gaze out the window at my neighbor mowing his lawn. Second, theoretical knowledge is the capacity to think in terms of concepts that designate some shared nature among perceptible or logical things. I have the idea of "roses"; I always smell a particular flower. We can also develop theories or models about things. Botany entails theories of life. One might also develop a theory of pure ideas—say, about unicorns or ideal numbers. The truth of a theory is its capacity to systematize and clarify phenomena as well as its logical coherence. The question is, then, do perception and conception provide a complete picture of the way we exist knowingly in the world? If so, we must either discover truth experientially or invent conceptual schemes to endow our world with intelligibility.

Hermeneutics insists that human understanding is not reducible to perception or conception and their forms of truth. The object of understanding—that is, "meaning"—is neither perceived as a "thing" nor grasped only as an idea. I do not sense the meaning of a text; the meaning of an embrace is not exhausted by our concept "embrace." Meaning is also not defined solely in terms of the ability to learn how to use certain words in a coherent and grammatically consistent way. To be sure, a moral idea, such as justice, is grasped in this way. All of us must learn to speak a moral language and to speak it cogently; we must know how to use the word "justice" in order to communicate with others. Moral reason is always dependent on some community and its moral discourse. Yet this obvious fact does not exhaust an account of "meaning."

The hermeneutical definition of "meaning" is not limited to cognitive or empirical "sense" and how this "sense" is culturally learned. Meaning as the object of understanding is the *connecting* of general thought and particular experience within a shared discourse; linguistically, it mediates concepts and images (symbols, metaphors, etc.). For instance, I understand the meaning of an embrace by connecting in my very being a distinct sensible experience with an entire set of ideas and beliefs held by my community about human interaction. The embrace's meaning is this event of connection. Linguistically, the event character of meaning is found most basically in the connecting of subject and predicate in a sentence. The meaning of the sentence is the *event* of connecting an idea (e.g., justice) and experience (our present social life); the event is not reducible to perception or conception. Language is the power to present or articulate this connective space, to manifest meaning. It is not simply a system of signs to depict the world and ourselves, a mirror of perceptions, or a storehouse of concepts. Language makes things manifest and thus helps to form life; it is expressive power. As Ricoeur puts this about texts, we are interested in the "world in front of the text" as a disclosure of a possible way of life.[4] That "world" is not sensed or reducible to a concept; the text presents something rather than merely depicting the world. Thus, most profoundly, meaning designates a space of significance and import in which human existence can knowingly transpire and in which we must orient ourselves.

For example, in one of Jesus' parables I do not "sense" the reign of God as a mustard seed; the parable also does not purport to offer a concept for that reality. By presenting possibilities for life, the text discloses human freedom and God's grace. And freedom—let alone grace—is not a sensible thing or an "idea." Freedom is the inner meaning of our being agents; it is how we exist knowingly as agents in the space called the "world." One can also speak of the "life-world," which is the domain of meaning manifest not in discourse but in a culture and its specific institutions and practices. The life-world is not a thing or a concept; it is a space within which agents must orient themselves. Meaning (life-world, or textual world) comes to presentation through some medium of communication, through some actual, natural language. And since we are partially constituted by our self-understandings, the language used to articulate this space of worth, our "world," helps to constitute that world and us. So, "meaning" has evaluative and cognitive components—it includes import *and* significance—because it concerns how we reflectively orient ourselves in some real or imaginary space of distinctions of worth (i.e., a world). It connects conditions of existence (e.g., freedom) and a unique situation of life. "Meanings" are synthetic or connective *events*: perceptible thing, image, idea, and the one thinking and perceiving are related in an event of import and significance that defines a space of life in which we must practically orient ourselves.

This is why, as Hans-Georg Gadamer notes, hermeneutics is heir to classical practical philosophy.[5] The understanding of "meaning" is practical, and not just empirical or theoretical, because it always involves trying to grasp the import of what is other than oneself for the sake of guiding further action in a shared space of life. This point is sometimes put rather cryptically by theorists: understanding is dialogical. Understanding involves an interaction through language between oneself and another in a mutually constituted arena of "reading" some message. As Charles Taylor has recently said, we exist in a moral space—a space defined by questions about how we will orient ourselves in the world and how rightly to live.[6] Our "world," the moral space of life, necessarily resonates with the kinds of persons we are, and thus we cannot know the world without acknowledging our deeply personal apprehension of it. The validation of an interpretation of moral matters is an ongoing process, always open to counterargument, and is less strict than "scientific" verification. As Aristotle knew, in the domain of practical reason we ought not to expect the same degree of precision—the same form of truth—as in empirical and theoretical sciences.

Hermeneutical inquiry examines within the act of interpretation the relation between understanding and meaning that constitutes consciousness of self, world, and other. The complexity of this point, we now see, is to realize that one of the media of communication is our historically and linguistically—i.e., culturally—funded experience, our own consciousness. Hermeneutical inquiry must then interpret the interpreter as an encoded cultural message. And this is what I mean by insisting that hermeneutics is heir to reflexive thinking. Stretching from Plato and Augustine to twentieth-century thinkers such as Martin Heidegger, Karl Rahner, Paul Tillich, H. Richard Niebuhr, Iris Murdoch, Paul Ricoeur, and Charles Taylor (to name but a few), reflexive philosophy explicates self-awareness with respect to the various media in which it appears (language, art, cultural forms, gestures, etc.). What this means is actually quite simple.

Consider some rather ordinary human activities. We can reflect on things and other people. We can, for instance, ponder and wonder about the meaning of a loved one's embrace. But more than this, we can also reflect on our acts of reflection—we can wonder about our wondering. In doing so, we reach a new level of self-awareness and consciousness. We grasp ourselves in our most basic actions of feeling, thinking, willing, and valuing. As H. Richard Niebuhr put this, "It is only by looking within and catching as it were the reflection of ourselves in act that we are able to achieve some degree of critical self-awareness."[7] Reflexive thinking aims at this kind of self-knowledge. And hermeneutical philosophy holds that the most basic human act we must explore in order to reach valid self-awareness is the act of understanding a world of meanings. In understanding, knowing and valuing interact for the sake of orienting human life; exploring the act of understanding is then the crucial clue for grasping our distinctively human way of existing in the world.

Critics of this line of thought contend that reflexive inquiry into human understanding means that the self is trapped within itself in an endless circle of self-reflection. Yet reflexive thinkers hold that when undertaken honestly and with rigor, such inquiry demonstrates that in trying to understand oneself, one also grasps a relation to what is other than self but inscribed in the self. This inscription of other in the self is found most obviously in historical consciousness. The past impresses itself on current awareness. To know oneself requires knowing the past that has funded experience. Traces of my parents, my cultural history, the long stretch of the Christian witness throughout the ages, and social patterns have all etched themselves, as Hans-Georg Gadamer puts it, into my effective historical consciousness. But, more radically, there may be an inscription of other persons, the good, or even God in the self that appears precisely as a prethematic, inarticulate openness to the world. In the act of understanding, I am always trying to apprehend what is not myself in relation to myself.

This radical reflexive kind of inquiry into self/other began in Christian thought with St. Augustine's claim that in reflecting on his thinking, feeling, and willing, he was directed beyond himself to God, a direction manifested prereflectively in his spiritual restlessness and desire for peace. Modern theologians in this tradition have struggled to make the same point against the critics of religion. As Søren Kierkegaard put it, when the self relates itself to itself it also has a relation to the power that establishes the self. This power is God. And Friedrich Schleiermacher, father of modern hermeneutics, says that the feeling of immediate self-consciousness is also a feeling of absolute dependence on a "whence," the divine. Still other thinkers could be noted. The claim is the same. In coming to self-awareness, the self in its most basic activities is a testimony to itself and to another. The human *is* an act of self-transcendence to its other; this defines the self as primordially in a world, a shared space of distinctions of worth. Reflexive thinkers differ over what is taken as the most basic activity of the self. Kierkegaard, for instance, sees this in the self-relation found in decision and choice; Schleiermacher finds immediate self-consciousness in the feeling (*Gefühl*) of absolute dependence on God; others, such as Descartes, take the basic act to be thinking. I argue that the basic action is found in our consciousness of being agents, our sense of releasing and undergoing power. Yet the basic point remains: the self is an act of self-transcendence.

The claim of reflexive thinking about the connection of self/other has been challenged in the postmodern world. Its denial might even define postmodernity. This is because "postmodern" thinkers no longer hold, as the ancients did, that our relation to the good is objective to the self. The postmodern claim is that the self directed inward is not directed beyond itself (to God or to the idea of the good) or another *in* the self, but to cultural practices, to the "nature" in which it participates (Nietzsche), to the chaos and energy of the unconscious (Freud), or to a system of signs productive of meaning (Derrida). This is why, as noted above, there is no easy way into and yet through the human to the divine. For many thinkers, self-reflection never seems to escape the inner-worldly and inner-psychic forces undergirding the self and its actions. Language seems to express, depict, or conceal only our meaning-making power. These are the deep roots of the forms of anti-realism and constructivism in ethics that I charted in previous chapters.

This insight brings us to a root issue in current thought and one step closer to hermeneutical realism. The deepest impulse in postmodern hermeneutics is to respond to these criticisms of reflexive thinking by reclaiming the "other" in relation to the understanding self. Contemporary theorists insist that human consciousness, informed as it is by language, cultural life, and the natural conditions of existence, is the inescapable *medium* through which we apprehend the meaning of our world and ourselves. Yet while this is true, the question becomes whether our desires, aspirations, and understandings are utterly self-referential in terms of their *meaning* or content. Is consciousness open to and defined by its relation to an "other"? Hermeneutical philosophy, in the strict sense in which I intend the term, is that mode of inquiry fundamentally committed to answering this question in the affirmative.

The self/other relation is developed in hermeneutics with respect to the dynamics of understanding, language, and meaning. Now we can see why this is the case. "Meaning" is the self-transcendence of the linguistic code. To understand something as meaningful is to grasp how some medium of communication (paradigmatically, language) intends what is other than itself and to understand oneself *in* that space of otherness. To recall an example, a parable of Jesus discloses the reign of God and calls for a response from the hearer. Or, when I embrace my parents, I intend not simply a physical act but, much more, an expression of love and thereby signal my abiding care for them. We live in a space of affection. But this fact actually raises anew the question formulated earlier. In what does the value of human beings consist? Does our worth consist of our capacity to recognize, wonder about, and respond to a world beyond us manifest in discourse, or is human value rooted in our power to create the meanings our linguistic practices express? In facing this question, hermeneutical inquiry must connect self/other with the question of value. This brings us to the second, axiological layer of our inquiry.

MORAL MEANING: CREATED OR DISCOVERED?

The problem contemporary hermeneutics seeks to address about self/other finds expression in the debates about "moral realism" charted in previous chapters of this book. We can further our reflection, then, by continuing to explore this debate in order to see what moral reflection contributes to a hermeneutical theory of meaning and understanding. Surprisingly enough, this contribution centers on the question of the *value* of power. Insofar as this is the case, it will mean that there is a moral dimension to all acts of human understanding, and, accordingly, that ethics must take seriously the character of human understanding even as hermeneutics will be seen as part of ethics. So, let us return to the debate over moral realism.

As shown in previous chapters, moral realism is the claim, or a theory developed to sustain the claim, that moral ideas and beliefs have truth value; they can be true or false.[8] A moral realist believes that in some final and irreducible way we discover the good: it is not *only* a human invention. Morality is not *only* a matter of group consensus, personal preference, or calculations of social utility. It dips into the nature of things. The morally good and right life is a matter of conforming one's existence to the real. Clarity of thought and veracity of moral perception are crucial to the moral life. Moral discourse strives to be faithful to something beyond itself. The enemies of human goodness are illusion, deception, and the willful revolt from conformity to the real.

Strict moral realism takes two forms in Christian ethics: divine command ethics and natural law ethics. Traditionally, divine command ethics holds that what God commands is morally right and thus the moral life is about obedience to those commands. In this century, theologians like Karl Barth and even some philosophers have tried to rehabilitate divine command ethics. Yet as we will see later in this book, problems continue to dog this form of moral theory. Assuming that God does command people, on what grounds ought we to believe that they rightly hear—perceive—those commands? Can we be sure that what authorities claim to be divine commands are not simply the means for the legitimation of their own power by appeal to the "reality" of God's will? Further, in order to think that God's commands must be obeyed, one must have some idea of what is worthy of human worship. How are we to account for that scale of values that itself is not a divine command? One cannot avoid the problem of interpretation unless one wants to reduce divine commands and the source of value to consciousness itself, or to hold that the command is as obvious as other perceptible things in the world. Both answers are unacceptable to divine command ethics.

Traditional Roman Catholic natural law ethics faces similar problems. Natural law classically linked an account of human reason with a claim about how nature indicates directions for action. This requires that one discern the nature of the being in question and then derive from that nature some claim about what ought to be done. For example, human beings are social animals, and, accordingly, the demands of social life are morally necessary. We can make the transition from *is* to *ought* because human reason participates in the divine mind (what Thomas Aquinas calls eternal law) governing the world. This participation (natural law) is known not through perception—as divine command theory has it—but because consciousness bears within the precepts of the moral law. Not only are these claims about human reason difficult to sustain, but, once again, problems of interpretation abound. How are we to understand the meaning of moral precepts in specific cases? How is it that we can know the ends and purposes nature indicates? Once we grant that human understanding is historically and socially embedded, what becomes of the claim of traditional natural law ethics to articulate universal precepts? And, just as for divine command ethics, must we not raise some suspicion about the use of the discourse of natural law to legitimate its claims by appeal to the "real"?

Revisions have been made in moral realism in order to take seriously the dynamics of historical understanding. A thinker can be a realist about a community's whole cognitive scheme, since it is this scheme, and not specific ideas or experiences, that is about the world. Internal realism, as I called it before, holds that people with different moral languages live in different moral worlds.[9] This follows from the fact that to understand any specific moral concept (say, justice) requires facility with the entire set of cultural beliefs about reality in which that concept makes sense. For this kind of realism, moral reason is blind without some framework within which to understand and articulate our lives. One insists on realism in ethics with respect to an entire set of moral beliefs.

Narrative theologians like Stanley Hauerwas, John Howard Yoder, and James McClendon hold this kind of modified realism.[10] As I have argued before, narrative ethicists insist that Christian moral identity and understanding of the world are functions of the Christian narrative. And this means that Christian beliefs are not definable in the terms of other forms of moral understanding. This saves Christian moral meanings from being reduced to claims about natural morality or the moral beliefs of the wider public. The truth of Christian moral claims can only be established internal to those beliefs; one cannot refer to the world "out there" or to natural moral reason to validate or to refute Christian moral beliefs. Those beliefs are validated with respect to communities whose lives and "worlds" they help to constitute.

Other theologians use existential and phenomenological methods to modify moral realism. Paul Tillich, for instance, argued for what he called "self-transcending realism." On this account, human reason truly apprehends reality only when it is grasped by the real in our own experience.[11] More recently, Thomas Ogletree has drawn on the work of the Jewish philosopher Emmanuel Levinas to center his ethics on the experience of the claim of other.[12] The other is not reducible to a conceptual scheme; we encounter the other in the sheer fact of his or her existence. The Roman Catholic moral theologian Josef Fuchs specifies the experience of obligation in conscience as definitive for the meaning of being a person.[13] These forms of modified realism ground morality in experience or self-understanding, rather than, as internal realists argue, the coherence and comprehensiveness of evolving moral traditions.

The difficulty with these various positions for hermeneutical ethics is that they can devolve into defining moral meanings in terms of perception or conception. The narrative theologian thinks that experience is the product of the stories we tell, our conceptual scheme. Some thinkers who insist on encounters with "the other" as morally basic believe that the other breaks through our systems of ideas. It is simply a brute fact. In each case, what is threatened with loss is the self-referential structure of the act of understanding meanings. The lost role subjectivity plays in valuing has fueled antirealism in ethics.

Antirealists hold that values are not ontologically grounded; morality is what we invent, not what we discover. As J. L. Mackie has put it, "Values are not objective, are not part of the fabric of the world."[14] Morality strikes no deeper than social convention and rules of convenience aimed at social cohesion. Moral goodness and moral obligation are functions of how we (whoever this "we" is) choose to think about them. Whereas people often believe that their moral values are part of the fabric of the world, the "world" is actually a function of language, culture, and social practices. Stripped of that discourse, we would not have any way of knowing what reality is and we would not have any idea of who "we" are as persons and communities. Communities and traditions see and experience the world differently because of their moral outlooks, and so we ought to explore those outlooks rather than try to peer through them to "reality."

Some contemporary theologians talk as if they were antirealists. They do so in order to further the cause of human freedom. The feminist ethicist Sharon Welch, for instance, argues that moral claims have no status beyond the linguistic and power relations of communities.[15] The concern is to expose the pretense to universality in all realistic forms of Christian ethics. A commitment to a feminist ethics of risk is grounded in nothing other than the sheer choice so to commit oneself. Yet while thinkers like Welch talk as antirealists, they have merely rejected traditional realism. Were this not the case, these thinkers would hold that not only our words about "God" but also the divine—or sacred—are human inventions. Yet Welch speaks of the power of relation as divine; others realize that the divine is transcendent, not reducible to the ongoing life of the community. Insofar as this is the case, few theologians are actually antirealists.

Other theologians insist on the constructed character of all belief systems but temper antirealism. They argue that human beings are always making meanings, but that we construct them for the purpose of coping with a world we confront. Gordon Kaufman, for one, contends that theology is an act of imaginative construction whereby the theologian formulates an image/concept of "God" in order to relativize human pretense and to orient human action for the purpose of humanizing the world.[16] The fact that God is an "image/concept" shows that Kaufman does not believe that the word "God" is reducible to an object of perception—in which case we could provide a sensible image for the divine (God is "mother," for example)—or a conception, such as, say, that God is "Being Itself." Kaufman is interested in how the theologian's construct *functions* to guide *meaningful* action. Moral reflection must take account of reality as we best know it. In recent work, Kaufman seeks to provide a theistic construct to account for the surprising creativity of the universe. Values might not be written into the fabric of the world, but morality must account for the world as we find it.

Christian feminist ethicists often speak in this way. Sallie McFague and Lisa Sowle Cahill draw on different sides of the Western Christian tradition (Protestant and Roman Catholic, respectively).[17] Each of these thinkers has modified the moral claims of her tradition (sovereignty of God; natural law ethics) in the direction of acknowledging the historical and shifting shape of moral discourse. McFague explores the roles of metaphors and models in theological discourse; Cahill is attentive to the variety of sources in moral theology. Yet each also insists that moral meanings are not invented: they are developed in response to a world in which we exist and which we must respect and enhance. We test moral and theological claims, Cahill and McFague argue, by the capacity of these claims to orient life. In moral reflection we do not discover or discern anything *morally* about the world, rather we try to orient ourselves in the world.

The debate in ethics about moral meaning ranges from positions holding that it is discovered to those insisting on human creativity. The realist holds to a basic otherness in moral consciousness not reducible to human creativity. Moral discourse and good people strive to be faithful to something beyond themselves. Antirealists ground human dignity in the power to create value; moral discourse manifests our response to our condition. For hermeneutics, problems arise in these moral theories because they define moral knowing in terms of perception or conception, try to bypass consciousness, or reduce the origin of value to the media of understanding (i.e., language). However, this debate in moral theory exposes the axiological dimension to the self/other question. And it exposes it in terms of power—the power to create or discover meanings. The question of realism at root is whether the human power to create meanings is morally basic or if there is some reality that thwarts human power. This poses a basic moral question: is the capacity to respond to, influence, and create reality—that is, power—alone constitutive of value? How, if at all, does hermeneutics deal with this basic question? This brings us to the third and final layer of our inquiry, and, surprisingly, the reality of God in current hermeneutics.

HERMENEUTICS AND THEOLOGICAL ETHICS

A hermeneutical approach to theological ethics must acknowledge that Christian faith entails some form of moral realism, because the source of morality (God) is not reducible to consensus, preferences, social utility, or the imagination. Christian consciousness, maybe all theistic consciousness, is defined by an irreducible otherness at the heart of self-understanding. One should expect traces, signs, of this otherness in the dynamics of consciousness. Theologically the problem is to show that these traces and signs testify to the God of all reality. But showing this means that we need an approach to ethics that takes seriously the self/other constitution of consciousness while acknowledging the mediation of all meaning and value through historical and linguistic understanding. If we can develop this approach in moral theory, we could call it hermeneutical realism.[18]

In order to outline this hermeneutical realist position we must return to basic anthropological matters and link them to ones about language and meaning. Recall that the basic claim of hermeneutics is that to be a human agent is to exist understandingly in a space of significance and import and thus one of distinctions of worth. The human agent exists in a moral universe—a culture—manifest in the apprehension of meanings. Language, as noted before, is not simply a tool we invent or learn to use for certain purposes, although it is also this. "What comes about through the development of language in the broadest sense is the coming to be of expressive power, the power to make things manifest. . . . What is made manifest is not exclusively, or even mainly, a self, but a world."[19] For ethics, this claim about language means that every moral tradition presents what I called in chapter 2 an axiology of power—i.e., some evaluation of power with respect to human life in the world—insofar as its moral discourse presents a background of possibilities and values within which to orient life. What, then, are we to make of the insight that meaning rests on expressive power? Does this show, as critics hold, that a hermeneutical theory of meaning is actually a form of moral antirealism, and, thus, is incompatible with the deepest impulses of theological ethics?

The relation of language and power warrants a *critical* stance toward claims to meaning; it requires an eye for the distortions that infest all human meaning-making. Specifically, it demands attention to how the worth of persons and the world can be defined exclusively by what or who exercises power in the making or ranking of values. In fact, it is exactly this concern to counter the reduction of value to power that is the reason for insistence on the "other" in so much contemporary thought. The "other" is taken to be the manifestation of a value beyond the range of subjective and linguistic power, whether that "other" is the past, a human face and its moral appeal, or the divine. This manifestation indicates that respect for others is basic to a meaningful human world; it founds the world morally. The will-to-power even in the form of meaning-creation is not the basic truth of life. And it is the desire to avoid the reduction of the other to the same that is the reason to insist on a hermeneutical account of "meaning," and, also, to continue and yet revise the tradition of reflexive philosophy. If it can be shown that the self/other relation is constitutive of consciousness and that language intends something beyond itself as a semiotic code, then the "other" cannot be reduced to our meaning-making power.

It is in this context of thinking about power/value in relation to self/other that we find the surprising return of God-talk in postmodern hermeneutics. God is the limiting case of otherness manifested *meaningfully* in language. The reality of God is affirmed by some hermeneutical philosophers in order to endorse the value of the world on grounds other than strict utility. Other thinkers insist that the being of God is manifest in the non-instrumental worth of others. Charles Taylor argues, for instance, that our perception of value is not devoid of our own creative meaning-making, but he also seeks something with which to thwart the triumph of power. "Put in other terms," he writes, "the world's being good may now be seen as not entirely independent of our seeing it and showing it as good, as least as far as the world of the human is concerned."[20] In this Taylor finds an analogy to divine *agape*, a seeing good that also helps effect what it sees. Otherwise the world is devoid of value, a simple object to be used as we wish. Other philosophers, notably Paul Ricoeur, argue that the self is constituted through its encounter with the "other."[21] Meaningful identity, the endowing of self with import and significance, transpires within our encounters with what is not self and also not reducible to our construals of life. For Ricoeur, the many ways of naming God in Christian faith are symbolic articulations of a primary affirmation of being against its negation. This affirmation is also manifest in the claim of the other not to be violated. Theological discourse provides the linguistic means of talking about the manifestation of worth not reducible to human power.

What are we to make of this return in postmodern hermeneutics to the classic, reflexive claim that self-consciousness is constituted by its other, even a divine other? Does this warrant the use of philosophical hermeneutics in theological ethics, or is it, once again, simply a God of the philosopher? Can a theologian accept what appears to be an anthropocentric endorsement of God for the purpose of backing human values? I have been arguing that hermeneutics enables us to examine the domain of meaning and human understanding in ways consonant with deep impulses in Christian thought. It pictures the human existing in a space of value that finds expression in human consciousness. Yet properly speaking, a theologian ought to demand theological reasons for the use of a philosophical position. Claims about God must come first in theological ethics, to preserve the freedom and integrity of theological reflection. So we must ask: are there theological reasons for endorsing the religious turn in hermeneutics?

Christian faith, as I showed in chapter 2, is an axiology of power. The diverse ways of naming God in Christian thought—from sovereign lord to suffering servant—manifest the divine being as value-creating power, but a power that respects and enhances finite reality as its other. To use traditional language, Christians trust that in God power and wisdom are ultimately one. The symbol "God" as the way Christians speak about ultimate reality presents a claim for the transvaluation of power in understanding self, world, and others by connecting the idea of ultimate power with an endorsement of finite worth. This "transvaluation" is the radical overturning of how power is valued in the creation of a meaningful world.[22] To believe that God creates, redeems, judges, and sustains the world is to insist that power is indeed axiologically basic to but not exhaustive of value. Religiously and morally, this means that one's faith, one's identity-conferring commitment, affirms that the ultimate power of reality is good. It means that God is love. Yet that faith also dethrones the works of sheer power as the substance of all value. A theological construal of the world thus demarcates a space of action—a world—defined by this affirmation and also by the dethronement of power. Such an outlook on the meaning of existence warrants a critical stance in ethics; it demands attention to the deceptions of power in all human activities. Yet this also signals that theologians must make the radical claim that the being of God is the ground of moral meaning. Can this claim be made?

Insofar as meaning is the manifestation of a world of significance and import expressed through but not reducible to the power of language, then the transvaluation of power—what Christians mean morally by their God-talk—is basic to an understanding of meaning and the human world. The power of language to manifest a world is seen theologically as a sign or trace of the divine. Language testifies to the being of God insofar as persons create a meaningful world through understandable discursive acts, but a world whose meaning is not reducible to that act of human power. Language and human understanding are signs of the transvaluation of power that Christians believe defines the reality of God. And insofar as language helps to constitute our self-understanding, consciousness shaped by this radical claim of Christian discourse about the divine apprehends the worth of reality enlivened by a higher source. Christian consciousness senses that we owe the meaning of our existence to something other than our power yet discoverable within our acts of meaning-making. The moral space of life from this perspective has its condition beyond itself even as it also bears the marks—tragically, comically—of human struggles with power and meaning. At issue morally is how we—we who wield and suffer power in the search for meaning—will orient ourselves in a world whose very condition entails the transvaluation of power. This transvaluation of power is bound to Christian conceptions of God, as I argued in chapter 2, and it is also, as we will see in the next chapter, basic to moral self-understanding. At this juncture, we can say that the moral requirement is that we transvalue our power to act in order to respect and enhance the integrity of life.

It is not possible in this chapter to trace the practical implications of these admittedly radical claims, nor even to elaborate them further. It is also not necessary to do so. My purpose has been to give the theological reason why hermeneutical inquiry is an important resource for theologians. The reason is that God is the source of moral meaning and so we ought to find some testimony to or denial of this in all apprehensions of meaning. Current hermeneutics and moral theory, I have shown, can be seen as addressing the question of the relation of human power to the source of value and thus posing the question of God as it is presented in Christian thought. Theologians have the symbolic resources needed to think and speak ethically about the connection of power and value. A hermeneutical form of theological ethics articulates and analyzes our self-understanding as agents and shows that in all meaning-making actions, all works of power, the divine is also encountered. This encounter with otherness can, may, and must transvalue how one understands and exercises power.

CONCLUSION

The purpose of this chapter has been to outline the possibility and also the importance of a hermeneutical approach to theological ethics. My deepest concern is to show *within* the dynamics of understanding—thus, meaning and language—the connection between knowledge of self and the source of value, the divine. The loss of this form of thinking, I believe, would herald the triumph of power and technical reason over all values. It would condemn Christians to an insufferable silence about their most basic convictions concerning human life and the divine. Thus, we have drawn on hermeneutics as an aid to articulating and analyzing the testimony to the divine within our moral meanings, and in so doing, we have found the theological reason for the use of hermeneutics in ethics. And yet, a question remains to be pursued. How ought we to articulate the connection between understanding and moral responsibility? The following chapters are dedicated to answering this question.

5

Radical
Interpretation
and Moral
Responsibility

Questions about responsibility are at the heart of most contemporary moral and political debates.[1] We ask, for instance, about who is responsible for decisions in medical care and the termination of treatments. Then again, there are debates that surround the responsible use of deadly force against aggression and oppression, or about the morality of intervention into the affairs of other nations in order to relieve human suffering. All of these pressing moral and political questions, and many others as well, hinge on the idea of responsibility. The idea of responsibility provides the means of articulating the moral demands on the exercise of power by moral agents. More specifically, responsibility is one of a select group of ideas in our moral discourse used to interrelate an analysis of the nature of moral agents with a theory of moral norms. In an age marked by the radical extension of human power through technology and also increased awareness of moral diversity, it is not surprising that the idea of responsibility should be so central to moral reflection and debate.

MATTERS OF RESPONSIBILITY

In this chapter I propose to explore contributions to the theory of responsibility open to theological reflection in ethics. Specifically, I want to draw the connection between moral responsibility and the dynamics of moral understanding and consciousness explored in the previous chapter. I will undertake this admittedly complex inquiry by examining the recent work of Charles Taylor on the question of moral self-understanding and Hans Jonas's well-known proposal for an ethics of responsibility in a technological age. My intention is to use this examination to develop a constructive proposal of my own for theological ethics, but I shall also be criticizing the accounts given by Taylor and Jonas. This inquiry will help us understand two important things: how care and respect are related in the moral life, and the way in which they are to be related through a distinctive practice of moral consciousness that I call the act of radical interpretation. Radical interpretation, in my opinion, is morally basic because it reforms consciousness, converts heart and mind, by relating care and respect for others and self. To use traditional language, radical interpretation is a hermeneutical account of conscience, and, thus, the struggle to become morally better. I argue that a genuinely radical interpretation of our moral lives, an examination of conscience, implicitly or explicitly entails theological claims—a point, we will see, confirmed by the works of Taylor and Jonas. Thus, what I am attempting, finally, is a theological account of responsible moral existence that can make better sense of our intuitions about responsibility than important philosophical positions have done.

My argument runs counter to three prevalent assumptions in much of contemporary ethics. I want to note these assumptions at the outset in order to highlight features of my argument. The first assumption is that we cannot and indeed must not attempt to articulate a substantive theory of the nature of moral agents. This is the case, some postmodern thinkers hold, either because forms of human life are so diverse as to disallow such an undertaking, or because any such theory might exclude from moral consideration those who do not understand themselves explicitly in terms of the theory. The theologian Stanley Hauerwas, for instance, contends that Christians ought not to compromise their distinctive understanding of life by redescribing it in general philosophical terms. Other thinkers, such as Jürgen Habermas and Seyla Benhabib, worry about the tyrannous and exclusivistic ends to which any substantive notion of the nature of moral agents might be put. In other words, a substantive account of moral identity risks endorsing policies of conformity.

The question of how to speak about moral agents divides much of contemporary ethics. Some thinkers, again Habermas and Benhabib, who hold the first prevalent assumption—call them liberal postmoderns—prescind from any discussion of moral identity in ethics in order to focus on the morality of acts rather than what kinds of persons we ought to be, or they concentrate on legitimating procedural norms of justice. Communitarian ethicists like Hauerwas and Alasdair MacIntyre—thinkers who can be called traditionalist postmoderns—are satisfied with explicating the beliefs about human existence and moral virtue found in their specific moral community. In distinction, I hold that what is common to moral agents is an act of self-interpretation that is basic to being responsible for ourselves. Human understanding is reflexive and practical, as I argued in the preceding chapter. Against the critics, my argument turns on what must be affirmed in order to pursue any conceivable way of life with a sense of moral identity and also care and respect for ourselves and others. I do not believe that this argument is open to the criticisms usually leveled against claims about the nature of moral agents. I take as given that human beings can reflect on their lives, realizing the diversity of ways of doing so, and then try to see this reflection as itself basic to what it means to be a person. This makes the question of what defines moral understanding central to a theory of responsibility.

The second prominent assumption I contest is that the norms of responsibility can be specified solely in terms of social practices of praise and blame. On this antirealist reading, questions about responsibility strike no deeper than our given social practices and institutions. These practices have no warrant or purpose beyond the demands of given social and institutional life. As a result, questions about how one construes the world as the context for human life and action need not arise in ethics. If the first assumption I am contesting forecloses inquiry into the nature of agents, this argument equally delimits moral inquiry with respect to how we understand the context of human life.

I am not denying the social character of responsibility. Yet I do contend that any adequate ethics of responsibility must entail claims about reality and our place in it. Responsibility is a complex idea we use to make sense of our lives and our world; it entails metaphysical and ontological claims. In fact, I want to show that interpreting life from a theological perspective affords us the insight that all human beings are members of a moral community wider than actual social practices and institutions. One can speak about this community in a variety of ways—for instance, as a kingdom of ends, the reign of God, or the community of being. The point, I take it, is to specify how the scope of the moral community exceeds those of local communities with their distinctive practices of praise and blame. In terms of my argument this means that the norms of responsibility and the moral worth of others and ourselves are defined in relation to the divine and not solely by more proximate relations and communities.

Third, my argument cuts against the prevailing attitude that moral discourse is free from theological claims, and also that Christian ethics is an utterly distinctive moral outlook rooted in a special community and thus ought not to trouble itself with debates about the grounds of moral responsibility. The validity of these arguments depends on particular and, in my judgment, erroneous ideas of the divine, the contention that religious claims are necessarily in conflict with moral discourse, or that the ethicist fails to admit the substantive overlap of topics and problems between theological and philosophical ethics. As we will see, Taylor and Jonas avoid these errors, and this is one reason why I want to examine their work. Yet in my judgment their arguments about moral responsibility are inadequate without a substantively different theological position than either thinker proposes. My contention is that once we properly understand what is meant in Christian faith by the symbol "God," it is required, or at least a functional equivalent to it is required, for an adequate ethics of responsibility.

INTERPRETATION AND MORAL INSIGHT

At its most basic level, responsibility implies that someone or some community can and must give an account, provide an answer, for what they have done or intend to do.[2] The use of the discourse of responsibility means that the capacity of an agent to be a causal force in the world is subjected to the demand that account be given of the actual or intended exercise of power.[3] This basic structure of responsibility is important for the following reasons. It means, first, that a moral agent, or community of agents, must respond to someone or something that makes a claim on the agent for the moral evaluation of conduct. Different answers are possible regarding the relation that is constitutive of moral responsibility. An agent might be responsible to a community and its practices of praise and blame.[4] One might also argue, as a good deal of Kantian-influenced ethics does, that agents are ultimately responsible for self-legislated maxims that, if they are to be moral, must meet certain tests, such as the test of universalizability. Theologians as well as some philosophers argue that we are ultimately responding to a Thou, even a Divine Thou, whom we encounter in the event of being addressed.[5] But whatever the case, any theory of responsibility must specify that to which or to whom we are responsible.

Second, an interpretation of responsibility also means that the identity of the agent is bound to the activity of responding or answering to that claim. Determining "who" an agent is requires that we ascribe an identity to someone or something that is a causal force in the world. The identity of the responsible agent is ascribed by someone answering for actions intended or undertaken. This means that an agent's identity, or the identity of some community of agents, is at issue in any dispute about moral responsibility. It is why, I imagine, we often avoid taking responsibility for our actions since in a profound sense we fear that who we are, our moral identity, will be called into question. And it will. In other words, an ethics of responsibility must chart the connection between who or what rightly makes a claim on an agent for the evaluation of their actions and the ascription of identity to that agent—that is, the act of specifying "who" is responsible.

The position I want to develop turns on the connection between a theory of the nature of moral agents and a theory of moral norms. What warrants an ethics of responsibility is an insight into the intrinsic value of the complexity of life as this makes a claim to determine moral self-understanding and a construal of the world. This insight is a reflective sense of the non-instrumental value of others and ourselves as that to which we are responding. The insight into the value, or good, to which we are responding is achieved, I further hold, through an act of interpretation that constitutes moral identity. Thus *who* we are as moral beings is defined by our affirmation or denial of this insight into value that arises in the interpretive act basic to self-understanding. To borrow from Paul Ricoeur, we can call the insight into moral worth a second moral naiveté about the world and others.[6] It is an insight into the worth of existence reached, if at all, by means of a critical act of interpretation that defines our self-understanding as agents. In this respect, I am developing further the idea of hermeneutical realism introduced in the preceding chapter. For the claim I now want to make is that through an interpretive act we come to a new perception of the moral worth of self, others, and the world. Radical interpretation is the practice of hermeneutical realism in actual life; it is how we are changed and enabled to see the goodness that founds all other moral commitments. No doubt, Christians rightly understand this practice and the change it brings in human life as sustained by God's grace even as it is an act of freedom.

My claim, then, is that a distinctive form of self-understanding and the insight into the value of life are mutually interdependent. How we think about the good and how we see the good, if I can put it so, are linked in complex ways that constitute the event of moral understanding. More specifically, moral insight and self-understanding are enacted in the act of what I call radical interpretation. Radical interpretation is the activity of self-criticism in which the values and norms a person or community endorses as important to her/his or its life are transformed by some idea, symbol, or event that rightly claims to guide conduct because it enables an insight into what founds the moral life. Thus, moral insight is not dependent on a special moral faculty or a unique moral intuition; it is dependent on a certain form of interpretive, self-critical reflection. We do not perceive the goodness of existence in the same way we perceive that something simply exists. An act of interpretation is involved in moral insight mediated by symbols and ideas about the worth of existence. The object of moral insight is not brute facticity, but rather existence understood in the light of what endows existence with worth.[7]

This brings us to the basic question I must address in this chapter, a question that will also be addressed in part 3. In order to make this claim about moral understanding, I must specify the idea or symbol we are to interpret in order to see that existence is endowed with such value. I want to show that if we are to make sense of responsibility in our contemporary situation, then the act of radical interpretation must be shown to be basic to moral self-understanding and ought to be undertaken with respect to claims about God. Understanding this point depends, of course, on some idea of "God." The name of God symbolizes the transformation of power, even ultimate power, with respect to the worth of finite reality. That transformation is the moral and religious meaning of the divine name for the Christian tradition. Accordingly, we are to respond to others by interpreting them, ourselves, and the world through the divine. More particular christological and pneumatological statements in theology are, in my judgment, specifications of this basic and radical claim about the divine identity.

My argument is crafted in order to retrieve within ethics two fundamental claims of Christian thought. The first claim is that we understand ourselves authentically only in relation to the divine. The knowledge of self and knowledge of God are intimately linked. Understanding ourselves through the name of God has the effect, I contend, of binding our power as self-understanding agents to specific norms that concern the recognition, respect, and well-being of finite life. The second claim is the moral correlate to the first. Theologians have long argued that the most basic moral precepts are the love of God and the love of neighbor, precepts that also entail, as Augustine noted, the proper love of self.[8] Taken together, these two claims mean that knowledge of the worth and dignity of others and ourselves is grasped through an interpretive act of understanding life from a theological perspective. We are to know and love others *in* God. Understanding oneself and the world from this perspective necessarily commits one to the moral life—that is, to respect and enhance the integrity of life.

I am arguing, then, that we apprehend the most basic claim of responsibility within an interpretive act that constitutes moral identity through understanding the reality of God. This act links a theory of the nature of moral agents with a theory of moral norms. Thus, I want to explore next the connection between self-criticism and moral identity.

CRITICISM AND MORAL IDENTITY

What constitutes us as moral beings, Charles Taylor argues, is that we can undertake the "radical evaluation" of our lives.[9] We are not constituted as selves in discrete acts of choice or brute acts of will. All of our choices depend on the values we endorse and also on the various cultural and historical sources that have funded modern identity. We cannot choose not to have some values that direct our choices. We are beings who care; human beings are valuing beings. All persons have some concern, even ultimate concern, as Paul Tillich put it.[10] This is not a simple psychological observation about persons; it is an ontological claim about human existence. We are beings whose existence is a matter of concern to us and thus we orient our lives by some framework of value. As Taylor puts it, we exist in a moral space of life with respect to some idea of the good that orients our lives. If we are properly to understand ourselves, we must then attempt to grasp the various, and often conflicting, values that have shaped our identities. To lack concern about which values ought to guide our choices is to live at best an impulsive life and at worst a chaotic one.[11] We are not creatures of radical choice. Rather, we are, Taylor says, self-interpreting animals. In the domain of ethics, this means, in his judgment, considering what we fundamentally value.

For Taylor, the specific values that form our lives are embedded in the moral traditions of the West. As a student of Hegel, he is clear that the moral life draws its substance from the mores of a tradition or community. This does not mean that these values impose themselves on us. We can evaluate the values that have shaped who we are and thus orient our lives and our actions. But in doing so we put ourselves into question in the most radical sense of the term. That is, because a tradition or community has shaped what we care about, to question that value orientation, to engage in radical evaluation, is to submit our lives to self-criticism. We are then responsible for ourselves insofar as we come to endorse the values that orient our lives. This kind of self-criticism allows us to formulate what some philosophers, such as Harry Frankfurt, have called "second-order" desires and volitions— that is, the desires and volitions we want to define who we are.

The ideas of radical evaluation and second-order desires and volitions are important for ethics. These ideas allow us to grant that we always come to moral situations with the values of our traditions in hand. Yet they also provide the conceptual means of exploring how we are responsible for ourselves through self-criticism without claiming that the "I," or ego, is the origin of all value or that our moral identities, as some existentialists argue, are defined by radical acts of choice. In other words, Taylor's theory refashions our understanding of moral autonomy. To be autonomous is not to act out of radical choice; it is critically to endorse the values by which we want our lives to be oriented. We are indeed free because we make critical evaluations and form second-order volitions and desires about who we want to be. But this freedom is compatible with the social and historical character of human life and the linguistic means we use to depict our lives.

Responsibility is linked to our capacity to reflect on and revise, or transform, our lives through the criticism of what we care about. Radical evaluation is what Taylor means by this process of self-revision. However, when we ask about the standard for evaluation, Taylor's project becomes problematic. He writes:

> Our attempts to formulate what we hold important must, like descriptions, strive to be faithful to something. But what they strive to be faithful to is not an independent object with a fixed degree of evidence, but rather a largely inarticulate sense of what is of decisive importance.[12]

Taylor's insistence on what we care about is important for a proper understanding of moral autonomy. We hardly want to claim that someone is responsible when they are coerced into adopting a certain way of life. Moreover, Taylor is right, in my judgment, to insist that moral descriptions strive to be faithful to something; they have, in this sense, a realistic intention. But therein lies the problem in his argument. How can our *moral* evaluations be faithful to what Taylor admits is our "deepest unstructured sense of what is important"?[13]

The problem is not, I believe, in Taylor's appeal to what is important to us; the problem is how what we care about can serve as the criterion for moral descriptions insofar as our sense of what is important remains inarticulate. Taylor tries to answer this by providing a history of the formation of our moral values. But why should that history matter to us? Can it actually ground our commitment to the moral life? Later we will see how Taylor tries to answer these criticisms of a historical grounding of moral values. He does so, interestingly enough, through theological discourse. But at this junction, I think we must connect the idea of evaluation with Taylor's own claim that we are fundamentally self-interpreting animals. In order to do so, I want now to develop the idea of radical interpretation.

FROM EVALUATION TO INTERPRETATION

I have explored Taylor's position because of the affinity between his idea of evaluation and what I call radical interpretation. It is my contention that an ethics of responsibility must insist on interpretation as well as evaluation. The operative distinction between the two is that interpretation renders explicit the relation of self and other in understanding, whereas evaluation, at least as Taylor specifies it, can rest on an inarticulate sense of what is important. This distinction is important for an ethics of responsibility because moral descriptions are intended to be faithful not simply to an inchoate sense of what is important, but also to the world and others to whom we are responding. The form of self-criticism that defines who we are as moral agents is not, as it seems to be for Taylor, Frankfurt, and others, a debate within the evaluator's personal life about personal desires and volitions. Rather, moral self-criticism is defined with reference to what demands and empowers some answer from us. More basically still, moral identity is constituted not only by care, as Taylor insists, but also by respect. Respect is the recognition of and regard for what is other than the self and its projects. It is the acknowledgment of what rightly thwarts all attempts of the ego to impress itself on others, on reality. The experience of respect discloses the fact that we are always interacting with others and our world, because "respect rests on the recognition of something as intrinsically worthy of it."[14] The feeling of respect, in terms used in chapter 4, is a testimony to an irreducible otherness at the core of our self-awareness. Accordingly, what our moral descriptions must be faithful to is that which is worthy of respect as well as what is of decisive importance for us, what we care about.

I can clarify this point about care and respect that is basic to the idea of radical interpretation by drawing a distinction. Taylor's idea of evaluation, as I understand it, actually pertains to a condition necessary for any physical movement to be understood as a human action. For a movement to be an action, it must be directed toward some end, toward what appears to be good; otherwise, we would be speaking of mere motion. Put differently, action entails choice, and choices are always made with respect to ends. Going to the store is an action in a way that the movement of my heart is not, because in the case of going to the store I could have chosen to do otherwise. Given this, the examination of what we value, and thus the dynamics of care, is an exploration of a condition for distinctively human agency. If we are to be responsible for ourselves, we must critically evaluate the ends or goods that orient our lives as valuing beings. And this is the point of Taylor's theory of radical evaluation.

However, examination of the conditions of distinctively human action, while important for genuine self-understanding, is not sufficient for an account of *moral* action and identity. This is because respect is basic to moral conduct. We do not need to specify why we care about respect, as Taylor seems to argue, because respect is a basic moral sensibility; it is the recognition of and regard for the noninstrumental worth of others. Moral conduct presupposes various conditions for action, such as the fact that we can evaluate what we care about, but then insists that we recognize what is an end itself, has intrinsic worth, despite what we might care about and value. A theory of moral agency must include both the analysis of the conditions for action, and thus what we care about, and also respect as a basic component of moral conduct. These are not, as Taylor seems to argue, grafted onto each other. One does not begin with what one cares about and then graft it onto a theory of respect. Care and respect, I contend, are equally basic experiences simply because human beings are always acting for ends we value and also interacting with others.[15] In fact, this constitutes the basic moral tension of our existence, the tension between what we care about and what makes a claim to our recognition and regard. Stated differently, human life is moved by multiple motivations and these motivations can conflict.

A condition for responsible human action is, then, some critical evaluation of the good or goods that ought to orient our lives. Human action in this sense is teleological; persons are, as William James said, fighters for ends. However, we must also isolate another kind of teleology basic to moral action. In this teleology the end for which an action is done is not a state of affairs to be realized, as in consequentialism, or, as Taylor argues, a good that orients action in terms of what we value. It is something that exists as an end in itself to be respected in all action.[16] Here the concept of an "end" is bound to an actual, existing being or state of affairs rather than something to be achieved, sought, or realized. It is an "end" because the existent being or state of affairs is valued in itself and not simply as a means for achieving some other purpose. Persons are "ends" in this sense; so is God and God's reign. The dilemma, again, is that these two ends can and do conflict in our lives. What we care about can and does conflict with our recognition of and regard for others. When it does, we seek some reason for living morally. After all, why not simply pursue one's own self-interest? To respond to this question we must engage in forms of moral self-criticism in regard to what we ought to care about and respect. Insofar as all of us experience this form of moral conflict, self-criticism would seem to be basic to moral identity.

Moral self-criticism, as opposed to the self-questioning Taylor highlights, aims at transforming what we care about through recognition of what rightly claims our respect such that care and respect become one. Its purpose is to attain some level of moral integrity in life. This requires us to make the principle of distinctively human action—that is, what we care about—the claim to respect that is perceived in others and ourselves. In other words, the morally good person or community is one that cares about what ought to be respected. This is what Christian faith means by love; *agape* is the radical, excessive bestowal of care based on the recognition and regard for the goodness of what simply is, irrespective of its virtue or merit. Put differently, love for Christians is a manifestation of grace; it is expressive of God's free, unmerited, and justifying grace for human beings given in Christ without demands of merit. Thus, if we are to speak of moral self-criticism in theological ethics we need to explore how it is, if at all, that what we care about as the basic condition for distinctively human action is transformed in light of what we ought to respect.

What I am calling radical interpretation is reflective, critical inquiry aimed at the question of what has constituted our lives in terms of what we care about and what ought to guide our actions under the demand of respect for others. Such inquiry becomes "radical" when it strikes at the root and the reach of who we are, what we most deeply care about and respect, and the conceptual frameworks or moral descriptions we have used to understand ourselves and our world. Radical interpretation is, then, a way to articulate how moral identity is constituted and transformed through an act of understanding. This means that what instigates the moral life is an act of understanding and sensibility and not evaluation. We do not evaluate the moral worth of others in terms of our interests; we understand the moral life and what we care about in terms of the experience of the recognition and regard for others. What I call radical interpretation is the activity of moral self-criticism in which a condition of our very acting, what we care about, is transformed through the recognition of a good that grounds the moral life and ought to be respected in all our actions.

There are specific theological reasons for adopting the idea of radical interpretation as central to a theory of moral responsibility. In the biblical texts, the Hebrew prophets called Israel to engage in this kind of interpretation through repentance and the remembrance of the covenant and God's fidelity. Israel becomes Israel through remembering and living out the covenant as definitive of its identity. The teachings of Jesus confront the reader with the same demand about the reign of God. When Jesus asks "Who do you say I am?" he forces his listener to undertake this activity. The self is radically interpreted in response to the demand for some answer to Jesus' question. That answer is to be a description; it is a claim about who

Jesus actually, not potentially, is. The description entails a prescription. If Jesus is the Christ, one ought to follow him.[17] The idea of radical interpretation is also, I suggest, how we must understand the divine name in the biblical texts. God names God's self and in doing so constitutes the identity of the community and the norms for fidelity, norms of justice and mercy. What is the ethical import of this idea of radical interpretation?

On this point, Taylor makes a suggestive but undeveloped proposal. He argues that in order to warrant our adherence to basic moral norms of justice and benevolence present in our moral tradition we must, surprisingly enough, draw on the biblical claim, in Genesis 1, that "God saw that it was good." In other words, one must apprehend the noninstrumental worth of others as ends in themselves if moral norms are to be genuinely compelling and thus guide our actual conduct. What is more, if we are to be morally responsible for ourselves, we must recognize the goodness of actual beings and the demands these beings place on us. And thus Taylor asks, "Do we have ways of seeing-good which are still credible to us, which are powerful enough to sustain these standards [of justice and benevolence]?"[18] The recognition of and regard for an end that solicits our respect must ground other moral beliefs and norms because it instigates the moral life, the requirement that we consider the rights and well-being of others in evaluating what we care about. This is what the idea of radical interpretation is meant to articulate.

On reaching this conclusion, we are, dialectically speaking, at the transition point between an analysis of the nature of moral agents and a theory of moral norms. We make this transition, interestingly enough, in terms of theological discourse. Given this, I want to turn to the problem of norms in an age that has witnessed the explosive growth of human power. By exploring the recent work of the Jewish philosopher Hans Jonas, we will see that theological questions are also entailed in a theory of responsibility.

POWER AND MORAL RESPONSIBILITY

For Hans Jonas, modern technology is an ontological event in history; it has changed the nature of action. Technology so extends human power that the future is our responsibility. This development is concomitant with the modern reduction of the human place in reality to one more "fact" in the causal world. Modern self-understanding denies that human beings are created in the image of God. As Jonas puts it,

> the paradox of the modern condition is that this reduction of
> man's stature, the utter humbling of his metaphysical pride, goes

hand in hand with his promotion to quasi-God-like privilege and power. The emphasis is on *power*.[19]

Technology is simply the working out of this shift from the intrinsic worth of human life as the image of God to the exercise of power. Not surprisingly, in the modern world religious discourse no longer serves to legitimate norms, values, and institutions because it does not make sense of self-identity.[20] The loss of religious faith, along with the change in the nature of action and the centrality of power in human life, creates a space of virtually unlimited human responsibility for life on earth. In Jonas's judgment, it moves the question of responsibility to the center of ethics. And it further means, as noted before, that how we understand the world and our place within it is crucial to a theory of responsibility.

Jonas begins to develop an ethics of responsibility for a technological age with a claim about freedom rather than, as with Taylor, the problem of self-understanding. As a condition for moral action, freedom is best understood as the self-affirmation of life against death. This is because, as Jonas writes, in "every purpose being declares itself for itself against nothingness."[21] Freedom emerges in the biosphere because of the capacity of human beings to differentiate themselves from their environment and make choices about how to act. Human freedom is a unique expression of the basic fact of purposiveness; freedom introduces complexity and increased contingency into the world, but it also entails an affirmation of life. Since we now have the power to end life on this planet, it is vitally important that human beings take responsibility for the contingency their actions have introduced into the world. Given this demand, human beings must continue to exist.

Based on this argument, Jonas formulates an imperative of responsibility for our age: "Do not compromise the conditions for an indefinite continuation of humanity on earth."[22] This means that we are "not responsible to the future of human individuals but to the *idea* of Man, which is such that it demands the presence of its embodiment in the world."[23] The idea of humanity ("Man"), the notion that humanity is an end-in-itself, is to guide action because it specifies what ought to be embodied in the world. The idea of humanity articulates a reality that ought to be respected and actualized. If one grasps the meaning of this idea, one understands that it must be embodied. This is, we might say, Jonas's ontological proof that humanity *ought* to exist. If we understand this *idea*, we do not know *that* humanity exists (as in the case of the ontological proof of God's existence), but, rather, that humans *ought to* exist. The proof is practical and prescriptive rather than theoretical and descriptive in character; it concerns norms and prescriptions for human action. The idea of humanity, we can say, specifies the end that ought to be respected in all action—that is, the conditions necessary for the continuation of human life on earth.

Granting the presence of human life in the biosphere, how is the imperative that there ought to be finite life in the future apprehended in the present so that it might move us to sacrifice present interests for future well-being? That is, how is it that our self-understanding can be transformed so that we recognize that future generations of human life make a claim on our present purposes and conduct? This is the inverse of the problem faced by Taylor: Jonas must specify how we are moved to care about what we ought to respect.

In order to address this problem, Jonas begins with how the imperative of responsibility is known. He argues that "a 'command' can issue not only from a commanding will, for instance, of a personal God or a Thou, but also from the immanent claim of a good-in-itself to its realization."[24] There are certain ends, goods that are to be respected, that demand their realization. For Jonas, this kind of end is paradigmatically seen in the face of the child. In every act of procreation, human beings affirm, at least implicitly, the goodness of continued existence. The imperative of responsibility rests, then, on the insight that for human life to exist is good. This designates knowledge of the objective character of the norm of responsibility. The moral imperative is universalized through the idea of humanity; humanity itself, and not specific individuals or groups, ought to be realized.

This objective norm must also be related to a subjective motive to act. A moral norm is irrelevant if it does not move agents freely to abide by it. In order to move agents to act on the moral imperative, being itself, Jonas contends, must be the cause and the object of reverence. We must have some recognition of the goodness of being that moves us to live by the moral law. So, Jonas writes,

> Being (or instances of it) disclosed to a sight not blocked by self-ishness or dimmed by dullness, may well instill reverence—and can with this affection of our feeling come to the aid of the, otherwise powerless, moral law which bids us to honor the intrinsic claim of Being.[25]

Jonas's contention is that perishable existence is the object of the feeling of responsibility. The feeling of responsibility manifests the intrinsic claim of being on us in terms of what we care about. While this claim is "heard" at the level of "feeling," it can move agents to act on the moral law formulated in the imperative of responsibility.

The plausibility of Jonas's ethics depends, then, on the assumption that being does in fact evoke reverence and binds us to live by the moral law. And therein lies the difficulty. Any realistic ethics must insist that agents are in fact selfish and that our moral perception is deeply distorted. As I previously noted, what we care about and what we ought to respect can and do conflict. Jonas recognizes part of the problem. Granting the fact of selfishness, he holds that one must appeal to fear, to imagined *malum*, and not awe or reverence for being as crucial to moving people to care for the future. The threat of extinction, of nonbeing, motivates an affirmation of life and care for the future of life. Moral motive is born of self-interest in the face of the threat to finite future life; we act responsibly out of fear. It is fear that instigates the transformation of our moral understanding—a fear, as I argued in chapter 1, deep within the postmodern psyche.

There are, of course, reasons to question this claim about fear as a moral motive. But the initial point is that if the idea of humanity (or "Man," as Jonas calls it) is to determine the will because it tells us what *ought* to be realized, then the idea itself must not dull our reverence for being as basic to moral motivation. It must enable us, as Taylor puts it, to "see-good." But the idea of humanity can do so only, I judge, if it draws on the moral force of something itself not threatened by the negative. Moral insight must be mediated by some idea, symbol, event, or name other than the idea of humanity, because, on Jonas's own admission, this idea rests for its binding force on some claim about being. On seeing this, we return to the other side of our inquiry. That is, we return to the problem of how we are to understand ourselves as moral beings with respect to some insight into the worth and goodness of existence itself.

In short, we are in search of a theory of responsibility that addresses the problem of moral blindness and the reality of power that Jonas rightly notes without regressing, as Taylor seems to do, simply to our inchoate sense of what is important to us. We need an ethics of self-criticism and also one that can specify the idea, event, or reality that will universalize an imperative of responsibility. This ethics must transform the recognition of the worth of reality into an imperative for action. And it must do so, it seems to me, without appeal simply to fear—the inverse of the experience of respect—or to our inchoate sense of importance as the reason for moral commitment. Let me conclude this inquiry by turning to these matters and thereby drawing together the strands of the argument of this chapter.

RADICAL INTERPRETATION AND THEOLOGICAL ETHICS

I have explored how Taylor's theory of responsibility and identity refashions our idea of moral autonomy in terms of what we care about. This situates moral freedom within our basic cares and also within the traditions that have formed our moral evaluations without thereby compromising the degree of autonomy needed for the moral life. And I have also shown how norms for the guidance of human power entail in Jonas's judgment some insight into an end that commands respect and ought to be realized. The norms of responsibility are socially mediated but find their warrant and purpose not simply in social practices of praise and blame. Their warrant lies in a claim about reality itself and what ought to exist in the future. The question before us now is the nature of the link between these two sides of our inquiry—that is, the analysis of the nature of moral agents and also a theory of moral norms.

The answer to this question is the activity of radical interpretation undertaken from a theological perspective. The possibility of this answer arises from what we have isolated by exploring the thoughts of Taylor and Jonas. What prompts us to step back and question ourselves, what instigates moral self-criticism and transformation, is not simply what is important to us, or even fear; it is what solicits our care and respect through its claim to exist, its intrinsic worth. This is, I submit, the founding experience of responsibility. We have, then, isolated a point of contact between reflection on moral identity and the question of norms for the exercise of power. The point of contact is an insight into the value of finite life—the integrity of life, as I call it—that solicits our respect and empowers the enhancement of life.

Significantly, for the thinkers we have explored any attempt at specifying this basic experience of responsibility entails implicit or explicit religious and theological claims. Taylor insists that the divine affirms the creature as good and thereby grounds the demands of justice and benevolence. And Jonas argues that the idea of creation can "take the form of *reverence* for certain inviolable integrities sanctioned by that idea."[26] Rather than insisting on the divine evaluation of creation (Taylor) or the *idea* of creation (Jonas), I want to propose a different and perhaps more radical theological claim. That is, I want now to develop the theological correlate to the theory of radical interpretation. In order to do so, I draw on the rich resources of the Christian tradition, its narratives, symbols, and metaphors. I am interested in the interpretive role basic theological symbols can play in moral understanding, especially the symbol of "God."

The task at this juncture in my argument is, then, to show how theological ethics can articulate the basic experience of responsibility and thereby provide a more adequate theory of responsibility than the positions we have examined. If this can be shown, our moral existence is better understood from a Christian perspective than from the perspectives of these other positions. The validity of a theological perspective in ethics will then have been dialectically established, granting that other questions and rival positions still need to be addressed.

The act of radical interpretation—what Christians used to call "conscience"—is the primal deed of moral identity. This is because it constitutes the self-understanding of an agent, or community of agents, who exercise power in terms of the claims of others and the world upon them. Radical interpretation is an expression of moral freedom because it informs and directs our choices on the basis of the critical assessment of value orientations with regard to a response to what solicits our respect. This enables us to affirm in ethics the degree of moral autonomy needed for the moral life. We can and must critically test our value orientations and endorse only those that meet the test of interpretation. That is what it means to be responsible for ourselves. The idea of radical interpretation makes moral transformation—or self-revision, as Taylor presents it—into an epistemological principle in ethics. Moral knowledge is a process of transforming self-understanding out of respect for others; it is to see others as good, as ends, and this entails the demand to realize life in others and ourselves. The moral life is then conceived of as nothing less than the ongoing transformation of understanding, care, and respect. It is what used to be called by John Wesley and many others perfection or sanctification.

However, if we are to specify the demands of moral responsibility, we must assess our actions and values by some idea that renders the recognition of the value of existence into an imperative for action. Radical interpretation, I have argued, enables us to articulate *how* this critical process of moral self-assessment takes place and thus constitutes identity. However, it does not of itself provide the idea or image for doing so. Does the idea of humanity provide it, as Jonas holds? Is what we hold, as Taylor claims, decisive of us? Maybe it is the idea of an ideal discourse community, as theorists like Jürgen Habermas and Karl-Otto Apel argue. In this light, can we make sense ethically of the Christian claim that we are to know and to love others and ourselves *in* God?

As I have argued in previous chapters, in the Christian tradition, ultimate power, the divine, is identified as "God" with respect to the recognition of the finite other as well as norms of justice and benevolence. God creates the moral order of reality insofar as the divine, or ultimate power, names itself with respect to the goodness of creation, the demands of covenant fidelity and justice, and the redemptive power of love. Outside of this name and the history of interpretation it entails, the meaning of the ultimate reality is the abyss of power. "Who" God is, the divine identity, is interpreted in the Christian tradition through specific values, norms, and the person and work of Christ: God is identified as creator, sustainer, and, in Christ, redeemer. The name "God," in a trinitarian faith, is thus the radical interpretation of ultimate power. This name symbolizes the transformation of power with respect to a recognition of and regard for finite goodness and derivative claims of justice and benevolence. This is what it means to say, in the Gospel of John and for Christians throughout the ages, that God is love.

The name of God entails, then, a specific construal of the world that expands the scope of our moral community. It means that the requirement placed on us as moral beings is first and foremost to endorse as constitutive of who we are the subjection of our power to norms of well-being. It is the possibility and demand of genuine Christian love. The importance of this possibility in Western thought and life ought not be easily denied. Commonly we do not hold that the human good is found simply in the release of power, but in the exercise of human capacities with respect to specific moral norms. This belief signals the impact of the divine name on moral consciousness whether or not the religious commitment it entails is rendered explicit.[27] Explicit faith is a second-order commitment to understand reality and ourselves with respect to a trust in and loyalty to the triune "God." The task for theological ethics, then, is to specify what this faith means for how we should live. And this task returns us to the relation of care and respect in the moral life and also in moral self-understanding.

If one understands the meaning of the divine reality as the radical interpretation of ultimate power, one can grasp not simply what ought to be respected but why finite reality is imbued with moral worth that should be realized. The interpretation of the symbol "God" within moral inquiry enables one to attain an insight into the "seeing-good" of reality and others, an insight that also determines moral identity. This insight can be specified in two ways that bear on the actual conduct of life. First, it can be specified in what is sometimes called the first precept of practical reason: seek good and avoid evil. This precept concerns one condition for distinctively human action—that is, what we care about. Interpreted Christianly, this precept means that the condition for responsible action is that one seek to enhance and realize the integrities of finite life and to avoid their destruction. Second, the "seeing-good" that characterizes moral insight can be specified in terms of an imperative of responsibility: in all actions and relations, respect and enhance the integrity of life before God. The principles of moral character and conduct center, then, on a recognition of the claims of others on us (justice) and an active concern for others and for the world (benevolence). These are the norms of responsibility consistent with the very structure of care and respect in moral action when care, as a condition for action, and respect, as a moral experience, are radically interpreted from a theological point of view.

This argument departs from Taylor's position because it does not appeal to a divine evaluation of reality for the grounding of more specific moral norms, but to the norms endorsed in the divine name as fundamental to moral understanding and commitment. The idea of radical interpretation in a theological context means that what is important about the divine seeing-good is that ultimate power binds its identity to specific moral norms rather than trying to imagine what is important to the deity. The argument also departs from Jonas's work by providing the means of addressing moral blindness while affirming an insight into the goodness of being. What mediates moral insight, and thus moral understanding, is not an idea of what ought to be reverenced (creation; humanity), but rather a name that articulates the transformation of power in the recognition of the claim of finite reality to exist. Again, in classical Christian theological parlance, love for others is always defined in relation to the love of God. Our insight into the worth of others is mediated through an understanding of the name of God insofar as that name is itself the radical interpretation of ultimate power. The name of God provides a truthful insight into what is to be respected and enhanced through an interpretive practice that transforms moral self-understanding.[28] This is how we must understand the claim that we are to love ourselves and others in God. An insight into the worth of existence is constitutive of moral understanding. Any construal of the divine that fails to ignite and deepen that insight cannot claim ethical or theological validity. This is the consequence, it seems to me, of claiming that the name of God identifies ultimate power with moral norms. Theological discourse on its own terms is subject to ethical criticism and validation.

I have, then, specified in theological terms the point of contact between claims about moral identity and norms for power in a technological age. The basic phenomenon of responsibility is a response to the worth of contingent life that solicits our respect and even care; it is a sense of the intrinsic worth of the integrity of life. This experience is a second moral naiveté that transpires within an activity of interpretation. The moral self is not the starting point of value because the self is constituted and transformed through an activity defined by an insight into the claims of others on us. Radical interpretation as the activity basic to moral responsibility is the means by which the self-understanding of agents who exercise power is transformed in order to respect and enhance the integrity of life. An ethics of responsibility is then realistic and cognitivistic even as it insists on the centrality of the unique freedom to interpret who we are as basic to the moral life. Radical interpretation undertaken theologically aims at enabling us to interrelate an account of the nature of moral agents and a theory of moral norms. It does so insofar as it provides the means for agents, or communities of agents, to assess and to transform their self-understanding with regard to what they care about and the experience of respect. What instigates this assessment and transformation is an insight into the intrinsic value of being as that to which we are ultimately responding. Human beings, I hold, are creative responders to value who ought to respect and enhance life. But the insight into the goodness to which we are responding is, we have also seen, a mediated insight; it is achieved by interpreting ourselves and our world through the name of God. We are, then, self-interpreting responders, and this fact specifies some of the creativity and freedom of the moral life. To interpret our lives and our world through the name of God is to expand the scope of our moral community and thus also to deepen and expand our moral identity. It is to understand ourselves and all others within an inclusive moral community whose defining principle is the transformation of power with respect to the recognition of, regard for, and enhancement of life. This is why, we can now see, theological claims matter in ethics. The idea of radical interpretation, then, supports certain ethical criteria and ideals for valid theological discourse even as it specifies the contribution of theology to ethics.

CONCLUSION

I have sought in this chapter to clarify the current debate about responsibility with respect to the questions of moral agency and the norms for human power. The position I have presented addresses problems isolated in other ethical theories while accounting for their central concerns. My proposal for an ethics of responsibility is nothing less than a radical interpretation of Christian faith and the moral identity it engenders. This theological ethics articulates faith as a distinctive way of being moral in the world through respect and care. The moral life, theologically construed, is about binding our power to norms of justice and benevolence in order to foster viable life by interpreting our existence through the name of God.

The theological ethical task of radical interpretation is an act of freedom with respect to who we are and what we ought to become. It is the task of enabling us to understand ourselves and the moral order in which we exist as constituted not only by our moral traditions or our participation in the biosphere, but also in response to the God who endows reality with worth and solicits our responsibility. It is the freedom to know and value others and ourselves in God for the sake of the integrity of life.

6

Responsibility and Comparative Ethics

T he difficulties in understanding the moral lives of others are legion.[1] Not a day goes by without our reading, hearing, or wondering about the beliefs and convictions of others who are different from ourselves. We constantly make judgments about values, beliefs, and ways of life, comparing them and deciding which are better, higher, or more valuable than others. If we are undertaking ethical inquiry, we need to provide some reasons for our judgments. My task in this chapter, accordingly, is to explore problems of comparative moral understanding. What are the conditions that make such understanding possible? How, if at all, does comparison transpire? Faced with these questions, we must admit a troublesome fact. There is virtually no agreement among thinkers on the shape of understanding, let alone the relation of rationality to the substantive concerns of theological ethics. I want to provide an analysis of comparative understanding as another step in developing a hermeneutical approach to theological ethics.

GUIDING ASSUMPTIONS

As all arguments do, mine rests on certain guiding assumptions. My basic one is hardly novel: understanding is achieved through interpretation. The attitude and perspective of the interpreter are those of the participant rather than the objectifying attitude and perspective of the observer concerned with propositional statements about events or states of affairs. The attitude and perspective of the interpreter clearly bear on the status of claims that she or he can possibly make. As Jürgen Habermas notes,

> A correct interpretation, therefore, is not true in the sense in which a proposition that reflects an existing state of affairs is true. It would be better to say that a correct interpretation fits, suits, or explicates the meaning of the *interpretandum*, that which the interpreter is to understand.[2]

The problem I face in this chapter is that the *interpretandum* is interpretation itself and the form of understanding it enacts. The question then becomes how one is to construe interpretation.

I join those theorists who see interpretation as dialogical and dialectical in character. We understand through argument and conversation with others and ourselves; we are always engaged in some form of questioning and answering. This means that hermeneutical inquiry bears on (1) what someone says or something implies, (2) the interaction between the interpreter and what is said, and (3) that about which the subject matter, the "said," is concerned—its "referent." This requires modification of previous theories of understanding that, as I noted in chapter 4, take conceptualization or perception as the clue to knowing and to specifying criteria of truth. Such theories tend to concentrate inquiry on the third of the above-listed concerns—that is, the question of reference—while creating an observer's perspective and attitude toward the question of understanding. Hermeneutics contests the epistemological concentration of modern philosophy and its attendant cognitive attitude. As I have argued, understanding is thoroughly practical and reflexive in nature; we are participants and not observers of our world and our lives. This does not mean, as some critics might think, that the interpreter simply constructs the meaning of what is in question. On the contrary, the interpreter "has to explicate the given meaning of objectivations that can only be understood from within the context of the communication process."[3] We are concerned with that which calls for interpretation but which requires the participation of the interpreter in order for it to be understood.

The orienting assumption about understanding through dialogical interpretation clearly places my argument within the wider enterprise of phenomenological hermeneutics. The argument is phenomenological in the sense that I hope to specify the structure and intentionality of comparative understanding in terms of translation and insight. It is a hermeneutical inquiry, because understanding is reached through the interpretation of meaningful expressions, ones paradigmatically represented by linguistic forms (symbols, texts, etc.) but inclusive of actions and events as well. Thus, I consider the act of comparative interpretation in order to explore its shape and dynamic, what is disclosed in it, and what makes it possible. Hopefully this will show the plausibility of my guiding assumptions and the fruitfulness of this way of thinking about comparison in ethics.

Granting my agreement with other hermeneutical thinkers, I forward and defend a particular thesis about comparative understanding. It is certainly a contestable one, but is consistent with the thrust of this book as a whole. I claim that interpretation in comparative ethics is best seen as a performative activity analogous to the ritual and dramatic practices of religious communities. Interpretation is a human action; it is a praxis. My argument focuses, then, on what it means to say that for human beings understanding is bound to the exercise of power in action. Other hermeneutical positions are interested in the dynamic of traditions in the attempt to overcome historical alienation (Gadamer), the coordination of social interaction in a differentiated society (Habermas), or the interpretive mediation of self-understanding (Ricoeur). While drawing on these positions, my concern is nevertheless with the reflexive process through which communities and individuals are constituted by the enactment of a world of symbolic meaning.[4] Action and agency are the home of understanding. If this is so, then ethics becomes a fundamental discipline encompassing the work of hermeneutics. I believe this perspective is most fruitful for exploring our own moral and religious beliefs as well as the lives of others.

To offer this account of interpretation I will draw on the resources buried in the concept of mimesis or "imitation." I admit that this sounds odd. Mimesis is usually associated with poetics and aesthetics, or, in the Platonic tradition, with epistemology and metaphysics. As we will see, it holds resources for comparative ethics long neglected by philosophers because of its relation to ritual and drama. Yet, because of its ties to epistemology, aesthetics, and even metaphysics, mimesis adds to discourse about symbolic action the means of exploring understanding through linguistic forms. To make this claim about mimesis requires retrieval of its roots in ritual and dramatic practice, roots long understood by classics scholars but only now bearing historical, philosophical, and theological fruit.[5] Reclaiming those roots enables us to consider the complex relation of discourse and practice in understanding the moral lives of others and ourselves.

In order to demonstrate my thesis, I must elucidate it to the point that we can grasp the shape and dynamics of understanding in comparative ethics. This elucidation requires that the argument move in several steps while retaining a participant's perspective. First, I want to specify the debates in religious ethics that bear on the shape of comparative understanding. In the last analysis, these debates turn on the rational conditions for comparison concerning different ideas of the task of ethics. In order to move beyond this debate, we must take a hermeneutical turn in comparative ethics. Second, I examine interpretation as a mimetic practice and what this means for specifying the method, subject matter, and conditions for ethics. I conclude this section of the chapter by arguing that the formal and material criteria for adequate interpretation rest on the specific moral demand of responsibility. In this way, comparative ethics falls under its own moral norm since understanding is itself a moral task.

OPTIONS IN COMPARATIVE ETHICS

Comparative ethics finds itself amid a variety of challenges to previous ways of thinking about the moral life, the possibility of understanding others, and the validity of moral claims. Not surprisingly, there is intense debate about the subject matter and method of comparison. From this debate have emerged some basic options about how to proceed in ethics. In order to isolate them I want to specify the debate around *what* is in question, *how* thinkers hold that we should explore it, and also what they take as the *condition* for comparative understanding. I can do so by drawing a typology of positions, realizing that this serves heuristic purposes and is not meant as an exhaustive analysis.

At one extreme of our typology are thinkers who seek what Ronald Green calls a "deep structure" to religion.[6] These positions hold that we must understand specific traditions as expressions of universal, or nearly universal, structures of rationality. The ethics of particular communities are subsumed under a general concept of morality. The pattern of comparative thinking is formal and transcendental in character. That is, comparison seeks to isolate the formal structure of reason, later to be supplied with moral content from specific traditions, and also the conditions that make religious understanding possible—that is, the transcendental conditions of the possibility of understanding. In this way, these thinkers undertake a metapractical discourse in order to specify the conditions and criteria for the actual practice of comparative ethics. This requires us to explore the transcultural conditions of understanding, the origins and justifications for obligations of other-regard and human welfare, as well as possible responses to moral fault and failure. By examining other traditions we learn the various ways in which communities have addressed these issues basic to ethics.

In discernible continuity with Immanuel Kant's moral philosophy, this form of comparative ethics hopes to isolate how the "moral" transcends empirical conditions and cultural variation. *What* one seeks to explore are communities' obligations and rules, as well as their justifications, that demarcate the moral life. By undertaking such inquiry the moral philosopher or theologian hopes to provide the theoretical standpoint for comparative reflection no matter how much that perspective is subsequently enriched by sociological, historical, and anthropological investigation. Indeed, for Green this standpoint is grounded in the *sui generis* character of what he calls "religious reason" and its relation to morality. Such reason "arises because of an important conflict between prudential and moral reason, and it represents reason's effort to bring its own program to a coherent conclusion."[7] Reason and the problem it addresses provide the conditions for comparison. I will return to the matter of rational "structure" in comparative understanding later; it is important for the conditions of interpretation and thus of understanding. But initially we face a rather obvious question concerning this type of ethics: does it adequately acknowledge the diversity of moral communities as well as the historical-linguistic character of its own reflection?

It is this question that has provoked other scholars in comparative ethics to address the relativity of cultural worlds and belief systems. They attend to given forms of life and the discursive practices of traditions without assuming that there is a deep structure that makes up morality.[8] In this manner they signal the turn to language in moral philosophy, a turn shared by hermeneutics. Unlike hermeneutical thinkers, they are less concerned with the ontological question about language and our being-in-the-world. On the contrary, social-linguistic thinkers seek to explore the specificity of moral languages. They are suspicious of what Jeffery Stout has called "moral Esperanto"—that is, a supposedly universal language, like Green's, and perhaps of ontological reflection as well, which "rules the deep structure of morality as such."[9] These theorists contest any drive toward the complete translation of moral vocabularies through the construction of a metalanguage. This does not mean that there is no possibility for insight into the beliefs of others: we are not trapped in our own linguistic communities. The point is that this common ground cannot be specified in some set of moral principles based on the structure of reason.

The common ground or condition needed for understanding others is the simple fact that persons learn to speak moral languages despite the diversity of those languages. Inasmuch as there is no final moral language, we can expect that encountering the discourse and beliefs of others might enrich our own. As with the formalist concern for rational structures, I will also return to the insights of these social-linguistic thinkers. After all, interpretation is a social, discursive practice. But again we confront a question: is it not the case that the claims of religious communities about how to live are intertwined with other beliefs, beliefs about the world and the nature of human life? And if this is the case, must we not attend to these other beliefs precisely in order to carry out the task of comparative ethics? This is a substantive question and one that some thinkers hold ought to bear on the very method of ethics.

This conviction has given rise to yet another approach in comparative ethics. Between the *formalists* who seek deep structures and the *social-linguistic philosophers* who explore the diversity of languages are thinkers who argue for a revised form of *ethical naturalism*.[10] Like social-linguistic thinkers, the new naturalists reject the vision of reason found in ethical formalism. Yet against the concentration on moral language, the naturalist "treats a system of beliefs as a whole and refuses to isolate moral propositions for analysis from propositions about how things are in the world and how they come to be that way."[11] The task, in other words, is to explore beliefs about how individuals and communities should live in relation to other convictions concerning the world (its origin, ordering, and end, as well as its meaning and value) and the human's place in it.

These new naturalists readily grant the particularity and diversity of moral claims. Nevertheless, they insist that all communities have beliefs about the world that contextualize their moral ones. Naturalism is, in other words, a form of moral realism. The condition for comparative understanding is therefore neither an analogy of discursive ability nor a deep formal structure of reason. It is based in the dependence of particular propositions on an entire system of beliefs about reality. In exploring the morals of others, the scholar must not start with theory but must observe and describe a belief system and its import for moral claims.

This form of reflection begins with no a priori set of obligations, aims, or human purposes; it tries to understand how communities address these obligations, aims, and purposes in light of their convictions about the world. As Robin Lovin and Frank Reynolds note,

> The range of possible connections between norm, fact, and purpose shifts the attention in naturalistic ethics to substantive, rather than formal questions, and suggests that alternative norms must be evaluated in terms of their place in a complete way of life, including a set of beliefs about human persons and the reality in which they must live and may thrive.[12]

These thinkers are concerned with how given construals of the world and existence shape human life in a community or tradition. In the hermeneutic turn I advocate, the relation of the moral life to beliefs about reality will not be lost. This is what I have called hermeneutical realism. However, hermeneutical reflection also holds that understanding always enacts a world of meaning; we discover a world in part by our active participation in making meaning. This radicalizes claims of the new naturalism about the meaning of a moral "world." The condition for understanding others is precisely that we live our lives as interpreters of meaning.

This sketch of the options in comparative ethics shows that the debate is positioned along lines that have beset Western thought over the last few centuries. It pits descriptivist against formalist accounts of moral rationality in asking about *how* comparative work should be conducted; it traverses the range of ethical theories from naturalism to non-naturalism with regard to *what* ethics is all about. The reason for this dispute is perhaps obvious. Each of the positions in our typology explores forms of life, but each does so from the perspective of a different account of reasoning and a different idea of the task of ethics. Any move beyond the current debate requires us to consider the shape of comparative understanding itself. So we must ask a specifically hermeneutical question: what is happening when we understand others?

While a hermeneutic turn is needed in comparative ethics, the current debate helps to specify the demands that face an adequate position. Any contribution to the current discussion must provide some construal of moral rationality and detail the relation between moral convictions and the other beliefs that communities hold. It must also specify the very conditions that make comparative understanding possible within its account of *how* we are to approach the beliefs and lives of others. As a step toward answering these issues, I want to turn next to a phenomenological consideration of the dimensions of comparative understanding.

TRANSLATION AND INSIGHT

It has often been noted that any account of human thinking draws on some root metaphor, analogy, activity, or image as a clue to the meaning of understanding. A central problem in hermeneutical theory is, then, what image or act should be used as the entrance point for examining what it means to understand. And of course there is a paradox in all of this since the activity of understanding is transpiring in the very attempt to comprehend it. The only way to explore the event of understanding is to consider the symbols, images, or pictures we have adopted or invented for it.

In the West, common metaphors that have been taken to be crucial for thinking have been those of vision and hearing, and these metaphors have determined the criteria for truth claims. To understand is to "see" what is the case, to have an insight into what someone or something means.

Truth is, accordingly, a correspondence between perception and conception, thing and representation, reality and mind. Similar claims can be made for metaphors drawn from speaking and listening. We are interested in what people, texts, beliefs, and events "tell" us about themselves and the world. For these traditional epistemologies, knowing is a synthetic act of seeing or hearing something, an act in which the mind works on what is given to it. This means two things. First, knowing has receptive and active dimensions; it receives something (sense perceptions) which it makes sense of through ideas or concepts. Second, knowledge is born of the relation between these receptive and active dimensions. The condition of knowledge is not simply sense data or the construction of ideas and concepts but the synthetic act itself. This is why I argued in chapter 4 that "meaning," hermeneutically defined, is an event in which understanding and meaning connect in the medium of language.

This argument has also been made on nonhermeneutical grounds. For instance, critical idealism from Kant to Fichte found that condition of knowing in the synthetic act of the transcendental "I." That is, the "I" is the power to connect sense intuitions and concepts, thereby producing human knowing. But this also means that the "I," as the inner dynamic of the self, is always immediate to itself in all its acts. Given this, when the "I" acts it must apprehend its own being. "I think, therefore I am," as René Descartes put it. Hermeneutic reflection, which challenges the immediacy of the "I" to itself, finds this condition in language and the act of dialogical interpretation. It attempts to escape the narrow concerns of epistemology while acknowledging the active and receptive dimensions of understanding. Hermeneutics, as I have argued, always ties self-understanding to an encounter with what is other than self.

Given these observations, we can ask: what is the construal thinkers have adopted or made in order to speak about comparative understanding? Ironically, current comparative ethics simply lacks an answer to this question. This is the case even though there is a tacit agreement among scholars that understanding entails analogical insight and is reached through the act of translation. Adopting the participant's perspective, I want to explore what is meant by translation and insight precisely from the vantage point of interpretation. Translation is the active, even poetic, dimension of comparative understanding whereas insight marks its receptive, basically aesthetic, dimension. Their relation is found in the practice of interpretation, which is by the nature of the case communicative and intersubjective.

Comparison, at least for the West, often arose through travel and adventure, the act of moving between, or trans-lating, worlds. This historical fact is rich with phenomenological import. It is even seen, as I noted in chapter 3, in the image of the human presupposed in the information age. Comparative understanding entails some movement; it is an act of translation. This translation is present most simply at the level of linguistic systems, but more profoundly it entails a movement between cultural worlds thanks to the medium of language. Understanding is the act of making a movement—a translation—between the texts, beliefs, and activities of others and one's own world of meaning. Hans-Georg Gadamer has made this point.

> Reflect for a moment, if you would, on this: what is involved when we translate, when we transpose a dead thing, in a new act of understanding, from what was present as a text only in a foreign language into our own language? The translation process contains the whole secret of human understanding of the world and of social communication.[13]

This secret of understanding, we must note, takes place by means of what texts, beliefs, and practices of others have to say to us—their subject matter. This is so because language is the mediating structure of understanding. Thus in translation one finds a dialectic of linguistic mediation and understanding concerning what something or someone has to say.

In part, understanding others is translating or carrying over beliefs, practices, texts, and symbols into a language the interpreter can comprehend. It is to play the "Hermes," the messenger between worlds. Such movement is not foreign to religious communities. Through ritual, dramatic action they entail patterns of movement between worlds, between the sacred and the profane, between the temporal and the eternal, and through various liminal states, as Victor Turner calls them.[14] In these activities the participant is carried over, is translated, from one world to another by means of language and action. The simplicity of this observation ought not to fool us, however. It means that translation is a metaphoric process. To carry over or transfer meaning as a linguistic act is the movement metaphor entails.[15] It is poetically creative of meaning. Comparison is a metaphoric activity in and through translation. This is the active dimension of comparative understanding.

The metaphoricity of translation poses a genuine problem for comparative studies. To what do the translator's claims refer? Do they refer to the community's beliefs that are being translated and/or the meaning created through the clash between the interpreter's linguistic world and those beliefs? If translation is a metaphoric activity, it would seem impossible to control the creation of meaning and thus achieve any precise knowledge about the actual beliefs of others. This problem is behind the current debate about the need and possibility of a formal metalanguage for comparative studies and the attempt once again to achieve the observer's perspective. Some thinkers argue that complete translation is not possible in any ordinary language because it is fraught with polysemy and metaphoricity. The philosopher must therefore construct an artificial language—a denaturalized discourse, as Paul Griffiths calls it—in which to carry out comparison.[16] This discourse would be free of metaphoricity and thus the creation of meaning in its struggle for univocity. Other philosophers despair of this enterprise because we can hardly be certain that any constructed discourse actually accounts for what one is trying to understand. Likewise, it would seem impossible to escape the metaphoric shape of comparative understanding because understanding itself is an activity of translation.

What this dispute shows is that the formal criterion of comparison (i.e., representing accurately the beliefs and actions of others as they understand them) cannot be justified solely in terms of an analysis of language, since the very act of translation is metaphorically charged. The way to meet the problem, and thus to respect the independent status of what one wants to understand, is not to try to escape the metaphoric character of translation, the density of natural discourse, or the participant's attitude. Instead, it is to ask about what transpires in our own activity of translation. This means realizing that translation is related to another dimension of understanding.

The current debate in comparative ethics is instructive on this point. All contributors to the dispute seem to agree that what arises through comparative work is some analogical insight into one set of beliefs and values and another, for instance, between one set of claims about virtue and another.[17] And in fact, philosophers have long known that the ability to metaphorize well, to transpose meanings, requires that one see similarities in differences even as metaphoric discourse provides new insight, new discoveries of what was not previously understood. Insight, we might say, is the passive and even aesthetic dimension of comparative understanding that arises within the act of translation. Paul Ricoeur is correct, then, when he notes that invention (translation) is actually discovery (insight).[18] Just because analogical insight arises within the inventive activity of translation does not mean that we do not discover something true about how others see life.

Translation and insight are the dialectic at the heart of comparative understanding. That we gain insight through comparison shows us both the possibilities and the limits of translation as a metaphoric activity. There are enough similarities to enable us to carry over the beliefs and practices of others into our own discourse, realizing that this is also productive of new meaning. However, something is also lost or never transported precisely because of the productive character of the metaphoric act of translation. This fact founds the universality of the hermeneutical problem in comparative studies and thus the ongoing task of interpretation for such work.

What I am suggesting is that comparative understanding is an activity of translation within which arise insights into similarities and differences between traditions, communities, and thinkers by means of engaging the symbols, myths, and beliefs they have about human life and the world. This is not a novel suggestion. It coheres with common practice in comparative studies. What has not been addressed in the current discussion is how to think through the dialectic of translation and insight within interpretation. Scholars are in search of a construal of the act of understanding that is the synthesis of translation and insight, one that does not simply appeal to a transcendental "I" but itself is genuinely comparative. Mimesis, I contend, helps in this regard. In order to show this I must explore the way it enables us to consider the range of issues entailed in comparison.

MIMESIS AND INTERPRETATION

The terminology of mimesis arose in Dionysian cultic worship and Sicilian mime—in ritual and drama. Only later was it used by Plato and Aristotle for speaking about art, poetics, moral education, and even metaphysics. Before Plato's reading of it as "imitation," mimesis "meant not only imitation, but also 'to make like,' 'to bring to presentation,' 'to express,' 'to present.'"[19] To understand mimesis as a way of thinking about symbolic action is then to explore representation and the entire field of human action.

The roots of mimesis in ritual and drama as well as its philosophical use by Aristotle concerning narrative have all been reclaimed in contemporary thought.[20] There are several reasons why this retrieval of mimesis is attractive for my argument. First, a turn to performative action implies that the meaning of a text, symbol, or image cannot be understood solely in terms of its supposed "author" or of a "referent" that it seeks to copy. This challenges classic theories in which ideas and works of art imitate "nature" or eidetic forms. Hence it has import for *what* the comparativist studies since it frees her or him to engage the subject matter of the *interpretandum* rather than its supposed origin or author. As Ricoeur has put it, in hermeneutics we are concerned with what is disclosed in front of the text as a possible way of being in the world.[21] For the ethicist, this disclosure bears on individual and social conduct and character.

Second, a retrieval of mimesis allows us to say something about *how* understanding takes place. It enables us to see the activity of interpretation as a form of ritual and dramatic action. This shifts our account of understanding from perceptual metaphors (seeing/hearing) with relation to concepts to that of a kind of activity or practice and requires the participant's attitude.[22] As Gadamer and others argue, understanding arises within dialogical interaction. Dialogue must be seen as mimetic in character. What mimesis adds to current theories of dialogue is the centrality of practice, and specifically of performative action, in understanding.[23]

Finally, the turn to mimesis allows us to say something about the *conditions* for understanding: they are found in the relation between language and action in the activity of interpretation. Mimetic practices are the reflexive processes through which a community or individual gains an identity by engaging various construals of life. If we can show that interpretation is the scholar's mimetic praxis, we will have demonstrated two things. First, we will have isolated the analogical relation between the mimetic activities of religious communities and those of scholars. This relation is central to the very possibility of understanding. Second, we also will have shown why moral demands ground other criteria in comparative religious studies. This means that comparative work itself is a kind of moral task, with all the risks and responsibilities that such a task entails. Having said this, I want now to specify these claims and their importance for interpretation in comparative religious ethics.

The Conditions of Understanding

Any account of understanding must begin with a simple but vexing problem. To understand anything at all requires some pregiven relation to what one is seeking to understand. Without this relation, understanding is quite literally impossible, or, worse yet, there is the imposition of the interpreter's perspective on the thoughts and lives of others. This is a problem in comparative studies: what is the condition for understanding moral and religious beliefs that are radically different from one's own? As we have seen, there is virtually no agreement on this point among comparative ethicists. Some look to the deep structure of rationality itself, others hold to the minimal conditions of having the ability to speak a moral language, and still other philosophers construct denaturalized metalanguages as the condition for comparative work.

A turn to performative action, or mimesis, provides a redress of this problem. It suggests that one condition for comparative study is found in the feelings we have of ourselves and of the world that arises in action. As Hans Jonas puts it,

> Reality is disclosed in the same act and as one with the disclo-
> sure of my own reality—which occurs in self-action: in feeling
> my own reality by some sort of *effort* I make, I feel the reality of
> the world. And I make an effort in the encounter with some-
> thing other than myself.[24]

My task is not to justify this phenomenological claim. At best, we can con-
firm it by elucidating its heuristic import. The point is simply that a condition of understanding is found in human activity, because action has an in-
tentional structure that includes the disclosure of a relation among self, the
world, and others. And yet, this initial observation about action and the
disclosure of reality does not completely solve the problem of the conditions
for understanding. It fails to tell us about a shared horizon within which our
actions take place, or it assumes that self-action constitutes that horizon. If
the latter is the case, how can we be assured that *what* is being understood
is not finally the expression of oneself or, more generally, one's cognitive
system or even one's wishes?

Once we conceive of interpretation as a performative action, we can
grasp the spatial-temporal horizon that is the condition for understanding.
This horizon is disclosed by the interpreter's action but not constituted by
him or her. Again, Jonas puts this well:

> In miming representation (as in speech), the performer's own
> body in action is the carrier of the symbolism, which remains
> bound to the transient act itself. Thus the imagery, enacted in
> the space and time that actor and spectator share, remains
> merged with the common causal order in which things happen,
> interact, and pass. As a real event it has its allotted span within
> the common time, and is no more. It is indeed repeatable, and by
> this token its eidetic identity defies the uniqueness of real events;
> but it has to be repeated in order to be present, and it "is" only
> while being produced.[25]

Any mimetic action inscribes its participants in a common order through
the corporeal character of the interaction. Such corporeality—bodiliness—
is present whether we are speaking of scholars reading texts or participants
in a ritual. The participatory character of mimetic action provides a way of
considering the conditions that make comparative understanding possible.
By undertaking the act of interpretation the scholar enters a shared spatial-
temporal order through the effort of that action.

What constitutes the possibility of insight into similarities between
beliefs and ways of life is the common order enacted in interpretation. Yet
this is also the condition for apprehending differences, since what is dis-

closed in the act is the reality of the other and the interpreter as different. The interpreter feels the reality of others thanks to the effort of interpretation. In interpretation, this "feeling," as Jonas called it, has a cognitive dimension because it is a quality of understanding. We find it, for instance, in the dissonance we sense between the beliefs of others and our own, responses that can range from revulsion to fascination. Such feelings are to moral understanding what sense perceptions are to empirical knowledge.[26] It is hardly surprising, then, that comparativists agree that understanding is characterized by analogical insight. We gain insight into what always remains different even at the level of basic felt experience.

This also has bearing on ethical reflection. On the one hand, the spatial-temporal horizon presented through the incarnate character of interpretive action is the backing for a naturalist bent in comparative ethics. The moral life takes place within the structure and dynamics of reality, however construed. On the other hand, the irreducibility of others and the "feeling" of ourselves in relation to them disclosed in action requires a hermeneutical approach to ethics. The "world" of moral action is always an interpreted one, whatever else it might be. In sum, the event of understanding is not a transcendence of the world; it is a participation through interaction in the emergence of a common world of meaning in continuity with a shared causal order of action. And this is also why I have spoken of hermeneutical realism in ethics. However, *what* is being interpreted? To address this takes us into problems traditionally assigned to the discourse of mimesis: the status and meaning of representations.

Mimesis and Representation

For much of Western thought, the tactic taken to explore the meaning and truth status of representations was to isolate their cause. This assumed that "expression is the power of a subject; and expressions *manifest* things, and hence essentially refer us to subjects for whom these things can be manifest."[27] Imitation in classical and even nineteenth-century romantic thought was a way of conceptualizing the relation among representation, referent, and the representation's cause (e.g., "nature" or mind). The problem the comparativist faces is that the images, symbols, and myths religious communities use in interpreting and guiding their lives cannot easily be reduced to the expression of a subject. The aesthetics of expressivism simply fails to account for complex mythic and symbolic systems. How then are we to explore these systems? In order to address this issue we must consider two things: (1) the general problem of symbolic or linguistic expression and (2) the particular problems of expression that scholars explore.

It is the capacity of linguistic and symbolic forms to efface or transform their own causes that is crucial to their semantic effectiveness. A work escapes the intentions of its author precisely through its inscription as a text; it takes on a life of its own. What is disclosed is not simply the intentionality of a human subject. As Charles Taylor notes,

> What comes about through the development of language in the broadest sense is the coming to be of expressive power, the power to make things manifest. It is not unambiguously clear that this ought to be considered as self-expression/realization. What is made manifest is not exclusively, nor even mainly, the self, but a world.[28]

Current hermeneutical theory has capitalized on this point by freeing the interpreter from the search for the ostensive origins of a work. There is a difficulty in this, however. If we bracket the question of "authorship," how do we understand the representation relative to that to which it refers, to its subject matter?

This question is at the heart of any theory of text, symbol, or action. To answer it requires that we examine the audience, or the subjects, for whom things can be manifested and also what is being expressed in practices and texts aside from their supposed author. This is to suggest that the "subject matter" of ethics must include the lives of those for whom something is manifest in religious practices. Comparison cannot be constricted to the supposed "moral" discourse of a community, as if that discourse could be severed from the world enacted in the discursive and ritual actions of a community. As the new naturalists have seen, comparative ethics must consider the relation between beliefs about how humans can and should live and other beliefs about their world.

However, this naturalist argument must be modified by hermeneutical considerations. Comparative ethics needs to examine the ways in which persons and communities have a world of meaning as this bears on life and conduct. The ethicist approaches this issue by interpreting the images of life that communities make and use in shaping character and conduct through their own performative activities, everything from rituals to methods of interpreting sacred texts to specific ways of life. *What* the comparativist is exploring are the complex practices communities use to symbolize their own lives. The "referent" of these practices is their reception in a specific form of life as well as what they present as possibilities for life. The moral import of this is obvious: a basic ethical question concerns the formation of life and the actual or possible disparity between beliefs about how one ought to live and concrete modes of behavior. Exploring the mimetic dynamics of communities is an entry into this problematic. What makes this exploration possible is that the relation of audience, and thus interpreter, to subject matter transpires in language, not simply as a system of signs but as discourse, as the medium of the reciprocal, dialogical action *between* agents. The scholar enters this dialogical space through the unique effort of interpretation. By engaging the symbols, texts, and actions of other communities, the comparativist is presenting a new shared world of meaning.

Thus far I have made two claims and related them to the discourse of mimesis. First, I have argued that the condition of possibility for understanding others is action. The act of interpretation requires and presents a common spatial and temporal order even while it enacts the difference between interpreter and what is being interpreted. It is analogous to what happens in religious practices and can be thought about by means of the concept of mimesis, especially when we see that mimesis arose out of dramatic and ritual action. Second, I have suggested that whatever it is that comparative ethics wants to study, it is bound up with the images, symbols, and narratives a community employs to inform life. This means exploring the power of language through interpretive action to present a possible way of life. Put differently, I have briefly addressed the general problem of expression and representation through the metaphoric character of mimetic action. Can mimesis also help us to explore the more particular expressions that comparativists study?

Gadamer has shown that a symbol, image, or work of art is the transformation into figuration of its subject matter: human action in narratives, sacred origins in cosmogonic myths, and so on. In this transformation, the subject matter, whatever it happens to be, achieves a certain ideality beyond its momentary appearance in discourse or specific enactments, ritual or dramatic. The fleeting and fickle shape of human action, for example, enjoys an increase in meaning through its transformation into a drama. Through the transformation into figuration (say, a narrative), one is concerned not simply with the contingency of a happening but also with its ideality, its character and meaning.

This helps to explain the disappearance of mimesis as a concept in modern reflection on texts, symbols, and works of art. Modern thought entails a rejection of a stable nature or essence and looks instead to history and the realm of becoming. The criticism of imitation was that "mimesis as a poetic theory demands a very realistic ontology if it is to thrive or to occur at all. The first step in achieving poetic form is contact with form in nature."[29]

Aristotelian mimesis, in other words, meant that the interpreter had to grasp the ideality or form found in the nature of human action as it was represented by plot. Based on the argument above, this criticism of classical realism need not trouble us. The ideality grasped by interpreting a community's pictures of life is not the form or nature of the human as such, but precisely what that community is struggling to resemble, is using to inform its specific and historically contingent way of life. The ideality of these pictures is how they form and transform ways of being human by presenting a vision of what ought to be. The particular images, symbols, and myths of communities are transformations into figuration of some vision about life as this bears on the *ethos* and conduct of a community and its members.

By reclaiming the performative roots of mimesis we are then concerned with the creation and reception of meaning through particular symbolic forms and actions. Unlike modern expressive theories, the pictures that the comparativist interprets manifest a way of life in a world. Attending to the mimetic practices in which those pictures make sense requires that we not consider them as realistic imitations of nature, brute imaginative creations, or simple projections of collective or individual consciousness. Rather, they must be explored within symbolic interaction. The totality of a community's symbolic world is enacted in mimetic practices that inform its way of life. Particular figures must then be placed within the entire complex of the interpretive practices of a community.

On reaching this conclusion we return to the vexing problem of the conditions for understanding. How is it that the interpreter can come to understand the particular images, symbols, and myths of communities? It is here that we must attend to the shift from the active to the receptive character of understanding, from the poetic aspect of mimetic action to its aesthetic dimension. We need to consider the audience and thus the interpreter of religious communities.

Audience and Interpreter

Through the transformation into figuration, the symbols, images, and actions of others break beyond themselves for beholders, to any possible interpreter. Because a way of life has achieved some ideality through figuration, it is presented for someone, for an audience or reader, who thereby can seek to understand what is so presented. The figurations, we might say, have an intentionality; they call for interpreters to complete their meaning. The audience, through its interpretive engagement, is crucial to the very meaning of symbols, texts, and images. The participant's attitude is basic to the meaning of what one seeks to understand, to the very *interpretandum* in question. It is in the lives of the audience or the interpreter that the symbolic action breaks beyond the confines of a system of signs.

This observation leads us to the passive dimension of understanding. We should recall that the spectator, the *theoros*, was the observer at the ancient rituals. The "theoretical" stance of the interpreter in comparative ethics is then not a disengaged viewing, as Plato held. It does not require the observer's attitude, as if the claims of the comparativist were strictly reducible to propositional statements about states of affairs. Rather, a theoretic stance is an interaction with others in order to understand what demands interpretation. Understanding begins, as Gadamer has noted, with listening. And he insists that mimesis and "presentation (*Darstellung*) are not merely a copied repetition, but a recognition of the essence. Because they are not merely repetition, but a bringing-forth, the spectator is involved in them."[30]

This recognition, or insight, is a complex phenomenon. As thinkers from Aristotle to Ricoeur attest, amid interpretive interaction there arise various feelings, from pity to fear, that enable the audience to appropriate what is disclosed by those symbolic works. We claim what we interpret as our own in good measure through our affective responses to it. This feeling, as noted before, is cognitive since it arises in the act of interpretation. It is the moral analogue to sense data. Interpretation thereby allows moral self-knowledge to be linked to the understanding of others precisely through the feeling of one's own activity. This is the import of the phenomenological observation about action made above: self and other are disclosed in the effort and feeling characteristic of action.

The recognition of the relation of self and other is a good that is internal to the activity of interpretation, as Alasdair MacIntyre might put it.[31] The good of insight is possible because symbols, myths, and rituals intend an audience, beholders, who are taken into the event of understanding. The interpreter is finally not free from what is being interpreted even as *what* is being understood requires interpreters in order to be made manifest. The relation of interpreter to subject matter constituted amid interpretive action accounts for the contemporaneity experienced in the event of understanding. For instance, we understand the claim of ancient texts and we do so now, in the present. This is possible—again, as noted before—because of the spatial and temporal conditions of understanding disclosed by action. There is, as Gadamer calls it, a fusion of horizons (*Horizontverschmelzung*) definitive of genuine insight. The horizon of meaning of the interpreter—that is, her or his configuration of the temporal-spatial conditions of meaningful action, is transformed and widened by the *interpretandum* even as it is allowed to speak anew through the interpreter's performative act.

The involvement of the audience, and thus the interpreter, in symbolic meaning bears considerable import for comparative ethics. To interpret the figurations of a community is to understand how certain people's lives are taken into specific mimetic practices and come to resemble what is presented in them. By seeking to carry over or translate meanings, the interpreter is taken into an event such that one sees similarities and differences between the sets of beliefs in question. This insight, I am suggesting, is not grounded in the pictures or beliefs so translated since translation is never complete. Insight is an end, a good, of the mimetic action of interpretation; it is how the human good is tied to, if not exhausted by, rational activity. Insight is a form of understanding qualified by affective response born of effort and encounter. As the good internal to the practice of interpretation, insight emerges from the analogical relation between interpretation and the mimetic activities through which communities form and appropriate construals of how to live.

By using mimesis to explore comparative interpretation we see that interpretation is the comparative philosopher's mimetic praxis. Insight is its good. This means that the figures of a tradition that inform life are part of *what* comparative ethics explores. Interpreting a tradition is not simply a way of enriching the theoretical task of comparison, as Ronald Green and Charles Reynolds suggest.[32] Without engagement of these figurations, there would be nothing to compare.

Understanding and Responsibility

But what is being understood in specifically ethical terms and how does this relate to the criterion of interpretation? This is the last dimension of mimetic practice of immediate import for our argument. Obviously, what one seeks to study are the beliefs, images, stories, and other figurations of a community about its world and how people should live. And the formal criterion for interpretation is an accurate representation of the figures and life of a community as its members understand them. This criterion is formal, we must admit, because we must specify what counts as an "accurate" representation; how, if at all, we can grasp the way in which a community understands its own beliefs and images; and, finally, whether or not our own self-understanding is helpfully included in judging the adequacy of an interpretation of religious beliefs and practices.

I cannot address all these issues in this chapter. We must first specify the grounds internal to interpretation that justify adherence to this formal criterion and its specifications, whatever they are. These grounds must be internal to interpretation, because we are interested in a reasoned approach to the study of ethics. So far I have argued that mimetic interpretation is the shape of reason in comparison. Now I must show that it grounds the demand for adhering to the criterion of valid interpretation. The irony here, from the perspective of some philosophers, is that I am claiming that moral demands form the context for the more narrow epistemic claims of the scholar. The reason for this is actually simple: if understanding requires participation in the communicative activity of interpretation, then demands on participation and action precede the particular criterion for propositional claims.

I want to approach this question about the formal criterion for interpretation by exploring once again mimetic practices as clues to comparative understanding. First, we should note that ritual actions in religious communities surround those events in life that are determinative of existence (birth, death, initiation, etc.) and thus are responses to the disruptions and continuities in existence.[33] Mimetic actions are responses to powers—psychological, social, physiological, and even cosmic powers—that persons suffer and enact. Mimetic practices can be seen as patterns of responsibility in a twofold sense: they entail a response to something or someone, and they require accountability for actions intended, undertaken, and actualized.[34]

What comparative ethics must explore is the texture of responsibility in different communities expressed through mimetic practices. These practices—like cultic action (see chapter 2)—are basically ways of participating in the enactment of a world of meaning and relations of power. They are responses to the problem of world building and maintenance, as sociologists put it, and thus also to basic existential questions such as suffering and death, the problem of evil, and self-understanding.[35] Such problems are profoundly ontological in character: they concern evaluative, affective responses to a world. The question of responsibility, then, touches on how persons and communities envision and posture themselves as participants in their world and on how these visions and postures shape and inform a way of life. It concerns how they take part in the construal of beliefs, symbols, and myths that guide and judge life and also how they appropriate them in a way of life. Given this, responsibility cannot be limited simply to legal demands or to "the amelioration of the human condition by resolving the problem of cooperation."[36]

This does not mean that comparative ethics begins with an a priori concept of natural human aims or with the deep structure of morality. Rather, it explores how the human *need* to participate in its own formation is carried out through mimetic practices that transform personal and social powers by subjecting them to claims of responsibility (see chapter 1).[37] Different communities will figure power differently, through rituals and anti-rituals, myths, prophetic discourse, and so on, and thus will entail various patterns of responsibility, different worlds of meaning and ways of being human. What they share, and all that is needed for comparative study, is the dynamic of mimetic activity through which they respond to and participate in a world. Religious traditions fail or die when their mimetic practices no longer donate this sense of active participation.

If this is the case, we can grasp the justification for adherence to the formal criterion of interpretation. Interpretation is the scholar's mimetic praxis and as such serves as a form of responsibility for him or her. Interpretation enacts a common world, a world that permits and demands responses to others and accountability for one's actions. The formal criterion of interpretation merely specifies a way of determining this responsiveness and accountability. Scholars willingly submit to this criterion because it is grounded in the very shape of their own act of interpretation; it is not heteronomous but is an expression of the free exercise of understanding. For the very same reason, the criterion of interpretation is not simply generated from the subjective purposes of interpreters. Again, Habermas is correct when he notes that "a correct interpretation fits, suits, or explicates the meaning of the *interpretandum*."[38] We now see how the demand for a fitting interpretation arises and how it coheres with the common world of understanding enacted in the mimetic act of interpretation.

The mimetic shape of interpretation helps us understand the justification for the demand of respect, i.e., to represent accurately the beliefs, symbols, and lives of others. Interpretation is the scholar's mimetic praxis. It is our means of moving between worlds and thus gaining insight into our lives and those of others. Interpretation is also how we respond to and participate in the enactment of a shared world of action and discourse. The condition and the demand for understanding are found in action itself whose intentionality, I have argued, is the self-other relation it enacts.

A PROPOSAL FOR COMPARATIVE ETHICS

What is the significance of this argument about moral rationality and the point of comparative ethics? Most basically, I have sought to mediate the disputes found in comparative studies while charting different directions for thought. This has required isolation of the structure of mimetic action in which understanding transpires even though practices and their communities differ. This formal structure is marked by reciprocal action within a shared spatial-temporal order mediated by linguistic, symbolic forms. It is a condition for comparative, descriptive study and also a reason to question radical relativism in normative reflection. Just because cultures and religions enact different "worlds" that define and shape character and conduct does not negate the fact that to be human is to have a world presented through patterns of reciprocal action. It is this shared fact that makes complete moral relativism spurious. The differences between religions are not incommensurable ones, because, if my argument holds, comparative interpretation is itself the enactment of a common world of meaning. It is not of course a pregiven moral universe. Yet through interpretation a shared world of meaning allows us to understand what remains different and requires respect for that difference.

The approach to understanding I am advocating moves, then, beyond the formalist/descriptivist debate in comparative ethics. It does so by tracing a common, formal structure to mimetic action while insisting that one must think comparatively by engaging not only that structure but also the figurations, symbols, beliefs, and practices that mark a community's moral world. The dialectic of translation and insight characteristic of comparative understanding founds the demand for critical analysis and interpretive engagement in comparative ethics. In other words, the use of reason in comparative ethics is neither purely formal nor simply descriptive; it is interpretive in character.

The position I have sought to chart also circumvents the naturalist/ non-naturalist debate concerning *what* comparative ethics explores. It suggests that comparative ethics is concerned with moral worlds but that the question of a "world" must take seriously the discursive, symbolic forms enacted in communities that give rise to a sense of reality and possible ways of life. This requires examination of the relation between basic human needs and beliefs about reality and human life in descriptive and in normative inquiry. Of course, there is no assumption about what *ought* to be the shape of a moral and religious life. Here a comparative ethics must carefully engage, interpret, compare, and evaluate traditions, and yet it must insist that the problem of mimesis—the picturing, making, and forming of a life-world with reference to what is encountered in the effort and feeling of action— is found in all cultures and traditions. It must claim that religions can be seen as complex mimetic practices that construe and enact a world and a way of life. They are forms of radical interpretation. For comparative ethics, this means taking seriously the naturalist claim about the relationship between moral convictions and other beliefs, and yet a comparative ethics must examine this claim within the problem of a moral "world" and thus within the narratives, symbols, and practices that shape life.

The turn to performative action also helps answer the most disputed point in comparative ethics: the condition that makes comparative study possible. This condition cannot be simply the deep structure of reason or some specified metalanguage, because our only access to the structure of rationality is itself an interpretive one and, further, the practice of construing a metalanguage cannot escape the mediation of all human activity by natural linguistic forms. Likewise, the condition for understanding cannot be simply an analogy of discursive ability as social-linguistic thinkers seem to hold. This is so because, as noted before, one must also consider that in which linguistic activity takes place, its horizon, if one wants to grasp how it is we can understand what is and must remain different. What is more, the experience of action—the sense of self and other through effort and encounter—shows that language games break beyond themselves just because they are forms of action. Finally, the condition for comparative work cannot be simply the descriptive study of the myths, symbols, and practices communities make and employ in speaking about their world and their lives. These myths, symbols, and practices must be interpreted in order to be meaningful and thus are bound to our own act of understanding.

In short, the main options in comparative religious ethics offer deficient accounts of the conditions for their own interpretive activity. By drawing on the conceptual density of mimesis I have isolated the means of considering the condition for understanding. It is, as we have seen, a shared spatial-temporal order enacted through the interpretive activity of examining the figurations communities make and use to inform their lives. By considering what transpires in interpretation—that is, analogical insight within translation—we have seen that the common world of understanding is a metaphorized world that we invent in order to discover something about others and ourselves. This shared world is enacted in a practice (interpretation) characterized by a movement between worlds (translation) with its own good (insight) and under the moral demand (responsibility) to adhere to the formal criterion of comparison.

The task of comparative religious ethics on this reading is not simply the study of diverse moral traditions, although it is certainly that. More profoundly, the practice of comparative ethics contributes to the enactment of a shared moral universe in which the diverse ways of being human are preserved amid the claims of responsibility. Only by insisting on this do we avoid the tyranny of interpretation—that is, the imposition of the interpreter's perspective on what is under inquiry. To see interpretation as a form of responsibility means that the comparativist must respond to the claim of the other and be accountable for her or his actions. Formal and material criteria for interpretation rest on this moral demand. With this conclusion we reach as well what this argument contributes to the general task of the comparative philosophy of religions. Such work can begin with the simple fact that human beings fashion their lives by engaging various figures that disclose to them something about the meaning, value, and purpose of being human. It reaches its goal when through encountering others in the performative act of interpretation we experience some apprehension of the shape, texture, and direction of the lives of ourselves and others within a shared space of meaning and responsibility.

CONCLUSION

Comparative ethics seeks to understand other communities and traditions even as it hopes to say something about our moral and religious condition. It would be a mistake, therefore, to think that the argument made in these pages is not itself fundamentally concerned with answering the pressing questions that face us. Is it not the case in the West that the images, myths, and symbols we have used or made to guide our lives are now in serious question? Have we not in fact witnessed the decay of practices that shaped and animated life into repressive and manipulative forms of thought and discourse seen in technological, mass culture? Was this not the force of our inquiry in chapter 3 of this book?

In this situation we lack a norm for responsible existence because the "distinction between life and art, reality and appearance becomes impossible. . . . Life becomes the proto-type of the world of appearances and these the proto-types of life."[39] In response to this situation I have argued that interpretation is our mimetic activity. It is our way of responding to the questions that confront us even as it bears within it the good of understanding that insists on the reality of the other. In undertaking to engage the other, the interpreter struggles to understand how we should live. And this understanding emerges, if at all, within practices that enact the fragile claim of responsibility.

PART 3 MORALITY AND CHRISTIAN COMMITMENT

The final part of this book explores the connection between religion and morality by examining three forms of realistic ethics present in the history of Western ethics. In chapter 7, I engage the work of Dietrich Bonhoeffer on the centrality of Christ for understanding reality and also morality. This enables me to further my description of our postmodern condition, and also to specify the claims about God that I judge must be affirmed in moral reflection. Chapter 8 addresses one of the most pervasive forms of moral realism in the history of Western ethics. Divine command ethics—that is, the claim that what is morally right is what God commands—is important for my argument not only because it is a form of moral realism, albeit a form I judge untenable, but also because, as I show, it properly forces one to consider the relation between power and value. Finally, in chapter 9, I examine a current representative of what I take to be the main philosophical partner to Christian moral realism: Platonic ethics. I try to show that Christian moral reflection, while in substantive agreement with Platonism, offers a decided advance in thinking.

Part 3 develops and defends hermeneutical realism and an ethics of responsibility with respect to other realistic options in ethics. Yet in doing so, these last three chapters also reenact the pattern of thought found in previous parts of the book. In chapter 7, the question of how to understand reality, and so too the reality of value, is addressed in ways parallel to my previous account of our moral situation (chapter 1) and the nature of moral meaning (chapter 4). Chapter 8 treats the question of power and value in terms of the place of divine command in moral understanding. This relates to the earlier discussion of understanding our world (chapter 2) and also the idea of radical interpretation (chapter 5). Finally, in chapter 9, matters of the reality (chapter 7) and power (chapter 8) of God are linked to convictions about the goodness of God, a goodness understood in terms of the transvaluation of power. At that juncture I am exploring the deepest suppositions about morality and reality in a way consistent with the accounts given in my responses to skepticism (chapter 3) and to comparative moral reflection (chapter 6). Part 3 shows, then, that attention to the reality, power, and goodness of God—that is, to the central attributes of the divine in relation to us—has structured each and every chapter of this book.

7

The Reality
of Christ and the
Value of Power

The current world situation is marked by global perils, but also by possibilities for the emergence of new forms of thought and life.[1] Any adequate moral or public policy response to this situation requires international and cross-cultural cooperation on issues ranging from economic and environmental matters to population control. At the same time, our age has shown how previous political and ideological solutions to ethnic, cultural, and moral diversity have failed. This failure is attested to by the legacies of racism and economic disparity within market-driven democracies and, in former communist nations, by the memory of state-sanctioned tyranny. For those who think about religions, the question is the extent to which the world's religious traditions can provide resources for meeting the future in terms other than age-old hostilities. As shown in chapter 1, our world situation is one of moral and cultural diversity at the very moment when we face planetary problems.

RESPONSIBILITY AND BELIEFS ABOUT REALITY

In the light of this situation, the search by many thinkers for a global ethics of responsibility is hardly surprising. Theologians like Hans Küng and various religious leaders meeting at the World Parliament of Religions in Chicago issued a call for a global ethics.[2] Philosophers Hans Jonas, Karl-

Otto Apel, and others insist on the need for a global moral vision even though they disagree about the nature of that ethics.[3] Feminist theologians, communitarian thinkers, and others debate the possibility of a common morality after the waning of the so-called Enlightenment project and the current awareness of distinctive moral identities.[4] It is fitting that this debate about the possibility of a common, global ethics should come to focus around the idea of responsibility. An ethics of responsibility explores the exercise of power by agents within complex domains of value and social relations. This form of ethics is uniquely concerned with providing direction for how agents can and should respond to, create, and shape reality. In other words, an ethics of responsibility seeks to address the basic concerns of our time.

My task in this chapter is to contribute to the ongoing inquiry into moral responsibility. The focus of the argument is not directly on matters of public policy or even the question of the validity of a common ethics in a world of moral diversity, matters that rightly capture the attention of moral philosophers and theologians. Rather, my focus will be on the relation between responsibility and beliefs about reality as the context for human conduct. My reason for putting the inquiry in this way is quite simple. In an age of human power, we must understand how reality in all its diversity and complexity is to be respected and enhanced. As I stated before, *the* moral question of our time is about the integrity of life. If we do not grasp this point as basic to any viable public policy, course of action, or social organization, it is not at all clear that we will have a future on this planet. In the following pages, I hope to show some of the resources that Christian theological ethics holds for helping us address this pressing issue.

I want to begin the inquiry by explaining this point about the connection between responsibility and beliefs about reality. This returns us to themes first introduced in part 1 of this book. The question, again, is how divergent accounts of power are manifest in visions of reality. In this chapter, I explore this with respect to distinctly Christian claims about Jesus Christ, the one in whom power is made perfect in weakness. The next two chapters will continue the inquiry, but with respect to the discourse of divine command ethics (chapter 8) and the exchange between Platonic forms of ethics and Christian thought (chapter 9). Taken together, these three chapters represent a dialectical exchange between various kinds of moral realism in ethics and my own account of hermeneutical realism and its distinctive claims about the God of Christian faith. I hope not only to learn from these other positions in ethics, but also to offer a response to them that overcomes problems endemic to those kinds of moral realism.

In terms of the present chapter, our inquiry will progress through several layers of reflection. First, I will specify the lines of inquiry that currently characterize thinking about responsibility. My purpose in doing so is to show why the question of the moral significance of reality has reentered ethics after the rigid separation between moral and ontological claims that is characteristic of much modern ethics. The second layer of reflection is undertaken by exploring Dietrich Bonhoeffer's thought on Christ, "reality," and moral responsibility. This will enable me to focus on claims about the moral character of reality within a Christocentric ethics of responsibility. My reading of Bonhoeffer will undoubtedly be controversial. Scholars indebted to him will contest the criticisms I will level at Bonhoeffer's ethics; other moralists will dismiss any attempt to engage theological resources in order to address ontological questions in ethics. Be that as it may, the theological ethicist must use all available resources to address the matters at hand, and this is the tactic I take in this chapter.

The final layer of the argument is a theological ethical position that entails a revision in how we understand Christian faith and its claims about reality, a position that centers on the integrity of life. The validity of my position depends on its capacity to address ongoing problems in ethics, problems that center on the relation of power and value in beliefs about reality. Indeed, it is precisely these problems that propel the argument through the various layers of dialectical reflection.

THE MORAL SHAPE OF REALITY

Our current world situation demands a reconsideration within ethics of the place of claims about reality in the moral life. We simply must overcome the long-standing assumption in modern ethics that we can segregate moral values and norms from the beliefs persons and cultures hold about reality and human existence. For instance, the moral significance of reality is different if the world is conceived as created by God rather than as a purposeless confluence of emergent processes. These different accounts of reality warrant divergent moral outlooks. But this is merely to say that beliefs about reality are construals of the context of human existence rooted in experience. They must be interpreted and morally assessed. As stated before, one task of theological ethics is to isolate and explore the moral ontologies of contemporary thought and Christian belief. This means to examine how different pictures of reality and human existence entail constitutive beliefs about value and the source of morality.

In terms of moral theory, the reappraisal of the place of beliefs about reality within ethics falls, as we know, under the rubric of "moral realism."

Recall that "moral realism" simply means any theory which holds that morality and moral values are not simply or only human, social inventions. Moral realists insist that in some important and irreducible way we *discover* what is good and right; the right and the good are not simply *invented*. Realism in this strict sense holds that the ideal pattern of life is written into the structure of reality, the desires of individuals, or the fabric of reason. We do not choose the ideal pattern; we choose to live in harmony with or in defiance of it.[5] So defined, moral realism would seem to be required in any theological ethics because, whatever is meant by the symbol "God," the reality it designates always exists prior to acts of faith, imagination, and understanding. Typically, believers hold that in their reasoning about what to do and how to live, they are seeking to understand, discern, or discover what God wills or requires of them. For Christians, Jesus Christ reveals in some decisive way the divine will for us and also the true meaning of reality itself.

However, it is equally obvious that moral reasoning and action are creative in the sense that they respond to novel situations and cultural outlooks. In an important respect, we do invent what is morally right and also the shapes of our own lives. Taking these points seriously means that an ethics of responsibility must account for the limits and possibilities finite existence places on agents as well as genuine creativity in the moral life. Individuals and communities construe the world in certain ways on the basis of fundamental experiences; they do so by means of basic ideas, metaphors, and symbols in order thereby to discover the truth of a moral situation. I have called this position hermeneutical realism in ethics. My argument in the present chapter is an example, but not a defense, of this moral theory.[6]

Thus, I am arguing that a viable ethics of responsibility must insist on human action and creativity and yet also represent some form of moral realism. This brings me to the crux of my argument. I want to show that the kind of realism required in an ethics of responsibility centers on the precise relation of power and value in our construal of reality. Furthermore, I want to show that this is in fact not simply a philosophical matter, but a genuinely theological ethical question. In order to understand my claim, we must draw an extremely important distinction.

Classical forms of moral realism, such as natural law ethics, held that "reality" or "nature" indicated in various ways the ends and purposes we ought to seek in order to live morally. The purpose of the moral life was then to live in conformity with nature's dictates. The implications of this position are famous, or infamous, especially in sexual ethics. However, the form of moral realism I am advocating centers on the *vulnerability of reality* under human power and not nature's *indications*. The possibility of future life is bound to the exercise of human power in the present. With this shift of attention from the dictates of nature to its vulnerability, the central moral question becomes why reality itself is good and why we ought to respect and enhance it rather than try to isolate what goods nature supposedly indicates we ought to seek. The idea of the goodness of being must again become basic in ethics. Insisting on this goodness does not necessarily entail what Albert Schweitzer called an ethics of the reverence for life.[7] The goodness of life is not sacrality. But it does mean that utility alone—that is, the maximization of outcomes through the exercise of power—cannot justify the tragic choices we must make when life conflicts with life.

We can put the matter more sharply. What is the relation between power and the goodness of life? When we ask this question, we see that the moral outlooks of contemporary, technological Western societies and also Christian faith revolve around what I called in chapter 2 "axiologies of power." These moral ontologies entail different accounts of the value of power in understanding reality and the moral life. They claim, in other words, that the origin or source of the value of finite existence is power, and they conceive of this in terms of either God or distinctly human forms of power. The question of why the real is good, why finite existence matters at all and places constraints on the use of power, becomes then a matter of the power or powers that constitute or shape reality. As I understand it, this is a profoundly religious and theological question. It is a question about what human beings are responding to in the totality of their lives in the world.

Many have pointed out that the theological problem is that Christian faith too easily reduces all value to one central power (divine sovereignty) or, conversely, that it valorizes powerlessness in the figure of Jesus Christ. Christian faith is an axiology of power, but it is one, critics argue, that vacillates between the reduction of value to power or the simple negation of power (*kenotic* images of Christ). It is not clear whether these options offer much help in meeting the current challenge to ethics. Accordingly, theological ethics must redress the ambiguity about power in Christian faith. We will have to see later if Bonhoeffer's argument is adequate for the present demands of theological ethics.

I am arguing that an ethics of responsibility must address basic features of our world situation. It must first address beliefs about moral value in connection with the reality of power. And, second, an adequate ethics of responsibility must articulate the relation between human action and the environing world with which we interact and on which planetary life depends. These are, of course, deeply interrelated matters. As human power increases we have the capacity to subjugate the environment and the future to human purposes. Given this fact, it is of the utmost importance to determine what can and should direct the exercise of this newfound power. The moral dimension of power reopens the question of how we have thought about responsibility and also the moral significance of reality.

POWER, VALUE, AND REALITY

Any consideration of moral responsibility in our time needs to be carried out along different but intersecting lines of inquiry. We can usefully group these lines of inquiry under the headings of *value, power,* and *reality.* Taken together, these lines of inquiry also articulate the contours of our moral situation and the challenge facing an ethics of responsibility.

Under the heading of "value," responsibility ethicists are addressing two concerns that characterize contemporary life. First, most proponents of a global ethics of responsibility agree that the modern Western project of affirming human dignity, freedom, and self-determination remains an unfulfilled project, and, furthermore, that this project must be continued. For instance, at the United Nations meeting on population held in Cairo, the majority of participants agreed on the need to empower women. This is an apt symbol of the legacy of the modern quest for human dignity and freedom. On the eve of a new millennium, most people on this planet are hungry and have little control over their physical, political, economic, and spiritual lives. Women and children especially suffer this plight. Any global ethics must address this fact. In order to do so, it must reaffirm as morally basic a commitment to the dignity of all people and with this the need to empower them as historical agents. It is for this reason that the discourse of human rights, despite its problems, remains important in the international arena and in discourse about responsibility.

However, the affirmation of human dignity and freedom within the continuing modern project is not enough from the perspective of a new ethics of responsibility. This is attributable to the simple fact that human life depends on a fragile and endangered planetary ecosystem. Accordingly, the second concern under the heading "value" in present thinking about responsibility centers on overcoming the anthropocentrism of modern morality—that is, the claim that moral value centers on human beings alone and the projects they undertake. As Wolfgang Huber notes, the question is "whether humans alone are gifted with a specific dignity, or whether they participate in the dignity of all creatures, albeit in a specifically human manner."[8] A global ethics must address not only the possibility of human well-being and dignity, but also the demand for a viable future for life on earth.

The ethical question about planetary life concerns the moral status of nonhuman life and also the obligations, if any, we have to future life. The modern world, as we saw in chapter 5, has defined the domain of moral value in terms of rational agents—citizens, as Immanuel Kant put it, in the kingdom of ends—or, with utilitarians, around sentient life. But even taken most generously, it is not clear on either of these grounds what obligation we have for viable *future* life. The question of the moral status of the non-human includes the worth not only of sentient existence but also, surprisingly, of *future* life as well. Modern anthropocentrism collapsed all moral worth into human existence and, as I argued in chapter 2, construed the future as the empty horizon in which human beings fulfill their projects. Even the despair and nihilism of much twentieth-century philosophy, literature, and art confirms this point.[9] We were told by existentialists and pop artists that human beings are cast into a meaningless and valueless space to forge authentic existence in the face of death. One might imagine that this devaluation of nature and the future is in no small measure the consequence of the anthropocentrism of modernity and also the triumph of human power in understanding the world.

The problem facing ethics is that these two axiological concerns can and do conflict. How can and must we affirm the value of human dignity and self-determination when the demands for viable future life places limits on the expansion of human interests? Yet even this question about the conflict of values does not strike deeply enough. There is yet another element in the current thinking about responsibility. This element falls under the heading of power. No matter what form responsibility takes, power is basic.[10] We live in an age of increasing human power, and this fact moves responsibility to the center of ethics. The moral question is how, if at all, we can direct and evaluate the use of power.

On this score, theologians and philosophers face profound problems in ethics in terms of specifying principles for assessing power. If one looks to contemporary, technological culture, the basic premise, I have been claiming, seems to be that power simply ought to be maximized. Recall Hans Jonas's sobering words: "The paradox of the modern condition is that this reduction of man's stature, the utter humbling of his metaphysical pride, goes hand in hand with his promotion to quasi-God-like privilege and power. The emphasis is on power."[11] And yet, if one looks to traditional Christian belief, power is either asserted as ontologically basic in the creative action of God or divested of worth in the *kenosis* of a Christ who took the form of a servant. In other words, contemporary ethics is confronting the ambiguity of our religious heritage on the question of the value of power and yet must find some way to counter a simple celebration of the will-to-power by technological culture. It is for this reason that responsibility theorists are looking anew at the place of appeals to reality in ethics.

Virtually all forms of modern ethics have insisted on a strict fact/value, or is/ought, distinction. The force of this point was to contend that we invent morality, we do not discover it. I cannot know what I ought to do by exploring what is the case or what kind of entity a human being is. There is no ideal pattern for how to live, as classical realism held. And this is the case because words like "ought" and "good," when used morally, do not seem to refer to anything in the world. They are directives for actions or words of appraisal and not reports about reality. The upshot of this claim about moral concepts is that moral values are not part of the fabric of the world. Morality has no ontological status.[12] The passion motivating this position, as I argued in the introduction to this book, is the passion for freedom; it is to liberate human beings from all forms of tyranny that seek legitimation in appeals to the "real," to what is "natural."

Cracks have begun to appear in this distinctly modern consensus about fact and value. Moral theorists are once again asking about the ontological status of value.[13] In part, this can be attributed to the pressure of ecological consciousness on moral thinking and with it the challenge to modern anthropocentrism. Yet it is also a result of the fact that in moral reasoning we commonly think we are trying to arrive at a right judgment rather than simply inventing a moral outlook. Reality seems to pull on our commonsense moral intuitions. As Erazim Kohák has shown, it is not odd or counterintuitive to speak of a moral sense of nature.[14] This does not shackle us to current or classical ideologies about what is "natural." It merely means that human life transpires within a context of value and that come what may we must seek to understand and respond to this fact. In terms of responsibility, the question, then, is: to what reality or realities can and ought we respond in order to live morally?

Thus, current theorists of responsibility are exploring questions of human dignity, the moral standing of nonhuman life and the future, increasing human power, and the relation of convictions about moral value to construals of reality. In this way, the discussion of responsibility calls into question central features of the modern moral outlook—its anthropocentrism, the separation of fact and value, and how we ought to promote the dignity of all human beings. However, what has not been clearly grasped is the essential connection between, on the one hand, axiological concerns for the value of individuals and the moral standing of the ecosphere and the future, and, on the other hand, the reality of power. What is the connection between power and value? The fact that this question remains unanswered in ethics is indeed odd, since, as I have repeatedly noted, the modern account of the nature of human existence and traditional religious beliefs place the question of power at the center of a construal of reality. These modes of thought, despite their vast differences, entail an "axiology of power." Clarity on this point is thus essential if we are going to make any headway in thinking about responsibility.

In order to understand what I am calling an axiology of power, we must define some basic concepts. By the term "value" I mean simply what is esteemed or desired as important or useful by some agent or community of agents in their interactions with reality. Value is not reducible to subjective wants; it is also not a "property" or attribute of objects as are other natural attributes such as, say, color. "Value" specifies a *relation* between a desiring and appraising agent (or agents) and that which is desired and appraised. Most simply put, there are two general types of value: (1) what is called intrinsic value, meaning any thing, person, or practice that evokes respect and care as an end-in-itself; and (2) instrumental value, by which is meant anything that can be used to attain other ends or purposes. These are, of course, fluid distinctions; in some situations the thing or person that has intrinsic value is used for or instrumental to some other end. Such use is morally acceptable only if the person or thing is still recognized as an end-in-itself. But the more general point to be made is that value is the quality of beings in relation to each other, a quality characterized by what respects and enhances those beings. This is what H. Richard Niebuhr and other thinkers would call a relational theory of value.[15] Responsibility, on this account, is how one rightly lives and acts in patterns of relations, in dimensions of value.

However, without the capacity of agents or some community of agents to respond to, influence, and also shape reality, the discourse of responsibility makes little sense. This capacity to respond to, influence, and shape reality is the most basic meaning of power. As theorists such as Michel Foucault and others have shown, power is not simply a matter of overt domination.[16] We misunderstand the reality of power if we assume that it can be easily localized in social structures or even individual agents. Power can be exercised coercively but also through persuasion, cooperation, and collaboration. But power itself is the ability or capacity to influence, respond to, and shape reality. In this way, ideas, as well as persons and institutions, have power insofar as they constitute some reality. In terms of morals, responsibility is a matter of how we evaluate and direct exercises of power.

With these definitions in mind, we can recall again the deep structure of the moral outlook of contemporary technological societies. The most basic supposition of these cultures is that power—the ability to respond to, influence, and shape reality—is the source, the origin, of morality and thus the most basic value, because power constitutes the qualitative *relation* between beings. Without the capacity to respond to, influence, or shape reality, it is difficult to speak of value. Accordingly, that which has the most power—that is, that which can most widely, richly, and deeply respond to, influence, and shape reality—constitutes real value. This claim about the source of morality is the backbone of the contemporary construal of the world. It grounds a worldview in which power is desired as ultimately important and is believed to be that which endows worth to all else. The technological age is simply the working out of this axiology, impressing it, as it were, onto space and time—onto the environment and the future. The underlying reason for this is the distinctly modern construal of reality, a construal that shifts the grounds of value from being to power, from reality to human freedom. The moral meaning of reality is reducible to the medium of the distinct way in which human beings interact with their environments—i.e., to freedom.

The reason why the contemporary axiology of power poses a radical challenge in ethics is that it is actually rooted in the fact that human beings act. Whatever else we want and need to say about human beings, we are agents interacting with a world. This means that human beings do not simply see the good and respond to it; as agents we also purposely bring about a world of meaning and value. Human beings are always engaged in the task of world-making, the formation of culture. Yet in the act of bringing about such a cultural world, we always risk the reduction of value to power.

The connection between power and value in cultural production is an area of genuine moral ambiguity. To deny human beings the capacity of value-creation through action is to deny them the most basic form of dignity. This is why the demand for the empowerment of women at Cairo was not only important but essential for any viable response to population problems. But in the modern world this insight into the character of human agency has itself backed a construal of reality. The contention is that it is not "being" but rather freedom—the distinct human power of responding to, influencing, and shaping reality—that is the origin of morality and human self-understanding. The axiology of power centers on human power and its capacity to construct a meaningful world within a reality devoid of value.

The challenge to an ethics of responsibility in our time is, then, how to affirm the exercise of power by agents in the creation of value as basic to human dignity without making this power the sole content of the good. In this light, modern Western ethics leaves us without moral bearings. While preserving the moral dignity of persons as agents, these forms of thought nevertheless collapse value into human power and divest nature and time of worth. Stated differently, the only form of realism possible in modern ethics is a realism of power confronting power; it is some form of political realism.[17] What is needed, therefore, is a different account of the origin of value. Despite the dismissal of religious traditions by most moralists, we must ask in this light whether or not these traditions might hold resources for addressing this question. This brings me to the theological layer of my argument, for which I want to turn to Dietrich Bonhoeffer's ethics of responsibility.

CHRIST, POWER, AND RESPONSIBILITY

The question before us is how to understand the source of morality in realistic terms so that we might speak about responsibility for viable life on this planet. As I understand him, Bonhoeffer in fact focuses the discussion of responsibility in terms of our existence as agents, the character of moral knowledge, and also reality. In a well-known passage from his *Ethics*, he wrote:

> Already in the possibility of the knowledge of good and evil Christian ethics discerns a falling away from the origin. Man at his origin knows only one thing: God. It is only in the unity of his knowledge of God that he knows of other men, of things, and of himself. He knows all things only in God, and God in all things. The knowledge of good and evil shows that he is no longer at one with his origin.[18]

The origin of ethical reflection, Bonhoeffer insists, is a shift in the unity of knowledge from God to the human. It is a shift from finding the unity of knowledge about self and world in the divine to having that unity constituted by humans. Morality testifies to the fact that all things are now understood and valued only in reference to human existence.

Bonhoeffer grasped that the deepest challenge to Christian ethics is the claim, as I have put it, that human beings invent, rather than discover, morality. Finally rid of the idea of a creator God or a divine commander, we rush in as the creators of value. The primordial act that constitutes the human as a moral being is a falling away from our true origin in God. In this falling, human beings in the sheer possibility of action, in their sheer power to act, become the origin of the knowledge of good and evil. From this perspective, the source of good shifts from the being of God to human possibility and action—from ultimate reality to the nothingness of human possibility. All subsequent moral reflection, Bonhoeffer insists, moves within the wake of this fundamental shift in the origin of good and evil.

This shift also dictates the contours of Bonhoeffer's ethics. Christian ethics, he insists, must take up and transform the knowledge of good and evil with respect to Jesus Christ. It must reconsider the meaning of our being human in terms of the true origin of good and evil that is the being and choice of God, the divine election manifest in Christ. By insisting on Christ as life itself, Bonhoeffer hoped to challenge the reduction of good and evil to a matter of human self-knowledge and to refocus it in terms of reality. The revelation of Jesus Christ places the question of reality, and not self-knowledge, at the center of ethics. Already in his dissertation *Act and Being*, Bonhoeffer insisted that "revelation is its own donor, without preconditions, and alone has the power to place [thought] in reality. From God to reality, not from reality to God, goes the path of theology."[19] The revelation of God in Christ—the unity of God and humanity—is the donation of reality. Reality is the personal. This means that "the problem of Christian ethics is the realization among God's creatures of the revelational reality of God in Christ."[20] The ultimate principle of reality is Christ and not the self or nature. In terms I have used in chapter 5, the revelation of Jesus Christ is what backs and enables a radical interpretation of self and world within Christian ethics.

What then defines responsible life? For Bonhoeffer, responsibility is a matter of deputyship. It is to act for and on behalf of others just as Christ acted. Not only is Christ the real, but the action of Christ is the pattern for right action. The Christian is to conform her or his life to that action. Ethics is formation, Bonhoeffer insists. That is, ethics is about how Christ takes form in human life. We can then call this *Christological realism* in ethics. And this means that Bonhoeffer has countered modern beliefs about human existence. First, he understands human life from the point of unity between God and humanity in Jesus Christ. This counters the modern negation of the idea of the human as created in the image of God. But, second, by defining responsibility in terms of "deputyship," Bonhoeffer also claims that the *moral* identity of any agent is constituted in his or her relation to the concrete other person. The self is understood within a Christological, symbolic framework of acting for and on behalf of others. This move to an insistence on the connection of self and other counters the modern attempt to understand persons simply from our capacities for thinking, feeling, and willing. Responsibility is acting in accordance with the reality of Christ and in accord with the concrete, relational nature of human existence.

What then of power? Bonhoeffer isolates a dynamic analogous to the origin of morality in the reality of power. Power, especially technological power, is rooted in what he calls a "mysterious correspondence" between the laws of thought and the laws of nature. When human reason emancipates itself from its origin in God, when it knows itself and its world only through itself, it is no longer in the service of some wider purpose. "The technical science of the modern western world," Bonhoeffer writes, "has emancipated itself from any form of subservience. It is in essence not service but mastery, mastery over nature. . . . This is the spirit of the forcible subjugation of nature beneath the rule of the thinking experimenting man."[21] Technical power manifests the same structure as the origin of good and evil. In sin, the human mediates reality through itself; in technical reason, this means subjecting nature to human purposes.

Responsible power, we might surmise, is the capacity to respond to, influence, and shape reality exercised in accordance with reality, with Jesus Christ. Responsible power is a matter of deputyship. This is seen in the limits placed on responsible action. Responsibility, Bonhoeffer writes, "takes into account the responsibility of the other man who confronts it. [This means that] responsibility differs from violence and exploitation precisely in the fact that it recognizes the other man as a responsible agent and indeed it enables him to become conscious of his responsibility."[22]

Thus, Bonhoeffer's ethics centers on the unity of God and humanity in the revelation of Christ, a revelation that donates reality. In this ethics we confront a distinctly Christian axiology of power quite different from that found in the modern world. For Bonhoeffer, responsible existence is the divestment of power as defining the content of the good. One is to act for and on behalf of others. Responsibility is acting in accordance with reality rather than the imposition of a law on reality. This is backed by a Christocentric account of reality in which the personal is central. The force of this revelational position is to answer what I discern in Christian belief as a vacillating assessment of power. In the revelation of Jesus Christ, power is valued both as constituting or donating reality *and* in a model of service for others. This means, we must now see, that value is defined in terms of the divine power of self-revelation, since it is this power that constitutes, influences, and shapes reality. This is why Bonhoeffer can claim that the "world, like all created things, is created through Christ and with Christ as its end, and consists in Christ alone."[23] Revelation—the power of self-disclosure to constitute reality—is axiologically basic. The event of revelation is the confluence of power and value in reality. Stated otherwise, Christ is the revelation of God because the being of Christ is the unity of power and value. The Christian must interpret reality from this perspective.

Bonhoeffer's ethics isolates and answers the modern moral outlook by shifting the question of good and evil from our self-understanding to the revelation of the being of God in Jesus Christ. This dislodges the question of value from dependency solely on human power. In doing so, Bonhoeffer also provides an important response to the ambiguity of power found in Christian thought. Behind these aspects of his thought is what I have called a Christological realism in ethics. If space allowed, we could show how this realism is developed by Bonhoeffer with respect to what he calls the four mandates and also ethics as formation. Prescinding from that discussion, we must think beyond Bonhoeffer's ethics in the search for a viable ethics of responsibility.

GOD, REALITY, AND POWER

My argument has progressed dialectically through various layers of reflection. What has propelled the argument on its way is the question of the relation of power and value in a moral worldview. I showed first that the moral ontology of technological society entails a specific picture of human existence and articulates a theory of value rooted in human power. Based on that theory it is unclear how we are to specify norms for the use of power on grounds other than the maximization of power, and, institutionally speaking, the checking of power with power. The only realism possible is a form of political realism. This is why, we might guess, appeals to norms other than utility have little compelling force or currency in technological societies. It is why claims about human rights or the need to empower persons as agents quickly get lost in the reality of a market-driven global economy. The rationalization of society analyzed by thinkers from Max Weber onward is the institutionalization of the modern axiology of power.

The move to the second, theological layer of my argument was provoked by the question of whether or not we can provide a different account of the source of value that would make realistic claims about the goodness of reality and thus limit the wanton extension of human power. By exploring Bonhoeffer's ethics, we found such an account, and one that also addressed the ambiguity about the value of power found in much traditional Christian thought. I tried to show that Bonhoeffer understands the origin of value in terms of the power of God's self-disclosure. Responsibility is then the exercise of power in accordance with revelation; it is the realization of the form of Christ in the world. According to Bonhoeffer, Christian ethics "speaks of the reality of the world as it is, which possesses reality solely through the reality of God. . . . In Jesus Christ the reality of God enters into the reality of the world."[24] This is what I called his Christological realism.

It replaces the anthropocentrism of modern ethics with a personalistic view of reality.

This brings me to the third and final layer of my argument. What provokes this move in our dialectical inquiry is a distinctly hermeneutical question. In contemporary, Western technological societies, we have conflicting accounts of how to understand reality morally. The challenge we face at the end of the twentieth century is simply the problem of which picture or construal of reality will factor centrally in how we assess the moral status of finite reality and provide orientation for action. Is our moral outlook to be determined by the technological axiology of power, or might the Christian vision still provide needed moral guidance? More profoundly, we must ask what it means for moral theory that we have the power to interpret our existence through conflicting accounts of the connection of power and value. How is our capacity to respond to, influence, and shape reality—that is, our distinctly human form of power—bound to the act of understanding? This question has been present throughout this book. Yet when we make it explicit, what comes to light?

Asking this question means that the connection between being and goodness we are seeking in ethics must be shown to be basic to our experience of being agents who seek to understand ourselves and our world. The theologian must show how the question of the good is not simply reducible to our structures of self-understanding, as Bonhoeffer feared, but without negating our experience of being agents as a clue to understanding the good. If this hermeneutical and yet realistic position can be shown to be true, then the power to act cannot be the sole value even as human efficacy will be endorsed as integral to human well-being. In other words, we avoid the reductionistic claim that we simply invent morality but do so without recourse to the revelationalism that seems endemic to Bonhoeffer's ethics. How might we make such an argument?

Recall that I argued in chapter 5 that every act to bring about some state of affairs in the world implicitly affirms the goodness of being over nonbeing. This is the case simply because, in acting, something is brought into being against a horizon of limits and possibilities. When I act, I alter the world. Yet I do so in such a way as implicitly to affirm that it is good to exist. To act at all is to endorse the relation of goodness and being as basic to one's self-understanding as an agent. We can call this the sense of responsibility intrinsic to our consciousness of being agents, and it can be formulated as a maxim for action. In all actions and relations, we ought to affirm the possibility of continued action and thus also human responsibility. This is a moral maxim because it arises from the connection between some causal agent and the effects of action, the state of affairs brought about by human action. But the question is whether or not this point about the experience of acting can be rendered intelligible without something like a theological claim. Is the affirmation of being over nonbeing, reality over destruction, written as a moral demand into the fabric of reality?

Stated differently, can the goodness of being endemic to the consciousness of being an agent be conceived without endorsing the reality of an unconditional good—that is, the divine? Without this claim, it is hard to understand how the source of value could be anything other than simply our acts of consciousness, our work of meaning-making. The irony of human existence is that in the very moment of action, in the very moment when we unleash power to alter reality, we sense, tacitly no doubt, that we are enlivened by a higher source not reducible to our power. The sense of responsibility intrinsic to the self-understanding of agents—that is, the sense of the identity of goodness and being manifest in the power to act— is an implicit testimony to some reality that is the condition of finite being. Insofar as any act brings about some state of affairs—even the terrifying act of the denial of existence—one endorses in every action a reality that is the condition for the power of human action. But this "reality," we must further note, must be one in which finite existence is itself respected in its finitude. How then might we best conceive of this reality?

The idea of God in Christian faith conjoins power and value. Ultimate power, when it evokes gratitude and reverence, is identified as "God" insofar as it respects and enhances finite reality. God is the name for the self-interpretation of power so that power is transformed in relation to the worth of contingent reality. God is love. Is this not what Bonhoeffer means by Christ as the revelation of reality? Is it not the moral meaning of Christian faith? This faith is a distinctive axiology of power. In other words, the central symbol of Christian faith is the means for the interpretation of our own existence as agents in the context of temporal life. By interpreting human life and the world theologically, one articulates the most basic ethical claim: value is not reducible to power, and yet the capacity or power to act is a basic human good that ought to be oriented toward respecting and enhancing the integrity of life.

I am arguing, then, that whether or not we explicitly sense the presence of God, every human act endorses that which is designated by the symbol "God" in the affirmation of being against its negation and fragmentation. If we think of the identity of God as presented in the polysemic ways of naming God in Christian faith, we grasp the affirmation of the divine reality in our consciousness of being agents. In Christian faith, God is the symbol for the unconditional source and possibility of moral responsibility. This means that an imperative of responsibility must be formulated theocentrically: respect and enhance the integrity of life *before God*. Acting on this imperative is an endorsement of the very condition of action and with it an affirmation of the being of God. The imperative of responsibility as I have now formulated it articulates the central claims of Christian faith in terms of a directive for action.

This allows us to see, finally, the meaning of the claim that we are to respect and enhance the integrity of life *before God*. In all actions and relations, we affirm the condition for responsible existence as this entails an interpretation of life through symbols of Christian faith. The divine reality as the condition for all existence is the ground of a hermeneutically realistic ethics of responsibility. Interpreting our life through Christian beliefs about the identity of God—the belief that "God" is the symbol for the self-interpretation of ultimate power—is the means of discovering the moral truth of our existence as agents. Understanding the imperative of responsibility in this way means that the human good is to be found in a moral project that does not flee worldly life to a transcendent goal but is a response to the goodness of existence in it.

The challenge to a theological ethics of responsibility is to demonstrate what this claim about God entails for our self-understanding as moral agents. To interpret our existence and the existence of the world theologically means to affirm the imperative of responsibility as the principle of moral identity. What this chapter has shown is that a theological ethics of responsibility can articulate a claim implied in, but not made explicit by, an ethics developed to meet the challenge of a technological age. It can show us, in other words, why power is morally basic but not morally determinative. Theological ethics makes sense of the connection between action and human dignity needed in current life without falling into the problems isolated in the modern axiology of power.

Why then do I insist on a theological move in ethics against Bonhoeffer's Christological realism? The reasons are simple. First, while his Christological realism escapes the axiology of power found in much modern thought, it must still speak of the value of nonhuman life in personalistic terms. The theological move I have advocated, centering as it does on the transformation of power, does not require a personalistic account of moral value.[25] This is important, I judge, for any viable ethics in our time. We must find ways of speaking about the moral status of the natural world in terms other than personalistic ones. Second, the theological position I have outlined means that the vulnerability of finite reality to the workings of power becomes morally central rather than the distinctly human problematic of sin. Sin and redemption are not the clues to the meaning of reality; sin and redemption concern how human existence transpires within reality. These two reasons for a theological turn in ethics mean that the *integrity of life* and not only the unity of divinity and humanity in Christ is the reality we ought to respect and enhance. In other words, we have important reasons for thinking about power, value, and reality theocentrically simply because the proper object of Christian faith, God, is the transformation of power with respect to finite reality. And these are, after all, matters basic to any viable ethics of responsibility.

CONCLUSION

Although my argument is perhaps too brief and tentative at its conclusion, I have in fact returned to matters that provoke this inquiry. An ethics of responsibility explores the exercise of power by agents within complex domains of value and social relations. It attempts to provide direction for how agents can and should respond to, influence, and shape reality. In an age of human power, we must understand how reality in all its diversity and complexity is to be respected and enhanced. If we do not grasp this point as basic to any viable public policy, course of action, or social organization, it is not at all clear that we will have a future on this planet. In this chapter I have tried to assess one resource of the Christian tradition, Christological realism, for meeting questions of genuinely global import.

8

Divine Command Ethics and the Otherness of God

Much Christian reflection on the moral life has claimed that moral norms and the source of morality are to be understood in terms of divine commands.[1] This is seen in the prominence of the Decalogue in Christian thought and life. It is also true that the teachings of Christ, especially the command to love, as well as the principles, precepts, and counsels of perfection found in the New Testament are taken to be expressions of God's will. Indeed, the sum total of Christian morality is usually expressed through the interlocking commands to love God and to love one's neighbor as oneself. This vision of morality as a matter of divine commandments satisfies the religious requirement that God is the supreme focus of trust, loyalty, and the human good. It also answers the genuine need to know the depth and truth of morality. Thus, if a theologian hopes to think about God and human existence within the Christian tradition, she or he must, in one way or another, contend with the claims of divine command ethics.

In this chapter I want to explore the meaning of divine commands for understanding our lives as agents. While I finally reject divine command ethics as a moral theory and as definitive of the whole of theological ethics, the question I hope to answer is this: What, if anything, does this discourse contribute to moral understanding? Any answer to this question centers on the transcendence of the divine with respect to the problems of human existence. As a moral theory, divine command ethics insists that the otherness of God, God's transcendence, is morally central and, in fact, constitutive of morality. What is important, in my judgment, is that this form of ethics has pictured God's relation to human life in terms of omnipotence. The divine will is not bound to or moved by a good beyond itself. The focus of my inquiry, then, is the content that the image of absolute power gives to the concept of divine transcendence. Put as a question, what does it mean for us morally to conceive of God's transcendence in terms of power? In this way, the argument of the following pages continues themes explored in the preceding chapter.

THE AIM OF THIS INQUIRY

The aim of this chapter is to explore how an account of divine transcendence functions to inform the evaluation of the world, others, self, and communities by moral agents. My deepest concern is to combat the glorification of power as defining the good by reconstructing divine command ethics, since it has too easily and too often been identified with just that form of human devotion.[2] In an age of technological power, worldwide ethnic conflict, systemic violence, and ecological peril, surely the most pressing challenge we face is the task of charting the connection between power and finite goodness in understanding human existence. Only in this way can we surmount the threat to the integrity of life that defines the postmodern situation.

My argument has two interrelated aspects. I want to state them at the outset and then use the chapter to develop them. Like other critics I argue, first, that divine command ethics cannot formulate a claim needed for its validity from within its own discourse. In order for a divine command ethics to be valid and to avoid an excessive, even horrific, glorification of power, it must assert that God is good or loving. Yet, as we will see, such a claim, strictly speaking, cannot be formulated within the discourse of divine commands. Divine command ethics is dependent on another form of reflection. Any ethics must formulate an axiology, a theory of value, as well as define principles of right conduct.[3] Based on this conclusion, I will argue, second, that divine command ethics does articulate a crucial insight. That insight is to pose the question of the value of power in the constitution of an agent's identity with respect to what is other than the agent. Divine command ethics, as it is developed in the Christian tradition, a development I briefly trace, is finally not about the glorification of omnipotence, a worship of brute power, that springs from deep within the human heart. This discourse is about the reconstitution of power in terms of what respects and enhances finite existence. The symbol or name "God," as I have previously argued, identifies the transformation of power with respect to the worth of finite existence. Thinking within the Christian tradition means holding this reconstitution of power as critical to moral understanding and thus to moral identity.

The claim I am defending is that divine command ethics must be seen as a moment of critical distanciation within the arc of moral understanding. Isolating this "arc" will deepen the discussion of the place of radical interpretation in moral understanding presented in chapter 5. By the phrase "the arc of moral understanding" I mean a scheme for interpreting our moral being in the world.[4] The act of interpretation requires, first, that we examine the embeddedness of life in a domain of natural and social values as the presupposition for asking about the moral value of forms of life and how to live in the world. Yet insofar as we are agents, any interpretation of moral existence and forms of life must also include a critical assessment of how we ought to exercise power so as to respect and enhance the integrity of life. This critical assessment potentially entails the radical interpretation of one's existence, or a form of life, when it asks about what values and orientations *ought* to characterize an understanding of the world and human beings. Finally, a hermeneutics of moral existence aims at the reconstitution of moral understanding and thus what one values on the other side of the critique of value and power. In this act a moral hermeneutics reaches its proper goal of informing a way of life. What one values or what a community values is reconstituted through the demand of what is right, but this demand contributes to a higher form of moral goodness aimed at the flourishing of life. The purpose of the moral life is to respect and enhance the integrity of life in all actions and relations.

What I argue, then, is that if divine command ethics is to be of any use to theological ethics it must be seen as a means for what I have called the radical interpretation of power with respect to the domain of values. Only in this way will the discourse of divine commands contribute to the reconstruction of moral understanding. My argument thus contextualizes a theory of moral rightness and wrongness, a deontology, within a wider, more complex axiology or theory of value. In this chapter I am concerned mainly with this deontological moment in moral understanding and ethical reflection. I will not be able to elaborate in detail on the axiology implied in the argument, although in the next chapter I will return to the question of value first examined in chapter 1. But in making the present argument, despite its limitations, I am obviously transforming divine command ethics. I want to show that a moral theory that insists on the otherness of God must finally take seriously what is other than God—that is, the value of finite, nondivine existence—in a construal of the world and how we should live. Theological ethics examines this twofold otherness in providing an account of the world or the moral space in which we exist, and in trying to provide meaning and guidance for life.[5] Insofar as this is the case, theological ethics is not defined solely by the discourse of divine commands.

Now that I have established the purpose of my inquiry, I want to begin with the traditional conception of divine command ethics and note some of the usual criticisms of it. This will be followed by a review of some recent revisions in divine command ethics by contemporary philosophers and theologians. Based on this preliminary discussion, I will examine the work of the main advocate of divine command ethics during this century, Karl Barth. Finally, it will be possible to outline an alternative account of the meaning of the discourse of divine commands that is more adequate for the task of contemporary thought.

MORAL THEORY AND DIVINE COMMAND ETHICS

Divine command ethics holds that moral rightness or wrongness consists in the agreement or disagreement, respectively, of an action or intention with the command or will of God. In its most extreme form, this means that if God should command what seems immoral—say, that the purpose of life is to inflict suffering on innocent persons—it would be wrong to disobey the divine will. What we call murder would be a virtuous act if it were commanded by God. This follows from the fact that the purpose of this extreme version of divine command ethics is to assert the difference between the divine will and our will in that God is determined only by God's own will. God is not bound by morality; the divine is the source of morality for human agents. As medieval theologians put it, God is the first uncaused cause and, insofar as this is analytically true of the idea of God, the divine will is necessarily the rule of justice.

This extreme position has been attributed to William Ockham, but it is more properly credited to his student Gabriel Biel.[6] But regardless of the historical problem of who did or did not hold this position, its exponents were sure that God would not really command cruelty for its own sake. This conviction was an article of faith based on revelation. Yet in terms of the moral theory, it is not a logical impossibility that God might command cruelty and thus make cruelty a just purpose of life. Insofar as moral rightness or wrongness depends on the will of God, what is right or wrong depends simply on what God commands. The perfection of God is such that God is not moved by goods or rules external to the divine will. Divine command ethics is thus a normative ethics; it tells us what we ought to do. It is also a meta-ethical theory—that is, a theory about the meaning of moral terms and also the truth of morality.

In the history of ethics, the question of the validity of such an ethical position has been formulated as the problem of the Euthyphro, taken from the Platonic dialogue by that name. Recall that in bringing his father to trial for the death of a slave, the young man Euthyphro tells Socrates that the gods commanded him so to act. Socrates is shocked to learn that the gods would command anyone to violate familial obligation. He then raises the question of whether the gods command something because it is pious or something is pious because it is commanded. The Socratic claim is that there is a principle of Good that is higher than the will of the gods. A divine command theorist cannot accept this conclusion. We ought to obey the command of God because God is God. The critics from Socrates onward hold that some idea of what is good is required in order to determine whether or not God is worthy of our obedience. If this is the case, divine command ethics fails as an ethics.

In light of this long-standing debate, theologians and philosophers have argued that divine command ethics enjoys two advantages over rival moral theories.[7] Clarity on this point will help us better understand divine command ethics as well as the problems it entails. First, divine command ethics asserts the objectivity of morality and moral norms. It is a form of moral realism. It stands against antirealist theories which contend that morality is simply what we invent or, in so-called emotivist ethics, that moral terms express our moral preferences and recommendations for actions. Intuitively, we sense that moral claims are binding on us outside of our subjective wants and desires, and this sense of what is obligatory, the argument goes, is difficult to explain on the grounds of constructivist or emotivist theories. In the medieval discussion, as Janine Idziak has shown, the binding power of law was held to be dependent on God's will as the origin of law. As Thomas Aquinas puts it, law emanates from the will of a ruler. God is the ruler of reality through the eternal law. Law as such is dependent on the divine.[8]

Other forms of objectivist ethics, such as Kantianism, seem to run aground on this point about obligation from the perspective of divine command ethics. How is it, the divine command theorist asks, that pure practical reason is the source of moral obligation from which to judge the claims of divine commands? Is it true, as Kant argues in *Groundwork for the Metaphysics of Morals*, that an a priori concept of reason can evoke the feeling of moral respect? Similarly, if one attempts to ground moral values and norms in a claim about being, how is it that being backs moral obligation? Hans Jonas has recently argued that "a 'command' can issue not only from a commanding will, for instance of a personal God or a Thou, but also from the immanent claim of a good-in-itself to its realization."[9] But what is the validity of that claim? The point is that divine command ethics asserts the objectivity of morality in such a way, so its proponents hold, that it makes better sense, or at least no worse sense, of our moral sensibilities than theories of practical reason (Kant) or a metaphysical grounding of morals (Jonas).

Second, divine command ethics is a form of non-naturalistic moral theory. Non-naturalism in ethics means that moral terms cannot be defined simply through forms of discourse that describe natural states of affairs, such as physics or biology. What we mean by moral goodness is not simply the same as, say, what gives physical pleasure. In this way, divine command ethics addresses a problem we isolated in chapter 3—namely, the status of moral claims when we do not sense them having a place in the world. The command of God is simply the "place" where moral rightness and wrongness are to be found. The problem for divine command ethics, accordingly, is how to relate moral claims in this restricted sense—that is, in the sense of what is obligatory—to nonmoral goods and virtues such as, for instance, the good of pleasure or the virtues of love and kindness.

The relation between moral rightness or wrongness and value is a problem of any non-naturalistic ethics. The divine command theorist argues that other main options for non-naturalism in ethics—that is, intuitionism, as in the work of G. E. Moore, or Platonism—are themselves fraught with problems. What exactly is an intuition of the moral good? What is the vision of the Good?[10] In this respect, divine command ethics seems in no worse shape than other forms of non-naturalism in ethics while having common cause with them in avoiding a reductionist account of moral terms. These negative arguments do not prove divine command ethics, but they do clear the ground for a debate about the plausibility of this moral theory.

As a normative ethics and a meta-ethical theory, divine command ethics is objectivist (realistic) and non-naturalistic; it is a theory about the ground and meaning of what is morally obligatory for agents and what we ought to do. It provides a way to understand the categorical character of moral obligation within a nonreductionist account of morality. However, it is precisely these features of divine command ethics that have been seen as its central shortcomings. Objections first arose within Christian thought in terms of problematic cases in the biblical texts, some of which have been called the immorality of the patriarchs. Recall just a few biblical passages that have been the focus of centuries of debate: (1) in Genesis 22, the command to Abraham to sacrifice his son Isaac; (2) in Exodus 12, the seeming command to Israel to plunder, or steal from, the Egyptians in the Exodus; (3) the command to the prophet Hosea to commit adultery; (4) Samson killing himself; (5) the polygamy of the patriarchs; and (6) Jacob lying with his father. Theologians have long wrestled with the morality of God's commands that seem to endorse murder, stealing, and adultery, as well as the behavior of biblical figures. Theologians have answered this problem in several different ways. Let me note these answers, because they specify problems of divine command ethics from within Christian theology.

The first response to these hard cases is the extreme form of divine command ethics noted previously. For these theologians, an act—any act—is morally right or wrong depending on the command of God. Insofar as Abraham was commanded to kill his son, it would have been right and meritorious for him to sacrifice Isaac in obedience to the divine law. This position is not as simple as it might seem at first blush. The contention is that the command of God justifies a redescription of the act outside our usual framework of moral evaluation such that it is no longer rightly defined or evaluated as an act of murder; it is, in light of the divine command, an act of sacrifice. The divine command supervenes on the act in such a way as to justify a different description and evaluation of the act. The fact that the command supervenes on a human act as the principle of its moral meaning is crucial not only to judge the virtue or viciousness of the act, but also to ensure that the analysis of the act and the good or ill it brings about in the world is not morally definitive of its meaning. God's command is definitive of its meaning. But this also requires that the will of God, the divine power, is not constrained by the dictates of morality or the analysis of the consequences of actions. If this were the case, the will of God would not define moral rightness and wrongness. God is externally related to the realm of moral values because the divine power, as first cause, can be evaluated only on its own terms.

Second, some theologians, such as Thomas Aquinas, argued that what is morally right and wrong is independent of God's will and, furthermore, that God always does right by the necessity of the divine nature. Thomistic ethics centers on the divine mind, not on the will of God, and asserts that it is impossible for God to command what is contrary to the divine nature. Even the eternal law is simply the mind of God, which is promulgated through the natural law, the human rational participation in the eternal law. On these grounds Aquinas addresses the problem of the immorality of the patriarchs. In *Summa Theologiae* I/II q. 94, a. 5, ad. 2, he argues that all persons die as the just desert of original sin, marriage emanates from the law of God, and all things ultimately belong to God as creator. Given this, a command of God to inflict death, engage in adultery, or take something against the will of the human owner is not ultimately wrong if in fact it was commanded by God. Specific commands of God are grounded in the eternal law, or the mind of God, and the relation of all things to God; therefore these commands do not violate the divine nature.

A final, more contemporary, example can be noted. Søren Kierkegaard examines the Abraham story in *Fear and Trembling*.[11] He argues that in the command to Abraham to sacrifice his son there is a teleological suspension of the ethical in which the individual's relation to God is made higher than fidelity to universal moral principles. Viewed morally, Abraham's act is murder because its meaning as an action falls under the dictates of morality; the command of God is about a good beyond the ethical. The command does not supervene on the act itself to change its meaning; the command is rather the condition for the good of faith. Abraham's existence is constituted in faith in the divine. The crisis of faith is precisely the question of whether or not to suspend the ethical and assert the good of the individual's relation to God over the universality of the moral law and obligations to others. This undercuts usual schemes for judging human life and reconstitutes existence on the objectively uncertain demand of faith.

These arguments about the morality of specific divine commands are counterintuitive from the perspective of contemporary ethics. First, the arguments seem to assert a form of moral heteronomy, the claim that human beings are morally bound by a will or mind not their own. But the question is why we ought to obey such a will or mind. Second, traditional arguments seem to undercut the values morality seeks to promote and preserve. Arguments aimed at defending God's commands seem to undercut basic social institutions needed for human relations, institutions that protect the values of human sexuality, property, and life by making them subject to an arbitrary will or divine nature or the crisis of faith. The objectivity and non-naturalistic character of divine command ethics in whatever form it takes seem to endorse heteronomy and render morality arbitrary. Insofar as this is the case, divine command ethics severed from an axiology seems, again, difficult to sustain.

We now have some of the main features of divine command ethics in hand as well as what are seen as its advantages and disadvantages. What has become clear from this examination is that the plausibility of divine command ethics rests not on a claim about rightness or wrongness but rather on a claim about the being of God with respect to natural needs of human life and the values they entail. It would seem that only if God is good or loving is there (1) reason to obey divine commands on grounds other than the glorification of omnipotence, (2) the means of countering the arbitrary and heteronomous nature of extreme forms of divine command ethics, and (3) a way of judging whether or not a specific command is consistent with what is morally right. It is the problem of God's goodness that contemporary divine command theorists are addressing.

A LOVING GOD AND MODIFIED DIVINE COMMAND ETHICS

In its traditional extreme form, divine command ethics contends that the will of God is the necessary and sufficient condition for actions to be morally right or wrong. Within the recent debate, modifications have been made in the theory such that the command of God is the necessary but not sufficient condition of rightness or wrongness.[12] Exponents of divine command ethics have modified the theory so that its implicit assumptions about the character of God are made explicit aside from claims of divine omnipotence. This has been crucial for countering criticisms of the most extreme form of divine command ethics.

Robert M. Adams, along with others, has proposed this modified form of divine command ethics.[13] The theory centers on the meaning of ethical wrongness. Adams puts it in this way:

> According to the modified divine command theory, when I say, "It is wrong to do X," (at least part of) what I *mean* is that it is contrary to God's command to do X. "It is wrong to do X" *implies* "it is contrary to God's command to do X." But "it is contrary to God's command to do X" implies "It is wrong to do X" only if it is assumed that God has the character I believe Him to have, of loving His human creatures. If God were really to command us to make cruelty our goal, then He would not have the character of loving us, and I would not say it would be wrong to disobey Him.[14]

The force of Adams's argument is to contend that if there is not a loving God, then nothing is ethically wrong, obligatory, or permitted.[15] Adams notes that while it might be logically possible for God to command cruelty as the purpose of life, this would entail the "breakdown" of the believer's concept of ethical right and wrong. In other words, the believer values and disvalues things—valuing kindness and pleasure while rejecting hatred and cruelty, for example—independently of God's command. The norm of ethical rightness and wrongness is coordinate with values and disvalues. Adams admits that "the acceptability of divine command ethics depends in part on the believer's independent positive valuation of the sorts of things that God is believed to command."[16] But does this admission mean abandoning divine command ethics altogether, because the validity of a conception of rightness and wrongness is dependent on nontheological valuations?

Adams and other modified divine command theorists contend that such an admission does not require them to abandon their position. Adams insists that "divine command theories, including the modified divine command theories, need not maintain that *all* value concepts, or even all moral concepts, must be understood in terms of God's commands."[17] This is because one can and must draw a distinction between nonmoral values and a conception of ethical right and wrong. That is to say, a modified divine command theory rests on the cogency of a distinction between the moral and the nonmoral where moral is defined by obligation—rightness or wrongness pertaining to actions—and not by attitudes, consequences, or states of affairs. We might value happiness, but this does not mean that it is always right to seek our own personal happiness. Egoism, for instance, asserts the ultimate value of personal happiness, but it is not necessarily ethically right always to act egoistically. Stated differently, a modified divine command ethics fastens once again on the non-naturalistic character of what is ethically right or wrong with respect to the moral meanings of actions. What is right or wrong cannot be defined simply in terms of what we value on other grounds, values related to the goods of human life.

The modification of divine command ethics centers then on three interrelated claims. First, it asserts that believers hold certain beliefs about the character or nature of God. Since God is believed to be loving, God cannot command cruelty as the purpose of human life. What is central is not merely the possible commands of God, but the actual commands of God consistent with beliefs about the character of God. God's revealed will and not absolute will is morally central. Second, the modified theory draws a distinction between nonmoral values and ethical rightness or wrongness and restricts the focus of divine commands to the ethical in this sense of the term. And, third, rightness and wrongness are properties of actions, and the assessment of actions is the business of ethics. The character of God, and presumably of persons, is surprisingly enough not the subject matter of ethics. Yet it is precisely the connection between character and action, the being of God and the command of God, that a divine command ethics must address. While it has not been pointed out before, the main shortcoming of a modified divine command ethics, I contend, is that this connection between the being and act of God remains unthought, even unthinkable, within the confines of the theory itself.

A modified divine command ethics must show that God is loving or good and, furthermore, must trace the connection between the ethical and nonmoral values in judging actions. This follows from the fact that, without addressing these questions, divine command ethics in its modified form cannot avoid the criticisms of extreme forms of divine command ethics or specify the relevance of norms of rightness and wrongness to the goods and virtues that morality as an institution seeks to protect and promote. Modified theories of divine command ethics properly shift the discussion of the character of God from power to goodness. And yet, given the distinction between judgments about moral rightness or wrongness and inquiry into nonmoral values, this means, oddly enough, that reflection on the being of God as good is not properly part of theological ethics. This is why I have insisted that divine command ethics cannot specify the condition for its validity from within its own discourse. It leaves open the question of how we are to think about the relation between God's goodness and judgments about actions. In order to address this problem, I want now to explore the ethics of Karl Barth. Barth fastens on the question of the being and act of God as the ground of what is right and good. His account of divine command ethics moves it beyond traditional and modified forms by addressing problems endemic to those theories. But Barth's answer, I hope to show, cannot finally be sustained. Given this, theological ethics must seek another path, a path beyond divine command ethics.

COMMAND AND THE WORD OF GOD

Karl Barth's theological ethics encompasses the normative and meta-ethical conceptions of divine command ethics. He also understands that ethics cannot be removed from the domain of dogmatic theology, since what is at stake is precisely the relation between God and the question of the good. Barth's tactic is to explore the act of God being God for humanity as the necessary and sufficient backing of divine command ethics. In this move, the right and the good are theologically defined. In fact, the good is defined in terms of the right.

Barth argues that what one ought to do is to obey the divine command. The command of God confronts the moral agent in every situation of decision and thus in every instance in which the moral character of human life is determined. This is because, as Barth writes, the "problem of ethics is the critical question under which the human being sees placed his action, but that is his entire temporal existence."[18] To be sure, Christians can place themselves in a better position to hear the command by attending to the preached Word of God. And there are also various spheres of life, as Barth calls them, that can guide moral reasoning. These spheres are specified with respect to the action of God as creator, redeemer, and reconciler.

For instance, the ordered relations in creation, man and woman being the most basic, are one sphere in which to hear the command of God. In this sphere, we should note, the command of God oddly enough valorizes wifely obedience and male superiority in the marriage covenant.

Thus, for Barth, one acts rightly if and only if one acts in obedience to the divine command. He writes:

> When God confronts man with His command, what he wills is purely *ad hoc* actions and attitudes which can only be thought of as historically contingent even in their necessity, acts of obedience to be performed on the spot in a specific way, pure decisions the meaning of which is not open to discussion, because they do not point to a higher law, but is rather contained in the fact that God has decided in this way and spoken accordingly, so that human decisions can only obey or disobey the divine decision.[19]

The command of God does not point to a higher law, principle, or good by which to judge its validity. The only possible response to the command is not a moral assessment of its validity but obedience or disobedience, which constitutes the rightness or wrongness of an act and thus one's existence. The Christian acknowledges, endorses, and conforms to the good who is Jesus Christ. The basic command for Barth is then really permission; it is freedom for life, for others, and for obedience, a permission that allows us to live our lives free from anxiety over the goodness of our existence.

Basic moral concepts are also defined by Barth through the command of God. He claims in *Church Dogmatics* II/2 that the ethical problem is the question of the good of human existence over and above all other goods. The problem is distinctively ethical insofar as for human beings to act is to exist. The good must be defined with respect to the problem of right action. In making this claim about action and existence, Barth collapses the question of what is valuable for human life and the question of what is morally right. Barth disallows the distinction between the good and moral rightness that modified divine command theorists are at pains to draw. Axiological claims, claims about the good, are specified within the discourse of divine commands. This is the case because, for Barth, to exist is to act; the rightness of human action is then the good of human existence.

What, then, is the good of human existence? The good of human existence is Jesus Christ, the Word of God, as God's being-in-act. The being of God is understood with respect to the act of grace grounded in divine election and not the exercise of power. The essence of God and the operation or act of God are one. As Barth writes, "God gives Himself to man entirely in His revelation. But not in such a way as to give Himself as a prisoner to man. He remains free in operating, in giving Himself."[20] Yet Barth insists that the freedom of Jesus Christ "does not correspond to the meaningless idea of a divine *potentia inordinata*, but to the *potentia ordinata* which is the real freedom and omnipotence of God. Like God, He lived in the freedom of One who is law to Himself."[21] Barth further argues that by "deciding for God [the human] has definitely decided not to be obedient to power as power."[22] Thus, for Barth, "God calls us and orders us and claims us by being gracious to us in Jesus Christ."[23] The meaning of God's freedom, the mystery of God, is manifest in God's being God for us, being gracious in Jesus Christ. This means that the essence of God, as Barth puts it elsewhere, is lordship.

Knowledge of God's essence, the divine lordship, is found in the revelation of God's grace that commands obedience. It is the actual Word of God, not the supposed possibility of divine power, that is the command of God. For Barth, we cannot reason behind the Word of God into the abyss of divine election. But it is not necessary to think behind the event of grace in order to ground the ethics. God is loving in the act of being God for us; this is the inner meaning and ground of the command of God. In Barth's terms, the Law is the form of the Gospel; the command of God is simply the form in which we hear and respond to the human good, the Word of God. Thus, the meaning of the good, as a question in meta-ethics, and the actual command of God, the content of the normative ethics (moral rightness), are one and the same—that is, Jesus Christ. All moral concepts must then be defined with respect to God's election to be God for humanity in Jesus Christ. Any other definition of the human good is for Barth simply an expression of human sin, the human attempt to determine its good outside of or as other than God.

For Barth, a divine command ethics asserts the otherness or mystery of God in terms of the meaning of the good and also in determinations of what one ought to do. What we think is good cannot be definitive of the good; what we decide to do is only right if it is in obedience to the divine command. The Word undercuts independent moral knowledge and thus all rational ethics outside of the divine command. Yet it also grounds an ethics of command in the being of God revealed in the Word, in Jesus Christ. The axiological question first raised by Socrates of why God is worthy of our obedience is collapsed into the act of God being God for us and the command to obedience this necessarily entails. The reason is that only in this event is the essence of God, the divine lordship, knowable in terms of human existence or action. The divine good, we might say, supervenes on human action in Jesus Christ. To support the radical character of Barth's ethics is to insist that one cannot know the meaning of the human good outside of the actual command of God.[24] This ethics is, as he says, divine ethics; the focus of moral attention is the action of God and not human action. The question of the human good is taken into the act of God being good for human beings. Ironically enough, an ethics that seemed to begin with the claim that for human beings to exist is to act, ends by negating a focus on human action as the domain of ethical inquiry.

POWER, GOODNESS, AND THEOLOGICAL ETHICS

I have argued that in order to be plausible a divine command ethics must specify the relation between axiological claims and judgments about moral rightness and wrongness. An extreme form of divine command ethics, we have seen, risks the reduction of goodness and rightness to the sovereignty of power. A modified form of divine command ethics avoids this conclusion, but it does so at the cost of making it impossible to consider within ethics the connection between the being and the act of God. Barth insists on the unity of goodness and rightness, divine being and act, in order to ensure that all valid moral reflection falls within the purview of dogmatics. The transcendence of God is the freedom of God to be other than the abyss of power; it is the freedom of God to be God for us.[25] Christology functions in Barthian ethics as a theological axiology while also being the content of the divine command. But this means that the sovereignty of God's grace, not God's power, ironically effaces the domain of natural and social values as central to ethical reflection. What is other than God is valorized in terms of God's self-othering in Jesus Christ. Given these problems in the forms of divine command ethics, what, if anything, can we take from the discussion?

By tracing movements within the Christian tradition, we have seen the backing for divine command ethics recast from power to the graciousness of God's being-in-act of self-disclosure. This form of theological ethical discourse specifies grace as the inner meaning of omnipotence. And this can be formulated as a basic principle of ethics—that is, a principle with which we apprehend and judge our existence. To interpret human existence through this principle dethrones power or the extension of power as definitive of the human good. And from this follows the critique of all systems of thought that define the good in terms of power, systems of thought that are, we should admit, all too pervasive in our current situation. It is this insight that theological ethics ought to grasp and articulate in its reflections on the being of God. It must attempt to formulate the grounds of moral understanding with respect to a transvaluation of power.

The price of this insight on Barth's part was the need to identify, at some ultimate level, power and goodness. By doing so Barth provided a theological axiology and a principle of moral rightness but at the expense of necessarily transforming ethics into divine ethics. What then becomes of finite human life and conduct and the finite world? What is the moral status of what is other than God? While it might well be the case that in God power and goodness, act and being, are convertible terms, this is decidedly not the case with our lives. The deep problem of human life is that our action and our character are not one, that goodness is not always powerful or human power always good. What we must grasp in distinction from Barth's ethics is that claims about divine commands do not simply answer the human problem; they also expose its depth and reality. This is the critical function that divine command ethics can play within a hermeneutical realist account of moral existence.

Divine command ethics taken in its most plausible form provides a means of interpreting the moral problematic of human existence. It constitutes a distinct form of thinking and valuing that centers on the clash of power and goodness in human existence. The divine being is conceived as the equivalence of power and goodness, act and being, in the light of which one evaluates, understands, and judges the moral shape of human life. Seen in this way, divine command ethics is a discourse that revolutionizes our conceptions and assessments of power and goodness, action and existence, because it insists that the disclosure of ultimate power is what creates, redeems, and sustains finite existence; power is made perfect in goodness. But if this is the case, must theological ethics be equated with divine command ethics? I do not think so.

Divine command ethics cannot encompass the whole of theological ethical reflection, because we can also conceive of a good beyond the conflict of power and goodness, the good of power that not only affirms its own causality but also respects and enhances what is other than itself—that is, the integrity of life in the variety of its expressions. "And God saw that it was good," as we have it in the creation narrative. This good is conceived theologically under the symbols of creation and the reign of God, or, in philosophical terms, a kingdom of ends. Moral obligations, systems of law, the exercise of power, and even divine commands exist for the sake of realizing, or at least approximating, this reality in which moral value is not defined by power or the extension of power but as ontologically basic. The language of divine commands is a critical moment within the task of articulating, criticizing, and revising beliefs about the moral significance of the world in which we exist and how we can and ought to orient our lives.

What this critical moment means is a judgment on any action or society driven by the attempt to reduce the meaning and content of the good to that of power in social and personal existence.

Theological ethics articulates a distinctive moral ontology, an evaluative construal of the world, within which to make sense of moral obligation and the discourse of commands. This moral ontology unfolds the claim that finite existence ought not to be subjected to the extension of power for its own sake. And this means that theological ethics is not simply concerned with the otherness of God, but is also about the moral standing of what is other than God. The recognition of finite otherness within divine command ethics, a recognition required if this form of ethics is to avoid the valorization of power alone, effectively reconstitutes this discourse and puts it in the service of a different theological ethical agenda. The reason for this is quite simple. As I have shown, one cannot conceive of the point of a divine command ethics without articulating a good it serves. It cannot serve the divine goodness, because, by definition, God in God's self is conceived in divine command ethics as being beyond moral determination. The service divine command ethics renders to the good of respecting and enhancing finite existence is an articulation of the moral problematic of human existence under its resolution. That is, divine command ethics, as I have reconstructed it, poses the question of the value of what is other than God within discourse about the otherness of God in such a way as to combat the glorification of omnipotence in human choices. The task of theological ethics is to show what this means in terms of how we understand and orient our lives in the world.

CONCLUSION

What I have argued in this chapter is that divine command ethics is not definitive of the whole of theological ethical reflection. It is a discourse for examining the moral life with respect to a conflict at the root of human existence. But, perhaps, in an age of human power this distinctive way of speaking about God and the moral life can and must again be deployed in thinking. For is it not the case that we must somehow and in some way come to understand and intend the goodness of existence in terms other than simply the exercise and extension of power? The central and radical claim of theological ethics is that in thinking about the being of God one grasps the insight that the exercise of power must respect and enhance the integrity of life as the very principle for understanding and evaluating human existence. But we must always think of God with respect to the integrity of life, what is other than God, lest we valorize yet again the glorification of omnipotence.

9

The Sovereignty
of God's Goodness

The most basic affirmation of Christian faith is the confession that God is good and that God's mercies endure forever.[1] Yet if we reflect on this confession, we immediately confront a deep and perplexing question: what is the relation between God and Good? This question lies deep within the history of ethics, especially the ongoing exchange between forms of Platonic ethics and Christian moral reflection. And yet, owing to the reality of Western secular cultures alongside the worldwide resurgence of the religions, it is also a pressing question in our day. The task of this final chapter is to address this question by engaging a powerful representative of Platonic ethics mindful of the current global context.

I want, first, to clarify what will be argued. Second, by drawing on the work of Iris Murdoch I will outline a basic problem that faces contemporary ethics. Third, I will turn to Murdoch and briefly explore how she pictures the human, her account of the Good, and the way she establishes the reality of the Good. Finally, I will forward a theological ethical response to Murdoch's version of Platonic ethics, a response that draws on, but also transforms, some of her insights.

WHAT WILL BE ARGUED

The inquiry of this chapter can be seen as another round in the long encounter between Platonism and Christian ethics. This is important to note for several reasons. First, each of these traditions insists on one supreme reality, Good or God, in relation to which human beings and the world are to be valued and understood. These traditions are, in other words, monistic or monotheistic forms of thought and life. Second, these forms of thought are realistic in the sense that they seek to understand a reality not reducible to how we construe the world. The real is not simply what we make or invent, even if our interpretations or pictures of the real are human constructions. Morally this means that we can choose to conform or not to conform our lives to the real. In other words, each of these traditions aims at finding some coherence between a view of reality and an account of moral goodness. What is morally good strikes to the root of things, and, conversely, the way things are is important for how we can and should live. These are forms of moral realism in ethics. Given these claims, Christianity and Platonism in their various expressions are, third, forms of ethical universalism. Thinkers within these traditions grant their particular, fallible, and historical starting points, but they seek, nevertheless, to specify the norms and goods that ought to characterize all human life.

These points of agreement between Platonic and Christian ethics are taken by their postmodern critics to be denials of the particular—a stifling, even tyrannous, monism unmindful of the obvious plurality of the world, hankering after some means of escaping the travail of history by adopting a God's-eye perspective on life, and a futile search for some way of reducing the anxiety and risk of the moral life. Morality, the critics argue, is not rooted in the way things are but in the power to bring about outcomes, social consensus, or creative imagination. As we have seen, antirealists assert that we do not discover morality, we invent it.[2] In this light, Platonic and Christian forms of ethics seem fantastic from the perspective of most current thought, because the point of these traditions is to articulate the unconditioned character and depth of morality. There are, then, good reasons for a Christian theologian to engage recent compelling advocates of Platonic ethics.

Throughout her many works, Iris Murdoch has presented a comprehensive moral philosophy indebted to Platonic thought. The good life, according to Murdoch, is a movement toward selfless care for individuals guided by ideas of perfection that are objects of love. In presenting this moral vision, Murdoch does not believe that we ought to expunge religious concerns from ethics, but she insists that we can and must replace God with Good as the central concept in ethics. In fact, at the end of *Metaphysics as a Guide to Morals*, Murdoch claims that we "need a theology which can continue without God" and then asks, "Why not call such a reflection a form of moral philosophy?" "All right," she continues, "so long as it treats those matters of 'ultimate concern,' our experience of the unconditioned and our continued sense of what is holy."[3] Presenting the task of moral philosophy in this way, Murdoch is explicit, even insistent, that the Good "is not the old God in disguise, but rather what the old God symbolized."[4] Murdoch is consistently Platonic in her moral outlook: the idea of the Good, not God, is morally basic. Engaging her work forces the theologian to address the most basic questions in ethics.

Thus, I do not engage Murdoch's work simply for historical or comparative reasons. The question I want to address about God and Good is nothing less than the question of first principles in ethics and thus how we speak morally about the real. By a first principle I mean the idea, symbol, or root metaphor that gives systematic integrity to an ethics. This idea, symbol, or metaphor is a principle insofar as it is the source of intelligibility within an ethics; it is first because the principle is irreducible and primary.[5] This way of putting matters ought not to distract us from the real human significance of the question. For what is at stake is how, if at all, one can show the intelligibility of a way of life in which respecting and enhancing things and persons is in fact primary and irreducible in existence.[6] In terms of the title of this chapter, the first principle of an ethics is that which is sovereign over all other moral concepts and, more importantly, sovereign over our lives. The judgment about which idea, symbol, or metaphor we use in speaking about the first principle of the moral life and how we should live is then of grave importance.

I aim in this chapter to specify the first principle of theological ethics through a critical comparison of Christian morality with Murdoch's ethics. The first principle of any ethics, I contend, has to do with the value and direction of power with respect to the world and others. This follows from the idea that we live as agents who exercise power, interact and suffer in the world, and also make evaluations about our lives, the world, and others in order to orient our lives in the world. Murdoch seems to agree with this insofar as she contends that the problem of the moral life centers on how to direct the energy of the psyche away from selfish fantasy and toward reality. Ethics must show, then, the intelligibility of a way of life in which values other than power, such as the value of other persons and the world, are irreducible and primary. If this is not the case, then the struggles and possibilities that characterize human life cannot be understood or evaluated in any other terms than the quest for power and the fantasies we use to promote our power. I want to isolate the error in the belief that power is the primary value, that it alone is sovereign in our lives because it is what gives value to our lives.

Christian faith is about sin and redemption. It is about creation and destruction, death and resurrection. It is about radical love and the hunger and thirst for the reign of righteousness and mercy in human life. This faith is about which power or powers one ought to serve in giving meaning and value to life. If this is so, then the question of God is the question of the first principle of morality. Theological discourse, a construal of the divine, symbolizes what must be affirmed in our actions and evaluations if the primacy and irreducibility of morality is to be intelligible. In other words, theological ethics critically and constructively uses the symbolic and conceptual resources of the Christian tradition in order to articulate and interpret the intrinsic moral structure of experienced reality. The wager is that its symbolic and conceptual resources will in fact prove their indispensable worth in just this way. And this, of course, is what I am attempting to establish by engaging Murdoch's theology without God, her moral philosophy.[7]

THE PROBLEM OF ETHICS

Iris Murdoch has sought to uncover the deep underpinnings of our current age and the grave challenges they pose to ethics. As she sees it, our situation is a product of the long process of the removal of value as metaphysically basic in an account of the world and with it the loss of the individual into vast nonhuman systems. The eclipse of God, the secularism of the modern West, is but one historical expression of this more basic shift in modern consciousness. Murdoch attempts to show how modern philosophy often merely reflects this deeper shift rather than critically assessing and responding to it.

Murdoch starts with recent developments in the philosophy of language, especially poststructuralist or deconstructionist thought. She reads these positions as accounts of the world as "a vast system or sign structure whereby meaning is determined by a mutual relationship of signs which transcends the localized talk of individual speakers."[8] As Jacques Derrida has put this, there is nothing outside text. All meaning is determined by the linguistic sign system, the "text." As I argued in chapter 4, unlike hermeneutical positions, poststructuralism does not see language as self-transcending toward its other, to nonlinguistic reality. This metaphysics of meaning, just like any total system, is one in which individual persons and the complexity of the interior life are forfeited in favor of an analysis of meaning systems and actions. "Meaning, then, is an internally self-related movement or *play* of language."[9] We explored this in chapter 3 with respect to the development of information technology. For Murdoch, it amounts to nothing more than linguistic determinism, since individual speakers, subsumed into the linguistic system, are players in the play of language. Insofar as this is the case, there is a loss of value as the background to the complexity of individual personal life.

In Murdoch's eyes, existentialists developed a picture of human beings that neatly fits this account of the world. In existentialism, the person is described as being randomly thrown into a meaningless world and condemned to create meaning for himself or herself. The focus of ethics becomes the creative act of the will; the self is manifest in action, sovereign in the moment of choice. Morality on this account "resides at the point of action. What I am 'objectively' is not under my control; logic and observers decide that. What I am 'subjectively' is a foot-loose, solitary, substanceless will. Personality dwindles to a point of pure will."[10] Once this picture of human beings is accepted, it is hardly surprising that ethics would focus on actions, norms of choice, and the meaning of public moral discourse—important words such as "duty," "ought," and "right." The complexity of the interior life, the depth and chaos of personality, and also what we love are simply beyond the pale of ethics. The world outside is discontinuous with the world inside, the unfettered will-to-choice. The human person, defined as a will, moves about in an alien world.

Any response to the reigning conception of the world and human beings requires that one rehabilitate the idea of transcendence, save the individual, examine the complexity of personality, and combat deterministic as well as voluntarist pictures of human beings. Murdoch undertakes this task by asking us to look closely at ordinary life. When we attend to actual experience, do we find the reigning theories of meaning and subjectivity confirmed? As creatures we live in and as our bodies and thus are part of the larger natural world. All of our linguistic and social actions, Murdoch notes, depend at some level on speaking and acting persons. We regularly have experiences of life saturated with value, experiences of beauty, and moral admiration of others. Not all our choices are aimed simply at maximizing self-interest, and human freedom is inherently limited by what we apprehend as good. The sun setting in streaks of red, orange, and purple over a tree-lined Wisconsin lake as the stars emerge in crystalline points of light evokes more than wonder about the physics of it all and the prospect of a new housing development. Its beauty, Murdoch would argue, is a sign of the transcendence of goodness. The embrace of a loved one deeply missed is the sense of what simply *ought* to be. The deaths of innocents sacrificed for political or religious ideologies evoke our grief and moral outrage.

It is incorrect to say that we are contingently thrown into a world devoid of value and left to find our way and to create value. We regularly have experiences of what transcends us and also the reality of value not definable in terms of wants and desires or acts of will.[11] This is what I have called the sense of responsibility basic to our consciousness of being agents. As Murdoch cryptically notes, the "ordinary person does not, unless corrupted by philosophy, believe that he creates values by his choices. He thinks that some things really are better than others and that he is capable of getting it wrong."[12] We are, for good reason, naturally moral realists. Murdoch challenges the current outlook by insisting that we cannot eradicate evaluative judgments from human existence; if one thinks away value, one thinks away what it means to be a human being. The Good is the source of intelligibility in life and it is primary and irreducible. Murdoch insists that what is at the root of our current situation is a loss of vision for the real and our desire for consoling fantasies driven by our natural egoism. A postmodern society is something like the ego writ large—a factory of self-serving illusions to help us escape responsibility.

Here we must press some basic questions. What comes to the fore morally when we consider the connection between power and value, as a dominant feature of the contemporary world? Seen from this vantage point, the problem of the loss of vision in the postmodern age is not, as Murdoch thinks, only an ego seeking omnipotence; it is an equation of power with value. The origin and ground of value, that which confers worth on persons or things, is believed to be power. Existentialism is a compelling picture of the self, because modern Westerners believe our acts of will somehow connect us with value-creating power. And contact with power is what gives value to our lives. Similarly, the poststructuralist account of meaning is not only about the loss of value; it is the analysis of the productive power of language to create meaning. There is nothing outside the "text," because the "text," and not nothingness, is productive of meaning. "Text" is a name for the matrixes of meaning-producing power. Finally, the loss of God from our picture of the world simply signifies the shift in the creation of value from God or nature to the domain of human power. The belief that holds together our current outlook is the equation of power and worth. We do not see value in reality because value is a matter of power, and power too easily conceals itself behind its workings—the workings of desire, political institutions, and economic systems.[13]

The problem we face in ethics, then, is that the ground of value has shifted from being to power, or, more precisely, that being itself, the source of value, is conceived only in terms of power. This is the axiology of power I have been charting and challenging throughout this book. Seeing this axiology does not require us to jettison metaphysical questions from ethics; it is not to champion will over mind, doing over being. But it is to realize that the metaphysical dimension of ethics has shifted. The modern world no longer sees nature as creation or the human as created in the image of God; we no longer dwell in the classic, mimetic universe wherein persons and things derived their value from a place in the system of being.[14] To recall Hans Jonas's pointed insight, the "paradox of the modern condition is that the reduction of man's stature, the utter humbling of his metaphysical pride [as the image of God], goes hand in hand with his promotion to quasi-God-like privilege and power. The emphasis is on *power*."[15]

Given this picture of human beings and our world, is it any wonder that current societies are characterized by unending conflict over access to the mechanisms of social, economic, cultural, and political power? We see ourselves not as creatures responding to a world of values but as value-creating actors (economic agents, for instance). Moreover, linguistic systems, as poststructuralists argue, are themselves productive of meaning. How surprising is it, then, that inner-city youth living amid racial injustice and poverty have developed gangs with moral codes based on the principle that respect and self-esteem are grounded in the power to defend oneself and, if necessary, to exercise lethal force on others? How surprising is it that the fragile integrity of life could be so deeply endangered in an age of increasing human power? In light of these facts, ethics must ask the question of the value of the power to create value.[16] And it is this question, as I insisted in chapter 2, that theological ethics has always addressed, because it symbolizes the real in terms of the relation of power and value—that is, in terms of the reality and agency of God.

This argument enables us to formulate the nub of the problem about first principles in ethics; it is the problem I will be exploring throughout the remainder of this chapter. Insofar as we are concerned with a principle in ethics, a first principle must specify how and in what way power is to be evaluated and exercised by agents and thus what confers value on things and persons. Two options are possible in trying to isolate the source of morality. These options explain why Murdoch thinks that the most crucial ethical systems in the West are those of Kant and Plato, and why, finally, she sides with Plato. We need clarity on this point in order to understand the unique stance of Christian morality about the source of value.

First, one can try to show that the constraints on power are internal to the agent—for example, in pure practical reason, as Kant argued. Formulating a principle of right action with respect to the well-being of others and acting according to it are themselves acts of freedom. The agent is sovereign over herself or himself and yet is also bound to exercise freedom in respect of others; the subjective act of self-legislation is the ground of objectively binding moral norms. Insofar as we recognize this in other persons, they evoke our moral respect. Conversely, we can argue that the principle of right action refers to what is other than the agent, as Platonists and Christians hold. This principle might be given by a divine command, as we explored in the preceding chapter; it could be understood in terms of the mind of God, the face of the other, or the Good. God or the Good is sovereign; the objective norm is to be subjectively appropriated by the agent in rendering life morally intelligible. These *externalist* positions, if I may refer to them as such, suspect that any purely *internalist* answer, such as Kant's, never really escapes the self and the drive to maximize its power. Because of this, Platonists and Christians look elsewhere. They seek a Good or a God that transcends the self but that nevertheless accords or resonates with the self.[17] In terms I have been using, they seek a norm beyond power—even the desire of love—that can constrain, direct, and even transform the power to act so that it serves good ends. But this norm, as I argued in chapter 4, must touch the depth of our consciousness and thus be open to reflexive thinking in ethics.

We have returned, then, to a basic point of agreement between Christian and Platonic ethics—specifically, the insistence that, given the nature of reality, morality is basic. Yet in spite of all of these agreements, we have also hit on a matter of continuing dispute in the encounter between these moral traditions. The dispute turns on how to conceive a norm beyond power, how it ought to be symbolized, how we are to make contact with it, and thus the formulation of the first principle of ethics. Put simply, what is at issue is how the real is symbolized, since the real is what morality is about; the real is the source of value. Christian theology claims that we can and must understand God, the divine goodness, as the first principle of ethics; Platonists speak of the Good beyond being and beyond the gods. In order to clarify this point of dispute and my own argument, I want to turn now to Murdoch's ethics, progress through levels of her argument, and end with how she justifies the reality of Good. This will allow me to explore the value of the individual in Murdoch's thought in a way that opens anew the question of God.

ON PERSONS, GOOD, AND GOD

Murdoch's understanding of what it means for us to be moral creatures is summarized in her claim that self-being or consciousness is the fundamental mode of moral being. "What we really are," Murdoch writes, "seems . . . like an obscure system of energy out of which choices and visible acts of will emerge at intervals in ways which are often unclear and often depend on the condition of the system in between moments of choice."[18] Consciousness is the means of organizing and directing the chaotic energy of the ego; the direction of energy is what the moral life is all about. Given this account of the self, an account indebted to Freud and Plato, Murdoch is interested in exploring the formation of consciousness that gives rise to right action rather than centering her account of agents on the capacity for willing.[19]

Not surprisingly, Murdoch contests any ethics that defines valuing as epiphenomenal to cognition by reducing it to an act of will and that construes the moral agent as a willing chooser rather than a knowing subject seeking contact with a world different from itself. The self defined by its capacity to will can picture itself and others only as substanceless wills that are self-identical in acts of choosing. If this is indeed the case, moral discourse refers to nothing in the world; it refers to the worldless act of the will.[20] Murdoch contends that "value, valuing, is not a specialized activity of the will, but an apprehension of the world, an aspect of cognition, which is everywhere."[21] The problem for Murdoch is that the ego in its quest for omnipotence easily and readily pictures itself in a world of its own making, a world of self-serving fantasy. But, in fact, other persons are transcendent to the self and so is the value of their lives. The moral life is about coming to see this fact and living by it; it is about constraining and directing the exercise of freedom by making contact with the reality of others. Perception is thus basic to self-being, to consciousness. Given this, sustained attention, serious contemplative perception, is central to moral betterment, the arduous struggle to see the world and others rightly.

Murdoch pictures the moral life as the conversion of the self to the real guided by some object of attention, a conversion that entails the redirection of psychic energy. Attention expresses the "idea of a just and loving gaze directed upon an individual reality." This form of perception, and not unimpeded freedom, is, Murdoch notes, "the characteristic and proper mark of the active moral agent."[22] Drawing on Plato's analogy of the cave, Murdoch describes persons as beings lost in illusions projected on the world who must, if they are to become morally better, turn and struggle from the cave in order, finally, to see the world, others, and the self for what they are in the light of the sun, the Good. The moral life is about progress, a process of perfecting the agent through attention to what is real. Morally understood, the core of consciousness is attention and its necessary object is the reality of the individual.

The heart of this position is Murdoch's claim that a person is compelled by obedience to the reality she or he can see. The real is sovereign over the self. Clarity of vision about the real organizes the system of psychic energy and thus enables the person to choose and to act rightly. The real is then the primary and irreducible source of intelligibility in life. And if it can be shown that the Good is real, then morality is irreducible and primary in human life. It is at this juncture that we are led to Murdoch's account of the Good and her defense of it as sovereign over all other concepts. If her argument is to hold, she must show that the Good is implicit in all acts of consciousness and that it is necessarily real.

In her famous essay "On 'God' and 'Good,'" Murdoch defines God as "a single perfect transcendent non-representable and necessarily real object of attention."[23] She takes this to be the idea of God that has dominated traditional theism; it is what the word "God" symbolizes. Murdoch wants to argue that the Good has these same attributes. Once we have grasped her account of the problem facing ethics, we can see the reason for this equation of Good and what God symbolized. She wants to show that what claims one's attention is a reality transcendent to the subject, a reality in which value is necessarily real and singular. This object is nonrepresentable and therefore not reducible to our systems of meaning or representation. The Good is also the transcendence of the singular against its reduction into a system of representations and manifests the metaphysical standing of value, that perfection is real. Insofar as all of this can be shown to be true, Murdoch will have established the unconditional character of morality and reclaimed value as metaphysically basic in our conception of the world and ourselves.

In order to establish the irreducibility of the Good in our lives, Murdoch begins with a claim about the perception of things, persons, and activities. The Good is a unifying idea in human life insofar as we understand anything at all in terms of degrees of perfection. We constantly grade and evaluate events, persons, and activities with respect to some explicit or implicit idea of better or worse. These evaluative acts are unified around some idea of the Good. Yet this also means that the Good as such is indefinable because of the inexhaustible variety of the world. In the moral life, centered as it is on attention to the individual, the Good is connected with the pointlessness of virtue—that is, the idea that moral virtue is good in itself and not a means to some other end, say the end of happiness. The Good spans our perception of the world and things in it and also the moral life. Murdoch's account of the Good unites in one grand vision an account of the world and the idea of virtue correlate to a claim about consciousness and attention. Her position, as she admits, is monistic. How, then, can we establish the reality of the Good?

Murdoch attempts to justify her claim about the Good in terms of the ontological proof of the existence of God. Recall that this is possible because she equates Good with the attributes of God as a real, transcendent, perfect object of attention. She tries to show that understanding the Good entails affirming its necessary existence. Consistent with what we have seen, Murdoch reads the proof of God—unlike Jonas did (chapter 5)—as rooted in our perception of degrees of goodness. As she puts it, the definition of God as noncontingent is "given body by our most general perceptions and experience of the fundamental and omnipresent (uniquely necessary) nature of moral value."[24] The proof is not about God but about the Good— that is, the necessarily real condition of possibility of our moral evaluations. "We gain the concept of this unique form of necessity," Murdoch argues, "from our unavoidable experience of good and evil."[25] In making this move to the reality of Good, Murdoch frees the proof from the burden of establishing the necessary existence of a personal God and understands it to be a claim about moral value. What the proof of the Good designates, then, is an unconditional structure that cannot be thought away in human life. Insofar as this is indeed the case, moral philosophy "accommodates the unconditional element in the structure of reason and reality."[26] Ethics is a theology without God because Good is what the old God symbolized.

Murdoch's replacement of God with Good rests on a series of interrelated claims. First, she contends that "God" is the name of a supernatural person and that confusion arises if we try to extend the word "God" to cover any or all ideas of spiritual reality. She believes, second, that nothing is lost spiritually or morally by forgoing the idea of a supernatural person in favor of the Good. In fact, the ontological proof works to this end by showing that the concept of an existing personal being cannot meet the demands of necessary existence. Third, Murdoch insists that the Good is what the old God symbolized, especially the absolute, necessary moral claim on humanity manifest in every experience of distinguishing degrees of perfection. And therefore, finally, Murdoch frees religion from theism and defines it as "a mode of belief in the unique sovereign place of goodness and virtue in human life."[27] This completes Murdoch's response to the problem of the loss of value as metaphysically basic and her proposal for a theology without God. She has shown the ubiquity of value in human consciousness and also the reality of Good.

As I argued about the idea of the agency of God in chapter 2, for Christian faith the word "God" is not simply a name of a supernatural person. We must now see that the idea of the Good does not exhaust the meaning of the divine. As a step toward formulating a theological response to

Murdoch's ethics that substantiates these claims, it is important to ask a basic but critical moral question. The question focuses on the object of moral concern—that is, the individual—and then forces us to consider the source of morality in order to make sense of that object of concern.

Murdoch insists that the focus of morality is love and knowledge of individuals. The "central concept of morality," she writes, "is 'the individual' thought of as knowable by love, thought of in the light of the command, 'Be ye therefore perfect.'" [28] She has noted that this commitment to the individual is also found in Christian faith. This raises our question: what is the source of this claim about the centrality of the individual? More pointedly, why ought the individual be an object of love and moral attention when any real, actual individual is always less than perfect? Was it not precisely the fact of contingency and imperfection that led Murdoch to reject a personal God in favor of the impersonal Good? Why does the same argument not fall on actual, existing human beings? In short, the question is about what confers value on individuals.

There are several well-known answers to this question; Murdoch endorses none of them. It is important to see why she rejects these positions. First, it could be argued that we are to care for and know individuals as a means to the end of knowing the Good for ourselves. An ethical hedonist might argue in this way. But if that were the case it would mean seeing persons as means to others' ends; virtue, despite Murdoch's protest, would have a point. Second, could it be that we are to respect and love persons only insofar as they approximate or represent perfection for us? Some versions of Kantian ethics seem to argue so, with their focus on the idea of *humanity in persons*—but not the individuals themselves—as evoking respect. But how would we know that our perception is without fault in making such evaluations? Murdoch is too aware of the delusions that infest moral understanding to endorse this answer about the value of individuals. So, we are left to ask, again, what it is about the imperfect, contingent, messy, petty reality of persons that compels, even commands, our love. As far as I can tell, an answer to this question within the strict confines of Murdoch's thought might entail affirming a claim that cuts against her whole moral philosophy. Clarity on this point is then absolutely crucial to what I want to argue about God and morality.

As we have seen, the mode of moral being according to Murdoch is consciousness. Human consciousness, she further notes, is a one-making activity. We always try to organize our lives and our world into some coherent, meaningful whole; this is the metaphysical impulse endemic to the human mind. As Kant saw, consciousness is a synthetic activity; Plato insisted that we understand with respect to the Good. Murdoch is trying to make both of these claims. This one-making act with respect to some idea of perfection is found in creative, artistic activity. This is why art is so important for Murdoch. We are all artists, she insists. Of course, Murdoch is aware of how the mind can fabricate and love false unities. She hopes to counter this tendency by establishing the reality of Good and exploring practices for transforming moral attention—practices such as meditation and prayer.

What Murdoch has not examined, and what I only intimated in chapter 4, is that the one-making of consciousness is itself an act of power. What are we to make of this fact with respect to what confers value on individuals and also the first principle of ethics? Two responses are possible: in terms I have used before, one is an internalist response while the other is an externalist one. First, we could argue that this act of power in consciousness, our cognitive one-making rather than willing, is value-conferring. The conferring of value must be understood as internal to the agent, this antirealist, constructivist argument would go, because otherwise we could not make sense of why individuals, imperfect as we all obviously are, are fit objects of love and respect. What compels our respect and love is the reality of individuals as one-making creatures, the fact that they have minds and thus some consciousness of the Good. To love individuals is to love the varied and complex ways in which the Good is known. What confers moral worth on persons is then an act of power, the one-making activity of the mind under the reality of Good. Power is creative of value, but it is the power of mind, not the power of will, that is central to this account.

Murdoch insists on love and respect for persons as such and not the one-making activity of consciousness. And this must mean, as an externalist response to the question, that consciousness as such does not confer value. Even the value of the self is in some respect external to it; the Good is sovereign here as well. This is, I take it, Murdoch's point in saying that the self is seen by the good person as nothing, as transparent to the Good. The self in its one-making activity must be effaced if it is to be morally good, realizing that every act of consciousness potentially, and maybe actually, works against this end. In other words, if consciousness were in fact value-conferring, moral attention would be directed to what individuals share rather than to the particularity of their existence.

We have returned, then, to the point of departure for this inquiry—namely, the relation between power and value as the root of morality and whether that relation is to be understood as internal to the agent, in willing or in consciousness, or as somehow external to the subject. Murdoch rejects existentialist and other antirealist positions on precisely this point; consciousness is directed toward the real, and human freedom makes sense only in that context. But then the question returns: what confers value on individuals? Murdoch has established the reality of Good, but what is the goodness of reality, especially the reality of individuals? This is the point, I judge, at which a residue of the Christian insistence on the created worth of individuals plays its role in Murdoch's thought. Simply by virtue of being created, persons are worthy of respect and love. In the light of creation, one affirms that *esse qua esse est bonum,* to cite Augustine. But can we make sense of this claim without a creator, without God?

Let me now take up this question and with it Murdoch's claims about God and Good. For if I am right, a realist ethics that holds to the dignity of the individual on grounds other than an act of power within the self—be that act will or consciousness—is possible only by appeal to some idea of creation and thus also a creator. But this would mean that we cannot replace God with Good. It would mean, in other words, that the Good is not all that God symbolizes. And it would also mean that we must endorse what I have been calling hermeneutical realism in ethics.

THE SOVEREIGNTY OF GOD'S GOODNESS

I have been arguing throughout this book that in our time the ground of value is increasingly defined in terms of power.[29] This means that value is understood to be rooted in the capacity to bring about states of affairs that fulfill some person's or community's existence, and this entails the further belief that value is increased through the increase of power, the capacity to respond to, shape, and influence reality.[30] Because, as far as we know, only human beings intentionally exercise power, this means that human beings, or at least human societies, are taken as the source of value. From this set of claims, ethicists have drawn several conclusions. Value, it is argued by antirealists, is not ontologically basic; power is basic. The constraints on power must then be found *internal* to those exercising power whether in will or in consciousness, or at least in terms of some consensus between agents who exercise power. Insofar as this is true, Platonism and Christianity, along with their most basic affirmations, are false. As we have seen, these are some of the deepest suppositions of postmodern cultures and also of contemporary ethics.

The question, again, is whether power is the ground of value in will or consciousness or if constraints are placed on the exercise of power by a Good other than power itself. This question is morally basic insofar as all human beings are actual or potential agents who exercise the capacity to act for certain ends and also suffer the actions of others. The connection between power and value is deep and cannot be eradicated from the human heart. It is the engine of human love, creativity, and conflict, and also, I believe, what religions are about. Persons seek contact with value-creating power in love, imagination, and action. This fact is basic to a realistic understanding of human existence. What Murdoch has contributed to this inquiry is a careful analysis of the place of vision and perception in moral life. She has tried to show that our power, our love and freedom, is constrained and directed by our perception of reality. But her argument, while indeed necessary, is not finally sufficient for ethics. The problem centers on how the Good symbolizes the real. In order to show this, I want to move through the levels of reflection we traced in Murdoch's thought—that is, a conception of the first principle of ethics, justifying it with respect to ordinary experience, and, finally, how we picture the fundamental mode of moral being without a lapse into will or consciousness as value-conferring.

If my argument to this point has been at all persuasive, the first principle of ethics must specify the relation of power and value in such a way that power is rendered subservient to the value of existing beings, beings such as human individuals. An act of power is then not value-conferring; power has moral value when it respects and enhances finite existence. An ethics of the Good, as Murdoch presents it, finally does not have the conceptual resources to make this argument. This is so because of the symbolism of the Good itself. What do I mean? Murdoch insists that the Good is that in which the "light of truth is seen; it reveals the world, hitherto invisible, and is also a source of life."[31] But it is absolutely important to note that as the source of life the Good does not bind its power to finite, created life. The Good does not recognize or respond to what is other than itself. In other words, the Good does not symbolize the transformation of value-creating power so that power respects and enhances finite life. And this is why, I believe, it is difficult for Murdoch to specify the ground for the value of the individual. In grasping this point we have isolated the inner limits of the Good as a symbol of the real.

As I have argued in various chapters of this book, the transformation of power is central to the Christian conception of God. God is ultimate value-creating power, a power that binds itself to the actual worth of finite existence. This account of the divine is not the God of the philosophers, Murdoch's "single perfect real object of attention." That definition, as we have seen, is already loaded with an idea of perfection geared toward the Good. Yet I also do not mean the idea of God in much popular piety with its all-too-anthropomorphic conception of deity. The point in saying that

God is personal and an agent is to make a claim about the irreducibility of creativity in our conception of life; it is not to designate a literal person. The God of Christian faith is believed to be the unconditional value-creating power. Yet, because faith in God is articulated through a complex set of concepts and symbols—such as creation, the human as the imago Dei, the priority of justice and mercy in the moral life, and, centrally, Christ—power *qua* power does not and cannot define the Good. The word "God" symbolizes the connection of power and value in the divine reality so that power is in principle rendered subservient to what respects and enhances the integrity of nondivine existence.[32] But this means that power cannot be the first principle of ethics; power oriented toward respecting and enhancing existence is that principle. The word "God" enables us to grasp this insight.

This brings us to the second step in the argument. How are we to show within ethics that this is what theological discourse symbolizes? We can answer this question in the first instance with respect to ways of life that explicitly understand human existence in relation to the divine. If one looks at Christian and Jewish faith, one finds that they are about a value-creating power that in the act of identifying itself binds power to respecting and enhancing, even redeeming, finite existence, and, what is more, that only this reality is the unconditional, the absolute. This was the point of the argument in chapter 2 and also chapter 8. The insight designated by the word "God" radiates throughout the whole of Christian faith and discourse. It is found in ideas of covenant, redemption, creation, and the final reign of God. In Christianity, as I argued in chapter 7, this insight comes to focus on Christ, the individual in whose life power is made perfect.

Claims about God designate, then, a valuation of power, of the divine reality that enables things—such as persons, moral values, and the world—to come to be and to continue to exist in complexes of interaction and thus is the very source of value. This is why God is irreducible and primary in understanding the world and human life. A theological ethics articulates the meaning and truth of the sovereignty of God's goodness—that is, the authority of value-creating power to constitute our sense of what is unconditionally good. To direct one's attention toward God, to engage in a radical interpretation of life, has the effect of transforming self-consciousness, one's construal of the world, and one's assessment of other persons. This is the claim of Christian and Jewish faith; it is the center of these particular ways of human life.

Theological ethics must show that this claim about God and how it symbolizes the first principle of ethics is true not only of Christian morality. Does the reality symbolized by the word "God," the divine reality that is objective to the self, in fact resonate within the self, to the depths of self-being? In order to answer this question we must grasp the moral meaning of a seemingly obscure theological point. Theologians have long insisted that God's work, the divine act of power or will, enacts the divine nature. Put in scholastic terms, God's essence and existence are one. The essence of God is to be. And yet the act of divine power, especially in creation and redemption, reconstitutes the identity of the divine—God is known as creator and redeemer. That is, we identify who God is with respect to a history of God's actions. God's goodness is the exercise of power that creates value but also reconstitutes the divine identity, shows who God is, by binding divine power to the worth of finite reality. This is why, in the biblical texts, the divine name is given within covenant relations. Who God is, the divine identity, is known only in a context that transvalues power and the source of value, such as covenant. Morally speaking, this means that any exercise of power is always a response to something real, but the act of power also reconstitutes the identity of the agent. And this is why theistic discourse resonates in the self. In every creative act of one-making, we too bind power of mind and will to the existence and continuation of a meaningful world and in so doing shape our own identities. In all actions and relations, we affirm or deny, implicitly at least, that power is always oriented, beyond itself, toward what is real and meaningful.

The problem, of course, is that the domain of the real and the meaningful, the world, can be limited to the ego. What then? By interpreting human existence theologically, one seeks to reconstitute the relation of power and value at the depths of human life. One engages in the act of radical interpretation. In this way, the power to act, the one-making power of human consciousness, and the power of human love and creativity are all transformed symbolically when God is the object of attention, because God symbolizes the real in terms other than the brute exercise of power. Moral progress or perfection can begin only with a transformation at the heart of human existence, with our longing for some contact with a value-creating power in our attempt to render our lives and our world meaningful and intelligible. This is why Christians speak of sanctification as basic to the moral life. Without this transformation, value is collapsed back into power, the world into the ego, and the purpose of life is to serve whoever or whatever seems to possess power.

The point I am making is that insofar as we are agents, we seek a meaningful and intelligible world through the exercise of power. Given this, one needs in ethics an idea or symbol that designates the transformation of power with respect to the value of existence. This symbol is necessary to ensure the worth of individuals and the world on grounds other than the exercise of human power and also to provide the symbolic means of transforming moral understanding and thereby reorienting human freedom. The modern age, as we have seen, found this symbol in humanity. But this modern faith in humankind has now strangely contradicted itself. Rather than respecting and enhancing life, we witness the apotheosis of the will-to-power. In Christian faith, the name "God" symbolizes the real as the depth of value. And all of this is missed if we assume that the Good is what God symbolizes.

Thus far in response to Murdoch, I have tried to show that the Good is not all that God symbolizes, that there are important differences in how God and Good symbolize the real, and that we can make sense of theistic discourse in terms of actual religious communities and human experience itself, especially our experience of being agents. The final step in my argument is to clarify what resonates in the self with respect to these claims about God. Murdoch, as we have seen, correlates Good and consciousness, the one-making act of mind with respect to our perceptions of grades of value. Is there anything analogous to this argument in the theological ethical position I have been presenting? There is, and yet we can designate it only by reclaiming a concept missing in Murdoch's thought and in much of contemporary ethics. But we must also rethink this concept, the idea of conscience, beyond its interpretation in existentialism and also social psychology. Making this point about conscience will complete my argument for the sovereignty of God's goodness, because we will see how God is sovereign over the self and its drive for omnipotence.

In terms of traditional Christian morality, by virtue of being created, human beings know the moral law. Conscience is the witness to this law. In the terminology I have been using, the core of consciousness, the one-making power of mind with respect to its evaluative capacity, is conscience. It testifies that power is ultimately in the service of finite existence. Conscience is not a faculty of mind; it designates our mode of being in the world as moral agents responding to the value of others. If we consider our experience as agents, we are grasped not only by our perception of better and worse; in our actions and relations, we are also grasped by the sense that some things simply ought to be and that what exists ought not to be wantonly demeaned or destroyed. The profound experience that some finite reality—a person, a child, a blazing sunset over a northern lake—ought to be and also ought not be demeaned or destroyed is a testimony to, an affirmation of, power's final, ultimate subservience to existence. This is an experience of the moral sense of creation, an awareness of the moral law; it is the witness of conscience. And the practice of conscience, as I called it in chapter 5, is that of radical interpretation. This spiritual and moral practice aims to deepen, reform, and even aid in sanctifying persons for the sake of respecting and enhancing the integrity of life.

Thus, conscience is not, as existentialists and thinkers like Martin Heidegger have argued, the call of the human to itself, authentic existence to the inauthentic self. That is a purely internalist position, one that any realistic ethics rejects. Similarly, conscience is not only a name for the ways in which people's moral convictions and identities have been formed by their communities. By conscience I mean the shape of existence as responsive to the noninstrumental value of others. Conscience recognizes rather than confers value; it is the grasp of the other on the self and thus the ground of our sociality itself. Conscience is the theological analogue to what Murdoch means by attention.

Once it is understood that experience testifies that power is ultimately in the service of existence, we find in the heart of human life, in conscience, a fundamental affirmation of the being of God. We can choose to conform our lives to this reality or to deny it. What has happened in our time—and possibly in all times—is not only the loss of a vision of the real; it is that conscience is blunted, deformed, through social and ideological means, such that the claim of finite life to be respected and enhanced does not resonate within the self in its exercise of power. And this is a failure to grasp what is primary and irreducible—the source of intelligibility of our lives as agents. Given this, the moral life is in good measure about coming to know the reality witnessed to by conscience and living in conformity to it. As St. Paul puts it in Romans 12:2, "Do not be conformed to this world but be transformed by the renewing of your minds, so that you may discern what is the will of God—what is good and acceptable and perfect."[33] Through this transformation of conscience, all things are valued in relation to God. The uniqueness of human beings, our irreducible moral worth, is that as created beings we may and do and must know what God symbolizes. Value is conferred in that we are created beings even as we are endowed with the capacity to respond to value other than the self, and, in so doing, transform and direct the exercise of power.[34]

CONCLUSION

I have been arguing that because we are beings who exercise power, make evaluations about how to live, and seek a meaningful existence, we need what the word "God" symbolizes if we are to articulate the first principle of ethics. Theological ethics symbolizes the real in such a way as to formulate that principle as the proper relation of value and power. I have tried to show this conceptually, in terms of our actual experience, and also with respect to how we are to picture the human. I have argued that God is the best symbolization of the real in ethics; conscience is the best picture of what it means to exist as a moral creature, the fundamental mode of moral being.

In making this argument, I have drawn insights from Iris Murdoch's thought. The argument of this book has centered, as Murdoch does, on the problem of how we understand the status of value as being other than the self and thus perceive the depth of morality. Yet, if I am correct, we cannot rightly understand our contemporary situation or Murdoch's moral philosophy without attending to the relation between power and value. The fact that she does not address these matters is not an oversight. The centrality of the Good in her thought effaces the depth of this problem about power and value. The current situation is also much more dangerous than Murdoch supposes; a correction of vision will not easily sever the equation of value with power. There are, in other words, limits to how the Good symbolizes the real.

Theological ethics has a complex set of concepts and symbols that addresses this problem and does so through the very organizing center of faith—that is, the divine. By speaking of God's goodness, one can formulate the first principle of ethics in terms of the relation of power and value. This provides us with a perspective from which to diagnose, criticize, and hopefully transform our situation. The point of this book has been that a theological perspective on the moral life isolates and addresses problems in other moral positions. And this is the case because theological ethics faithfully articulates the very structure of moral experience.

Murdoch has helped us see that we are in search of an ethics that is capable of considering the ways in which religious matters permeate human existence in terms of the experience of the unconditional claim of morality on our lives. In response to this search, Murdoch has proposed a theology without God. By engaging her work and the thought of other contemporary thinkers, I have sought to show that we need an articulate, critical theological ethics fully engaged with the deepest problems of our age, because an ethics committed to the worth of persons is possible only given some moral sense of creation that resonates in the core of human life. And it is in this way, I judge, that God's goodness is sovereign over all other concepts, a sovereignty to which our existence as agents testifies.

Notes

INTRODUCTION

1. I borrow this term from H. Richard Niebuhr, but it is clearly not limited to his own position. See H. Richard Niebuhr, *The Responsible Self: An Essay in Christian Moral Philosophy*, with an introduction by James M. Gustafson (New York: Harper & Row, 1963).

2. For a fuller account of this position, see William Schweiker, *Responsibility and Christian Ethics* (Cambridge: Cambridge University Press, 1995).

3. See, for example, Paul Tillich, *The Protestant Era*, trans. James Luther Adams (Chicago: University of Chicago Press, 1948). For his ethics, see *Morality and Beyond* (Louisville, Ky.: Westminster/John Knox Press, 1995).

4. I am not alone in putting the matter this way. This concern was voiced by Raphael Demos, H. Richard Niebuhr, and others in response to Tillich's work. On this point, see the supplement volume on his work in the *Journal of Religion* 46, nos. 1, 2 (1966). More recently, thinkers like Emmanuel Levinas, Charles Taylor, Iris Murdoch, Hans Jonas, Paul Ricoeur, Erazim Kohák, and Werner Marx have made varying arguments for the centrality of ethics to ontology. I deal with some of these thinkers throughout this book.

5. See Charles Taylor, *Sources of the Self: The Making of the Modern Identity* (Cambridge: Harvard University Press, 1990).

6. See John B. Cobb Jr., *Grace and Responsibility: A Wesleyan Theology for Today* (Nashville: Abingdon Press, 1995).

7. The task of theological ethics is to articulate the meaning and demonstrate the truth of Christian claims in the realm of the moral life in order to provide guidance for life. "Theological ethics," Douglas Ottati rightly notes, "is knowledge of God and ourselves as it connects with the wellsprings, contexts, and guides for human action." See Douglas Ottati, "The Reformed Tradition in Theological Ethics," in *Christian Ethics:*

Problems and Prospects, ed. Lisa Sowle Cahill and James F. Childress (Cleveland: The Pilgrim Press, 1996), 46.

8. For a helpful discussion, see Robin W. Lovin, *Reinhold Niebuhr and Christian Realism* (Cambridge: Cambridge University Press, 1995).

9. On this point, see Hans Jonas, *The Imperative of Responsibility: In Search of an Ethics for the Technological Age,* trans. Hans Jonas and David Herr (Chicago: University of Chicago Press, 1984); Erazim Kohák, *The Embers and the Stars: An Inquiry into the Moral Sense of Nature* (Chicago: University of Chicago Press, 1984); and Iris Murdoch, *Metaphysics as a Guide to Morals* (London: Allen Lane/The Penguin Press, 1992).

10. See William Schweiker and Michael Welker, "A New Paradigm of Theological and Biblical Inquiry," in *Power, Powerlessness, and the Divine: New Inquiry in Bible and Theology,* ed. Cynthia L. Rigby (Atlanta: Scholars Press, 1997), 3–20.

1. ONE WORLD, MANY MORALITIES

1. This chapter originally appeared in a different form in *Criterion* 32, no. 2 (1993): 12–21.

2. Paul Ramsey, *Fabricated Man: The Ethics of Genetic Control* (New Haven, Conn.: Yale University Press, 1970). Also see Hans Jonas, *The Phenomenon of Life: Toward a Philosophical Biology* (Chicago: University of Chicago Press, 1982).

3. For work in this area, see David Hollenbach, *Justice, Peace, and Human Rights: A Catholic Social Ethics in a Pluralistic Context* (New York: Crossroads, 1989); Jürgen Moltmann, *On Human Dignity: Political Theology and Ethics* (Philadelphia: Fortress Press, 1984); and Hans Küng, *Global Responsibility: In Search of a New World Ethics,* trans. John Bowden (New York: Crossroads, 1991).

4. Philosophers often note that we regularly engage in a variety of moral evaluations and judgments, which range from simple expressive statements ("My, that was a good thing to do") to considered judgments about what is good and right. This is hardly surprising. Human life is always situated among relations and actions we must evaluate and judge in order to get on in the world. On the idea of levels of moral discourse, see Henry David Aiken, *Reason and Conduct* (New York: Knopf, 1962), 65–87.

5. For an excellent discussion of this understanding, see Don S. Browning, Bonnie J. Miller-McLemore, Pamela D. Couture, K. Brynolf Lyon, and Robert M. Franklin, *From Culture Wars to Common Ground: Religion and the American Family Debate* (Louisville, Ky.: Westminster John Knox Press, 1997).

6. For example, see *Setting the Table: Women in Theological Conversation,* ed. Rita Nakashima Brock, Claudia Camp, and Serene Jones (St. Louis: Chalice Press, 1995), and also *Power, Powerlessness, and the Divine.*

7. For a helpful discussion on the necessary relation between ethical and sociological reflection, see Dorothy Emmet, *Rules, Roles and Relations* (New York: St. Martin's Press, 1967).

8. For discussions of pluralism in theology and ethics, see Schubert Ogden, *Is There Only One True Religion or Are There Many?* (Dallas: Southern Methodist University Press, 1992); Alasdair MacIntyre, *Three Rival Versions of Moral Enquiry: Encyclopaedia, Genealogy, Tradition* (Notre Dame, Ind.: University of Notre Dame Press, 1992); John

Hick, *God and the Universe of Faiths* (New York: St. Martin's Press, 1973); Paul Knitter, *No Other Name: A Critical Review of Christian Attitudes toward the World Religions* (Maryknoll, N.Y.: Orbis Books, 1985); David Tracy, *Plurality and Ambiguity: Hermeneutics, Religion and Hope* (New York: Harper & Row, 1986); and *Prospects for a Common Morality*, ed. Gene Outka and John P. Reeder Jr. (Princeton, N.J.: Princeton University Press, 1993).

9. For a discussion of this point, see Langdon Gilkey, *Society and the Sacred: Towards a Theology for a Culture in Decline* (New York: Crossroads, 1986), and also Gordon D. Kaufman, *God, Mystery, Diversity: Christian Theology in a Pluralistic World* (Minneapolis: Fortress Press, 1996).

10. For a subtle analysis of the pluralistic structures of postmodern societies, see Michael Welker, ". . . And Also Upon the Menservants and the Maidservants in Those Days Will I Pour Out My Spirit: On Pluralism and the Promise of the Spirit," in *Soundings* 78, no. 1 (1995): 49–67, and *Kirche im Pluralismus* (Kaiser: Gutersloh, 1995).

11. See Jeffrey Stout, *Ethics after Babel: The Languages of Morals and Their Discontents* (Boston: Beacon Press, 1988). For a discussion of this problem in comparative ethics, see William Schweiker, "The Drama of Interpretation and the Philosophy of Religions: An Essay on Understanding in Comparative Religious Ethics," in *Towards a Comparative Philosophy of Religion Volume III: Discourse and Practice*, ed. Frank Reynolds and David Tracy (Albany: SUNY Press, 1992), 263–94.

12. Mary Midgley, *Can't We Make Moral Judgments?* (New York: St. Martin's Press, 1993), 86.

13. In this chapter I am not exploring political realism. That form of realism is concerned with the realities of power and conflict in political affairs and thus the problems of justice. The ethics of responsibility I propose has these "realistic" concerns. For recent discussion of epistemological and moral realism, see Hilary Putnam, *The Many Faces of Realism* (LaSalle, Ill.: Open Court, 1987); David O. Brink, *Moral Realism and the Foundations of Ethics* (Cambridge: Cambridge University Press, 1989); and Geoffrey Sayre-McCord, ed., *Essays on Moral Realism* (Ithaca, N.Y.: Cornell University Press, 1988). Also see the essays from the D. R. Sharpe Lectureship on Ethics given at the Conference on Realism and Responsibility in Contemporary Ethics, which are to be published in the *Journal of Religion*. For a discussion of this conference, see Lois Malcolm, "Redefining Realism and Responsibility in Contemporary Ethics," *Criterion* 32, no. 1 (1993): 17–22.

14. See Franklin I. Gamwell, *The Meaning of Religious Freedom: Modern Politics and the Democratic Resolution* (Albany: SUNY Press, 1995).

15. Bertrand Russell, *Why I Am Not a Christian*, ed. Paul Edwards (New York: Simon & Schuster, 1957), 108.

16. See Taylor, *Sources of the Self*.

17. J. L. Mackie, *Ethics: Inventing Right and Wrong* (Harmondsworth, Eng.: Penguin Books, 1977).

18. Stanley Hauerwas, *Christian Existence Today: Essays on Church, World, and Living In Between* (Durham, N.C.: Labyrinth Press, 1988). Also see John Howard Yoder, "On Not Being Ashamed of the Gospel: Particularity, Pluralism, and Validation," *Faith and Philosophy* 9, no. 3 (1992): 285–300.

19. The literature on responsibility in ethics is immense. For positions I have found helpful, see Hans Jonas, *The Imperative of Responsibility*; H. Richard Niebuhr, *The Responsible Self*; Marion Smiley, *Moral Responsibility and the Boundaries of Community* (Chicago: University of Chicago Press, 1992); and Peter A. French, *Responsibility Matters* (Lawrence: University Press of Kansas, 1992). Also see Schweiker, *Responsibility and Christian Ethics*.

20. Thinkers from a variety of ethical positions capitalize on this fact. See, for example, Basil Mitchell, *Morality: Religious and Secular* (Oxford: Clarendon Press, 1980); John Finnis, *Fundamentals of Ethics* (Washington, D.C.: Georgetown University Press, 1983); Lisa Sowle Cahill, *Between the Sexes: Foundations for a Christian Ethics of Sexuality* (Philadelphia: Fortress Press, 1985), and her *Women and Sexuality* (New York: Paulist Press, 1992); and Paul Ricoeur, *Oneself as Another*, trans. Kathleen Blamey (Chicago: University of Chicago Press, 1992).

2. POWER AND THE AGENCY OF GOD

1. This chapter originally appeared in a slightly different form in *Theology Today* 52, no. 2 (1995): 204–24.

2. Of course, a post-theistic age does not mean that our time is necessarily postreligious. The contemporary interest in forms of spirituality and also the worldwide fundamentalist movement are evidence of the importance of religion in the postmodern context.

3. On the idea of a moral ontology and what it means for ethics, see Taylor, *Sources of the Self*. Also see William Schweiker, "The Good and Moral Identity: A Theological Ethical Response to Charles Taylor's *Sources of the Self*," *Journal of Religion* 72, no. 4 (1992): 560–72.

4. On the importance of this in ethics, see Murdoch, *Metaphysics as a Guide to Morals*. Also see *Iris Murdoch and the Search for Human Goodness*, ed. Maria Antonaccio and William Schweiker (Chicago: University of Chicago Press, 1996).

5. For an example of this form of inquiry, see William Schweiker, *Mimetic Reflections: A Study in Hermeneutics, Theology, and Ethics* (New York: Fordham University Press, 1990).

6. On the relation between naming and thinking God, see David Tracy, "Literary Theory and the Return of the Forms of Naming and Thinking God in Theology," *Journal of Religion* 74, no. 3 (1994): 302–19.

7. There have been a range of theological responses to the modern criticism of agential conceptions of God. Without examining these options in detail in this chapter, let me mention some of the most prominent. First, theologians such as Paul Tillich argued that religious symbols, such as "God," point to the depth structure of the self-world relation. Second, through the Word of God or through the use of the category of narrative, some theologians, like Karl Barth, have attempted to understand all of reality within specific discourse about God. Third, there are theologians who attempt to demythologize biblical discourse with respect to basic existential questions or understand claims about God as imaginative constructions for the purposes of orienting and guiding human action. These theologians, such as James Gustafson, Sallie McFague, and Gordon Kaufman, seek to accommodate nontheological construals of reality while des-

ignating the unique function of theological claims. Next, there are theologians, influenced by process metaphysics, who understand the divine as internally related to the world. This means, as Schubert Ogden puts it, that "God interacts with all, not only acting on them but also being acted on by them." See Ogden, *Is There Only One True Religion or Are There Many?*, 49. Finally, liberation theologians seek to understand the presence of God in solidarity with the oppressed and the struggle for liberation. Here an understanding of the social world is dependent on the perspective of the interpreter, and, so the argument goes, the theologically valid perspective is one in solidarity with the oppressed. Clearly, the question of agency and interpretations of reality is one point, and I think a crucial point, at which reflection on divine power and powerlessness intersects with consideration of human existence and action.

8. I should note that I am merely holding the classical Protestant insistence that we are concerned with God's bearing towards us, God pro nobis, for the sake of life and thus with practical, not speculative, claims about the divine. In my judgment, theological claims are fully practical in nature even as, as I try to show, these claims also entail beliefs and judgments about reality. This is the force of speaking of a "moral ontology" and also the moral meaning of ideas of God.

9. See Hans Jonas, *The Imperative of Responsibility*, 81. For Jonas's metaphysics, see his *The Phenomenon of Life*. Also see his *Philosophical Essays: From Ancient Creed to Technological Man* (Englewood Cliffs, N.J.: Prentice-Hall, 1974). For critical responses to Jonas's ethics, see Karl-Otto Apel, *Diskurs und Verantwortung: Das Problem des Übergangs zur postkonventionellen Moral* (Frankfurt: Suhrkamp, 1990), 179–218, and Wolfgang Huber, "Toward an Ethics of Responsibility," *Journal of Religion* 73, no. 4 (1993): 573–91.

10. John B. Thompson, *Ideology and Modern Culture: Critical Social Theory in the Era of Mass Communication* (Stanford, Calif.: Stanford University Press, 1990).

11. For a fuller account of this point, see chapter 4, "Understanding Moral Meanings."

12. Kaufman, *God, Mystery, Diversity*, 74.

13. Jean-Paul Sartre, *Being and Nothingness*, trans. Hazel Barnes (New York: Washington Square Press, 1966), 707.

14. For the classical statement of this position, see Friedrich Nietzsche, *The Birth of Tragedy and the Genealogy of Morals*, trans. Francis Golffing (New York: Doubleday Anchor Books, 1956).

15. Gerhard Von Rad, *Genesis: A Commentary*, trans. John H. Marks (London: SCE Press, 1961), 145.

16. See Samuel Terrien, *The Elusive Presence: The Heart of Biblical Theology* (New York: Harper & Row, 1978), 72–76.

17. Walter Wink, *Naming the Powers: The Language of Power in the New Testament* (Philadelphia: Fortress Press, 1984), 4.

18. See Tillich, *Morality and Beyond*.

19. See Donald Wiebe, *The Irony of Theology and the Nature of Religious Thought* (Montreal and Kingston: McGill-Queen's University Press, 1991). For a different, and I judge more adequate, account, see Gregory Vlastos, *Socrates: Ironist and Moral Philosopher* (Ithaca, N.Y.: Cornell University Press, 1991).

3. MORAL SKEPTICISM AND THE POSTMODERN AGE

1. This chapter was originally presented in a slightly different form for the conference "Computer Ethics and Moral Theologies" sponsored by the Computer Ethics Institute, Washington Theological Consortium and Virginia Theological Seminary, March 6–7, 1996, Virginia Theological Seminary in Alexandria, Virginia.

2. Mary Midgley, *Wisdom, Information, and Wonder: What Is Knowledge For?* (London: Routledge, 1989), 14.

3. Taylor, *Sources of the Self*.

4. See Schweiker, *Responsibility and Christian Ethics*.

5. Václav Havel, *Disturbing the Peace: A Conversation with Karel Hvizdala*, translated and with introduction by Paul Wilson (New York: Knopf, 1990), 11. For a similar argument by another Czech thinker, see Kohák, *The Embers and the Stars*.

6. On this topic, see Peter Berger and Thomas Luckman, *The Social Construction of Reality: A Treatise in the Sociology of Knowledge* (Garden City, N.Y.: Anchor Books, 1967).

7. Donna J. Haraway, "A Cyborg Manifesto: Science, Technology, and Socialist-Feminism in the Late Twentieth Century," in her *Simians, Cyborgs, and Women: The Reinvention of Nature* (New York: Routledge, 1991), 164.

8. See Alasdair MacIntyre, *After Virtue: A Study in Moral Theory* (Notre Dame, Ind.: University of Notre Dame Press, 1981). One should note the irony in my claim: despite his intention to follow Aristotle rather than Nietzsche, MacIntyre's position, like Aristotle's, has affinities with Nietzsche's ethics.

9. See Immanuel Kant, *Fundamental Principles of the Metaphysics of Morals*, trans. T. K. Abbot (New York: Liberal Arts, 1949).

10. For a discussion of these matters, see *The Is/Ought Question: A Collection of Papers on the Central Problem in Moral Philosophy*, ed. W. D. Hudson (New York: St. Martin's Press, 1969).

11. We can think about the *source* of value in three ways: (1) as arising from our acts of valuing, and thus subjective; (2) as somehow *in* what has worth and importance, and so objective; or (3) as designating the *relation* between the one valuing and what is esteemed as being of worth and importance, and so a relational theory of value. All of these accounts of the source of value seem right in some sense. It would be odd to say something is valuable if we could find no resonance for it in human interest and sensibility, but we equally doubt that all value simply is interest and sensibility. Value seems to have some hold *in* things or at least in the *relation between* beings, say, between persons. On this concept, see H. Richard Niebuhr, "The Center of Value," in *Radical Monotheism and Western Culture* (Louisville, Ky.: Westminster/John Knox Press, 1993), 110–13. Also see James M. Gustafson, *A Sense of the Divine: The Natural Environment from a Theocentric Perspective* (Cleveland: The Pilgrim Press, 1994).

12. See Mackie, *Ethics: Inventing Right and Wrong*, 30.

13. See Richard Rorty, *Objectivity, Relativism, and Truth*/Philosophical Papers I (Cambridge: Cambridge University Press, 1991). For a different position, see Midgley, *Can't We Make Moral Judgments?*

14. The force of the reality-is-solely-a-social-construction position is that finally nature itself is a matter of our writing, our systems of encoding meanings; what nature is

and means differs in different cultural worlds. Nature is translated into the encoded messages, the stories we tell about "nature."

15. See Hans Jonas, "Contemporary Problems in Ethics from a Jewish Perspective," in his *Philosophical Essays*. Also see his *The Imperative of Responsibility*.

16. See MacIntyre, *Three Rival Versions of Moral Enquiry*; Hauerwas, *Christian Existence Today*; and Jean Porter, *The Recovery of Virtue: The Relevance of Aquinas for Christian Ethics* (Louisville, Ky.: Westminster/John Knox Press, 1990).

17. Putnam, *The Many Faces of Realism*.

18. See Gordon D. Kaufman, *The Theological Imagination: Constructing the Concept of God* (Philadelphia: Westminster Press, 1981); Sallie McFague, *Models of God: Theology for an Ecological, Nuclear Age* (Philadelphia: Fortress Press, 1987); and Philip S. Keane, *Christian Ethics and Imagination* (New York: Paulist Press, 1984). The term "critical realism" is used in a variety of ways by a number of thinkers. For the purposes of this chapter, I limit the definition to those thinkers I am exploring.

19. Kaufman, *God, Mystery, Diversity*, 6.

20. See Schweiker, *Mimetic Reflections*.

21. Taylor, *Sources of the Self*, 449.

22. I want to thank David Schmidt for pushing me on the kind of claim I am making with respect to matters of moral and epistemic certainty.

4. UNDERSTANDING MORAL MEANINGS

1. This chapter appeared in a different form as "Understanding Moral Meanings: On Philosophical Hermeneutics and Theological Ethics," in *Christian Ethics*, 76–92.

2. See Richard E. Palmer, *Hermeneutics* (Evanston, Ill.: Northwestern University Press, 1969); David E. Klemm, *Hermeneutical Inquiry*, 2 vols. (Atlanta: Scholar's Press, 1986); and Schweiker, *Mimetic Reflections*.

3. Paul Ricoeur, *Interpretation Theory: Discourse and the Surplus of Meaning* (Fort Worth: Texas Christian University Press, 1976).

4. Paul Ricoeur, *Hermeneutics and the Human Sciences: Essays on Language, Action, and Interpretation*, edited, translated, and with an introduction by John B. Thompson (Cambridge: Cambridge University Press, 1981). Also see Charles Taylor, *Philosophy and the Human Sciences*, Philosophical Papers 2 (Cambridge: Cambridge University Press, 1985); Irving Singer, *Meaning in Life: The Creation of Value* (New York: The Free Press, 1992); and *Meanings in Texts and Actions: Questioning Paul Ricoeur*, ed. David E. Klemm and William Schweiker (Charlottesville: University of Virginia Press, 1993).

5. Hans-Georg Gadamer, *Reason in the Age of Science*, trans. F. Lawrence (Cambridge: MIT Press, 1981). Also see his *Truth and Method*, revised translation by J. Weinsheimer and D. Marshall (New York: Continuum, 1989).

6. See Taylor, *Sources of the Self*.

7. H. Richard Niebuhr, *Faith on Earth: An Inquiry into the Structure of Human Faith*, ed. Richard R. Niebuhr (New Haven, Conn.: Yale University Press, 1989), 23.

8. See Brink, *Moral Realism and the Foundation of Ethics; Essays in Moral Realism*.

9. See Putnam, *The Many Faces of Realism*.

10. See Hauerwas, *Christian Existence Today*; John Howard Yoder, *The Priestly Kingdom: Social Ethics as Gospel* (Notre Dame, Ind.: University of Notre Dame Press,

1984); and James Wm. McClendon Jr., *Ethics: Systematic Theology*, Vol. I (Nashville: Abingdon Press, 1986).

11. See Tillich, "Realism and Faith," in his *The Protestant Era*, 66–82.

12. Thomas Ogletree, *Hospitality to the Stranger: Dimensions of Moral Understanding* (Philadelphia: Fortress Press, 1985).

13. Josef Fuchs, *Christian Morality: The Word Became Flesh*, trans. B. McNeil (Washington, D.C.: Georgetown University Press, 1981).

14. Mackie, *Ethics: Inventing Right and Wrong*, 15.

15. Sharon Welch, *A Feminist Ethic of Risk* (Minneapolis: Fortress Press, 1990).

16. Gordon Kaufman, *Theology for a Nuclear Age* (Philadelphia: Westminster Press, 1985).

17. McFague, *Models of God*; Cahill, *Between the Sexes*; and Cahill, *Women and Sexuality*.

18. See Schweiker, *Responsibility and Christian Ethics*.

19. Charles Taylor, *Human Agency and Language*, Philosophical Papers I (Cambridge: Cambridge University Press, 1985), 238.

20. Taylor, *Sources of the Self*, 448.

21. Paul Ricoeur, *Soi-meme comme un autre* (Paris: Éditions du Seuil, 1990), and also his "Naming God" in *Union Seminary Quarterly Review* 34 (1979): 215–28.

22. The term "transvaluation" is first found in the work of Friedrich Nietzsche. He rightly realized that what is morally basic is how a culture develops a table of values with respect to the reality of power. I am arguing that the transvaluation of power entailed in Christian faith negates the centrality of the will-to-power in Nietzsche's thought and a world bent on the celebration of power. This is, in my judgment, the properly radical claim of Christian faith. See Friedrich Nietzsche, *Beyond Good and Evil: Prelude to a Philosophy of the Future*, trans. R. J. Hollingdale (New York: Penguin Books, 1973).

5. RADICAL INTERPRETATION AND MORAL RESPONSIBILITY

1. A version of this chapter originally appeared in the *Journal of Religion* 73, no. 4 (1993): 613–37.

2. An examination of the discourse of responsibility requires that we distinguish between causal and moral responsibility. Causal responsibility pertains to claims regarding events or things that bring about or cause a state of affairs but in which it is difficult, if not impossible, to impute any intention to those events or things. Moral responsibility, conversely, entails claims about an agent who is responsible, about what he or she is responsible for, and also about that to which or to whom the agent is responding. To speak of responsibility is then to identify an agent in the stream of events. My concern in this essay is obviously with moral responsibility but is mindful of the fact that human agents are causal forces in the world. And this is increasingly the case. The awesome extension of human power in our time now radically alters the forces of nature itself.

3. The question of whether or not one can speak of "corporate agents" is of course debated. For a recent discussion of these matters, see *Individual and Collective Responsibility*, ed. Peter A. French (Cambridge: Harvard University Press, 1972). Also see William Schweiker, "Accounting for Ourselves: Accounting and the Discourse of Ethics," *Accounting, Organizations and Society* 18, nos. 2/3 (1993).

4. On this point, see Smiley, *Moral Responsibility and the Boundaries of Community*, and French, *Responsibility Matters*.

5. See, for instance, Martin Buber, in his *I and Thou*, and also the divine command ethics of Karl Barth in the *Church Dogmatics*. Also see Emmanuel Levinas, *Totality and Infinity*, trans. Alphonso Lingus (Pittsburgh: Duquesne University, 1969), and Michael Theunissen, *The Other: Studies in the Social Ontology of Husserl, Heidegger, Sartre, and Buber*, trans. Christopher McCann (Cambridge: MIT Press, 1986).

6. See Ricoeur, *Interpretation Theory*. Also see his *Hermeneutics and the Human Sciences*, ed. and trans. John B. Thompson.

7. I am not arguing, as intuitionists such as Hutcheson and Shaftesbury did, for a special moral faculty—a moral sense—that apprehends *sui generis* moral values or duties. For a recent intuitionist proposal, see David Little, "The Nature and Basis of Human Rights," in *Prospects for a Common Morality*, ed. Outka and Reeder, 73–92. Furthermore, if I am correct that the insight reached through radical interpretation is, finally, that it is good to exist, then basic moral terms, such as "good," cannot be specified solely in non-naturalistic terms. What we mean by goodness is bound to the conditions necessary for the continuation and flourishing of existence, human and nonhuman. This does not commit me to a form of the naturalistic fallacy, as it is often called, because I am not arguing that "good" is the same as other natural properties of entities or persons.

8. Cf. St. Augustine, *The City of God* XIX, 14 (New York: Doubleday Image Books, 1958).

9. See Taylor, *Sources of the Self*, and his "Responsibility for Self," in *Free Will*, ed. Gary Watson (Oxford: Oxford University Press, 1982), 111–26. Also see Schweiker, "The Good and Moral Identity."

10. See, for example, Paul Tillich, *Systematic Theology*, vol. 1 (Chicago: University of Chicago Press, 1951).

11. Harry Frankfurt calls such persons "wantons." He defines wantons as "agents who have first-order desires but who are not persons because, whether or not they have desires of the second order, they have no second-order volitions." Harry Frankfurt, "Freedom of the Will and the Concept of a Person," in his *The Importance of What We Care About: Philosophical Essays* (Cambridge: Cambridge University Press, 1988), 16.

12. Taylor, "Responsibility for Self," 123.

13. Ibid., 125.

14. Alan Donagan, *The Theory of Morality* (Chicago: University of Chicago Press, 1977), 242.

15. On this issue, see Paul Ricoeur, *Oneself as Another*. Also see William Schweiker, "Imagination, Violence and Hope: A Theological Response to Ricoeur's Moral Philosophy," in *Meanings in Texts and Actions*, 205–25.

16. For a helpful discussion of this point, see Donagan, *The Theory of Morality*, esp. 57–66.

17. For a discussion of this point, see Robert P. Scharlemann, *The Reason of Following: Christology and the Ecstatic I* (Chicago: University of Chicago Press, 1991).

18. Taylor, *Sources of the Self*, 517.

19. Hans Jonas, "Contemporary Problems in Ethics from a Jewish Perspective," in his *Philosophical Essays*, 172.

20. See Hans Jonas, "The Concept of God after Auschwitz: A Jewish Voice," *Journal of Religion* 67, no. 1 (1987): 1–13.

21. Hans Jonas, *The Imperative of Responsibility*, 81. For Jonas's metaphysics, see his *The Phenomenon of Life*. Also see Strachan Donnelley, "Whitehead and Hans Jonas: Organism, Causality, and Perception," *International Philosophical Quarterly* 19, no. 3 (1979): 301–15, and T. A. Goudge, "Existentialism and Biology," *Dialogue: Canadian Philosophical Review* 5, no. 4 (1967): 603–8. For a critical response to Jonas's ethics from the perspective of discourse ethics see Apel, *Diskurs und Verantwortung*.

22. Jonas, *The Imperative of Responsibility*, 11.

23. Ibid., 43. See also James M. Gustafson, "Theology and Ethics: An Interpretation of the Agenda," and Hans Jonas, "Response to James M. Gustafson," *Knowing and Valuing: The Search for Common Roots*, ed. H. Tristain Engelhardt Jr. and Daniel Callahan (New York: The Hastings Center: Institute for Society, Ethics, and the Life Sciences, 1980), 181–217.

24. Ibid., 79.

25. Ibid., 89–90.

26. Jonas, "Contemporary Problems in Ethics from a Jewish Perspective," 179.

27. It was Nietzsche, of course, who claimed that the human good is found in the release of power. In this respect, his thought represents the gravest challenge to theological ethics, especially in an age of technological power. My argument here is analogous to that of Karl Rahner on the presence of the symbol "God" in Western thought. Rahner argues that the presence of this symbol in our culture signals the openness of human life to a horizon of absolute mystery. I am arguing that the presence of the name of God in our culture grounds a belief that the exercise of power itself is not the human good. See Karl Rahner, *Grace in Freedom* (New York: Herder & Herder, 1969), esp. 183–203.

28. For a discussion of the activity of understanding, see Schweiker, *Mimetic Reflections*.

6. RESPONSIBILITY AND COMPARATIVE ETHICS

1. This chapter originally appeared as "The Drama of Interpretation and the Philosophy of Religions: An Essay on Understanding in Comparative Religious Ethics," in *Discourse and Praxis*, ed. Reynolds and Tracy (New York: State University of New York Press, 1992), 263–94.

2. Jürgen Habermas, *Moral Consciousness and Communicative Action*, translated by Christian Lenhardt and Shierry Weber Nicholsen, with an introduction by Thomas McCarthy (Cambridge: MIT Press, 1990), 27.

3. Ibid., 28.

4. My approach is reflexive in character, but this does not mean that I am concerned simply with the act of consciousness and the attempt to grasp the generative power of its act, as in German idealism. By turning to interpretation as reciprocal action between participants I am suggesting that understanding is always social and linguistic in character. This does not preclude the exploration of the reciprocal activity constitutive of understanding in a reflexive manner, seeking to understand its dynamic and shape, what is disclosed in it, and even its conditions of possibility. On these issues, see H. Richard Niebuhr, *Faith on Earth*, and Otto Pöggeler, "Die ethische-politische Dimension der hermeneutischen Philosophie," in *Probleme der Ethik—zur Diskussiongestellt*, hg. Gerd-Günther Grau (Freiburg/München: Karl Alber, 1972), 45–82.

5. This is not to suggest that there is any agreement between thinkers. G. F. Else, for instance, contests Herman Koller's claim that mimesis relates dance and music in early Greek thought; Else himself concentrates on drama. Philosophers also disagree. Ricoeur is concerned with narrative mimesis while Karl Morrison takes mimesis to be a way of speaking about historical change and reform. Other differences and disputes could be mentioned. What is important is that, with the decline of romantic expressivism, mimesis is again considered basic to the task of understanding social existence, historical experience, aesthetic reality, and understanding itself. For works by classics scholars on mimesis, see G. F. Else, "Imitation in the 5th Century," *Classical Philology* 53, no. 2 (1958): 73–90; Herman Koller, *Die Mimesis in Antike: Nachahmung, Darstellung, Ausdruck* (Bern: A. Francke, 1954); and Göram Sörböm, *Mimesis and Art: Studies in the Origin and Early Development of an Aesthetic Vocabulary* (Uppsala: Svenska, 1966). For philosophical treatments, see Jacques Derrida, "Economimesis," trans. R. Klein, *Diacritics* 11 (1981): 3–25; Hans-Georg Gadamer, *Die Aktualität des Schönen: Kunst als Spiel, Symbol und Fest* (Stuttgart: Philipp Recalm, 1977); René Girard, *Violence and the Sacred*, trans. Patrick Gregory (Baltimore: The Johns Hopkins University Press, 1977); Karl Morrison, *The Mimetic Tradition of Reform in the West* (Princeton, N.J.: Princeton University Press, 1982); Paul Ricoeur, *Time and Narrative*, vol. I, trans. Kathleen McLaughlin and David Pellauer (Chicago: University of Chicago Press, 1984); Schweiker, *Mimetic Reflections*; and Christoph Wulf, "Mimesis," in *Historische Anthopologie: Zum Problem der Humanwissenschaften heute oder Versuch einer Neubegründung*, hg. Gunter Gebauer et al. (Hamburg: Rowohlt Taschenbuch Verlag, 1989), 83–128.

6. See Ronald Green, *Religious Reason* (New York: Oxford University Press, 1978), and his *Religion and Moral Reason* (New York: Oxford University Press, 1988). Also see Ronald Green and Charles Reynolds, "Cosmogony and the 'Question of Ethics,'" *Journal of Religious Ethics* 14, no. 1 (1986): 139–56; David Little and Sumner B. Twiss, *Comparative Religious Ethics* (New York: Harper & Row, 1978); and John P. Reeder Jr., *Source, Sanction, and Salvation: Religion and Morality in Christian Traditions* (Englewood Cliffs, N.J.: Prentice-Hall, 1988).

7. Green, *Religious Reason*, 4.

8. For different examples of this approach, see Charles Larmore, *Patterns of Moral Complexity* (Cambridge: Cambridge University Press, 1987); Stout, *Ethics after Babel*; and Bernard Williams, *Ethics and the Limits of Philosophy* (Cambridge: Harvard University Press, 1985).

9. Stout, *Ethics after Babel*, 5.

10. See Francis X. Clooney, "Finding One's Place in the Text: A Look at the Theological Treatment of Caste in Traditional India," *Journal of Religious Ethics* 17, no. 1 (1989): 1–29; Robin W. Lovin and Frank E. Reynolds, "In the Beginning," in *Cosmogony and Ethical Order: New Studies in Comparative Ethics*, ed. Robin W. Lovin and Frank E. Reynolds (Chicago: University of Chicago Press, 1985); and Lovin and Reynolds, "Focus Introduction," *Journal of Religious Ethics* 14, no. 1 (1986): 48–60.

11. Lovin and Reynolds, "In the Beginning," 3.

12. Lovin and Reynolds, "Focus Introduction," 57.

13. Gadamer, *Truth and Method*, 497.

14. See Victor Turner, *Dramas, Fields, and Metaphors: Symbolic Action in Human Society* (Ithaca, N.Y.: Cornell University Press, 1974).

15. For helpful discussions of metaphor, see Paul Ricoeur, *The Rule of Metaphor: Multi-Disciplinary Studies in the Creation of Meaning in Language*, trans. Robert Czerny, Kathleen McLaughlin, and John Costello (Toronto: University of Toronto Press, 1977), and Janet Martin Soskice, *Metaphor and Religious Language* (Oxford: Oxford University Press, 1985).

16. See Paul Griffiths, "Denaturalized Discourse," a paper presented to The Colloquium on Religion(s) in History and Culture, University of Chicago, 1989.

17. For an example of this claim, see Lee Yearly, "Aquinas and Mencius: Theories of Virtue and Conceptions of Courage," in *Towards a Comparative Philosophy of Religion(s)*, ed. David Tracy and Frank E. Reynolds (New York: SUNY Press, 1990).

18. See Ricoeur, *Interpretation Theory*.

19. Wulf, "Mimesis," 83. For a more extended discussion, see Koller, *Die Mimesis in Antike*.

20. There are thinkers who have reclaimed the roots of mimesis in ritual. Hans-Georg Gadamer, for instance, draws on mimesis in order to explore the power of texts, symbols, works of art, and thus language, to disclose the being of what they figure. René Girard charts how mimetic, ritual practices and their linguistic expressions conceal basic social processes—processes marked by violence and appeals to the sacred. There are also philosophers and critics, such as Derrida, who draw on the roots of mimesis in mime-drama. They do so in order to deconstruct Western aesthetics and epistemology because of its dependence on the idea of realistic imitation or the priority of speaking over writing. The mime is, after all, a mute signifier. For these theorists, language is not a set of ideas, words, and symbols that are imitations of some "referent" transcending them. It is a web of signs productive of meaning through the "play" of those signs when activated by an interpreter. Finally, there are theorists, such as Paul Ricoeur, who are concerned with narrative. They seek to reclaim Aristotle's insight that plot is the mimesis of human action. Narratives tell us something about human action because they configure action into a meaningful whole, a plot.

21. See Ricoeur, *Interpretation Theory*.

22. From my perspective, it is hardly surprising that some religious traditions, such as Judaism, have transformed actual ritual practices into textual strategies of interpretation. Historians of religion and anthropologists have also long understood the importance of symbolic action for claims about the world and the human. On this issue, see Turner, *Dramas, Fields, and Metaphors* and also Mircea Eliade, *The Sacred and the Profane: The Nature of Religion*, trans. Willard R. Trask (New York: Harcourt Brace Jovanovich, 1959). Kenneth Burke has explored dramatic action as a way of relating the hexad of terms central to any account of human activity: act, agent, scene, means, purpose, and attitude. See his *On Symbols and Society*, edited and with an introduction by Joseph R. Gusfield (Chicago: University of Chicago Press, 1989). What has not been done is to understand such action as the clue to exploring understanding within comparative religious ethics. That is the task of this essay.

23. In saying that interpretation is a form of enactment I am not, however, restricting the concept of "performative" to speech acts, as J. L. Austin and others have done. I am using it in an anthropological and sociological sense to denote those communal dramatic and ritual activities through which something (a myth, human action, a god) is pre-

sented in and for community. See J. L. Austin, *How to Do Things with Words*, 2d ed., ed. J. O. Urmson and Marina Sbisa (Cambridge: Cambridge University Press, 1975).

24. Jonas, *The Phenomenon of Life*, 148.

25. Ibid., 163, n. 3.

26. On this topic, see Habermas, *Moral Consciousness and Communicative Action*, 43–115.

27. Charles Taylor, *Human Agency and Language*, Philosophical Papers I (Cambridge: Cambridge University Press, 1985), 221.

28. Ibid., 238.

29. John D. Boyd, *The Function of Mimesis and Its Decline* (Cambridge: Harvard University Press, 1968), 54.

30. Gadamer, *Truth and Method*, 103.

31. See MacIntyre, *After Virtue*.

32. See Green and Reynolds, "Cosmogony and the 'Question of Ethics,'" 139–45.

33. For the scholar who has tried to develop a theory of mimesis to explore these events, see Girard's *Violence and the Sacred*. Also see William Schweiker, "Sacrifice, Interpretation, and the Sacred: The Import of Gadamer and Girard for Religious Studies," *Journal of the American Academy of Religion* 55, no. 4 (1987): 791–810.

34. For positions that have informed my argument at this point, see H. Richard Niebuhr, *The Responsible Self*, and Hans Jonas, *The Imperative of Responsibility*.

35. For an example, see Peter L. Berger, *The Sacred Canopy: Elements of a Sociological Theory of Religion* (New York: Doubleday and Co., 1967).

36. Little and Twiss, *Comparative Religious Ethics*, 28.

37. The recent shift in naturalist ethics has been from claims about the natural ends of the human, which seem difficult to sustain in light of the actual diversity of moral communities, to basic human needs. On this issue, see Mitchell, *Morality: Religious and Secular*. I am suggesting that one of those needs, and perhaps the crucial one for the human *qua* human, is the need to represent in order to come to be as a specific person or community. In this chapter I cannot explore the implication of this for naturalism in religious ethics.

38. Habermas, *Moral Consciousness and Communicative Action*, 27.

39. Wulf, "Mimesis," 119.

7. THE REALITY OF CHRIST AND THE VALUE OF POWER

1. This essay was originally delivered at the American Academy of Religion Annual meeting for the Bonhoeffer Social Responsibility and Public Policy Group held in Chicago, November 19, 1994.

2. See, for example, Küng, *Global Responsibility*.

3. See Jonas, *The Imperative of Responsibility*, and Apel, *Diskurs und Verantwortung*.

4. On this point, see *Prospects for a Common Morality*, ed. Outka and Reeder.

5. See Robin W. Lovin, "The Limits of Freedom and the Possibility of Politics: A Christian Realist Account of Political Responsibility," *Journal of Religion* 73, no. 4 (1993): 559–72. Also see Sayre-McCord, ed., *Essays on Moral Realism*.

6. See Schweiker, *Responsibility and Christian Ethics*.

7. Albert Schweitzer, *Out of My Life and Thought* (New York: Mentor, 1953). Also see James A. Nash, *Loving Nature: Ecological Integrity and Christian Responsibility* (Nashville: Abingdon Press, 1991).

8. Huber, "Toward an Ethics of Responsibility," 577. Also see his *Konflikt und Konsens: Studien zur Ethik der Verantwortung* (Munich: Kaiser, 1990).

9. On this point, see Murdoch, *Metaphysics as a Guide to Morals*.

10. This is not simply to make the point that responsibility and freedom are essentially linked, although many discussions of responsibility continue to center on freedom and determinism. To speak of power rather than of freedom is not to deny the unique human form of power called freedom. Rather, it is to provide us the means by which to speak of the moral status of other types of power.

11. Jonas, *Philosophical Essays*, 172.

12. Mackie, *Ethics: Inventing Right and Wrong*.

13. For different expressions of this concept, see James M. Gustafson, *Ethics from a Theocentric Perspective*, 2 vols. (Chicago: University of Chicago Press, 1981, 1984); Franklin I. Gamwell, *The Divine Good: Modern Moral Theory and the Necessity of God* (San Francisco: HarperCollins, 1990); and Schweiker, *Mimetic Reflections*.

14. Kohák, *The Embers and the Stars*.

15. H. Richard Niebuhr, "The Center of Value," 100–13. Also see Gustafson, *A Sense of the Divine*.

16. For a recent discussion of this point, see Thomas E. Wartenberg, *The Forms of Power: From Domination to Transformation* (Philadelphia: Temple University Press, 1990).

17. For a recent attempt to connect political realism with moral and theological realism, see Lovin, *Reinhold Niebuhr and Christian Realism*.

18. Dietrich Bonhoeffer, *Ethics*, ed. Eberhard Bethge (New York: Collier Books, 1986), 17. "Die christliche Ethik erkennt schon in der Möglichkeit des Wissen um Gut und Böse den Abfall vom Ursprung. Der Mensch im Ursprung weiß nur eines: Gott. Den anderen Menschen, die Dinge, sich selbst weiß er nur in der Einheit seines Wissen um Gott, er weiß alles nur in Gott und Gott in allem. Das Wissen um Gut und Böse deutet auf die vorgegangene Entzweiung mit dem Ursprung." Dietrich Bonhoeffer, *Ethik*, hg. Eberhard Bethge (München: Chr. Kaiser, 1985), 19. I will cite the German in the notes and amend the translation when necessary.

19. Dietrich Bonhoeffer, *Act and Being*, trans. Bernard Noble (New York: Octagon Books, 1983), 89.

20. Bonhoeffer, *Ethics*, 190. "Das Problem der christlichen Ethik ist das Wirklichwerden der Offenbarungswirklichkeit Gottes in Christus unter seinen Geschöpfen. . . ." (*Ethik*, 202).

21. Ibid., 98. "Die Technik des neuzeitlich Abendlandes hat sich von jeder Dienststellung befreit, sie ist gerade nicht wesentlich Dienst, sondern Herrschaft, und zwar Herrschaft über dies Natur. Es ist ein völlig neuer Geist, der sie hervorbringt und mit dessen Erlöschen sie auch weider zu Ende gehen wird, der Geist der gewaltsamen Unterwerfung der Nature unter den denkenden und experimentierenden Mensch" (*Ethik*, 104).

22. Ibid., 234. "Es gehört weiter zur Begrenztheit verantwortlichen Lebens und Handelns, daß es mit der Verantwortlichkeit der anderen ihm begegnenden Menschen rechnet. Eben darin unterscheidet sich Verantwortung von Vergewaltigung, daß sie im anderen Menschen den Verantwortlichkeit erkennt, ja daß sie ihm seine eigene Verantwortlichkeit bewußt werden läßt" (*Ethik*, 249).

23. Ibid., 207. "Die Welt ist, wie alles Geschaffene, durch Christus und auf Christus hin geschaffen und hat ihren Bestand alleine in Christus (Joh 1, 10; Kol 1, 16)" (*Ethik*, 220).

24. Ibid., 194. "Sie meint damit auch die Wirklichkeit der bestehenden Welt, dies allein durch die Wirklichkeit Gottes Wirklichkeit hat. . . . In Jesus Christus ist die Wirklichkeit Gottes in die Wirklichkeit dieser Welt eingegangen" (*Ethik*, 207).

25. In my judgment, this problem of personalistic accounts of value haunt all ethics of responsibility that are centered on the encounter between self and "other." For a recent argument for such a position based on "encounter," see Immanuel Levinas, *Totality and Infinity*.

8. DIVINE COMMAND ETHICS AND THE OTHERNESS OF GOD

1. This essay was presented in a different form at the conference "The Otherness of God" held at the University of Virginia, April 7–10, 1994. The proceedings have been published in *The Otherness of God*, ed. Orrin F. Summerell (Charlottesville: University Press of Virginia, 1998).

2. Ethics is reflection on human moral existence; it aims at determining how we should live. Ethical reflection arises from the fact that agents always face the problem of how to understand and guide their lives in relation to others and in terms of what kind of person one ought to be or in what type of community one should want to live. Furthermore, in exploring moral existence, any ethics articulates, criticizes, and (if necessary) revises beliefs held by a community or tradition about the world in which human beings exist and how they can and should orient their lives in that world. Moral reflection, in other words, is inescapable insofar as to exist in a human fashion requires that one seek to understand how one ought to live and act in the world. Theological ethics undertakes reflection on how to live from the perspective of the human relation to the divine. But this perspective is adopted within moral inquiry, and thus the focus of concern is not simply the Christian life but human moral existence. The theologian draws on the resources and beliefs of a specific tradition but for the sake of addressing the problems of human life. In this respect, I believe that long-standing divisions between moral philosophers and theologians are less decisive than they usually are thought to be. Contemporary theologians are less likely to make appeal to special moral knowledge or special revelation; many moral philosophers now grant the fact that moral discourse is always situated in some moral community and tradition. The fact that the theologian draws from the resources of the Christian tradition ought not to bar him or her from the general task of moral inquiry. At least this is how I am attempting to undertake the task of theological ethical reflection in this book.

3. For recent, if different, examples of this project, see Gamwell, *The Divine Good*; Gustafson, *Ethics from a Theocentric Perspective*; and Schweiker, *Responsibility and Christian Ethics*.

4. On the hermeneutical nature of theological ethics, see William Schweiker, "Hermeneutics, Ethics, and the Theology of Culture: Concluding Reflections," in *Meanings in Texts and Actions*, 292–313.

5. In other words, theological ethics must break beyond paradigms of thought dominated by voluntarism, as in divine command ethics, and reductionist moral naturalism.

6. See Janine Marie Idziak, "In Search of 'Good Positive Reasons' for an Ethics of Divine Commands: A Catalogue of Arguments," *Faith and Philosophy* 6, no. 1 (1989): 47–64.

7. See Philip Quinn, "The Recent Revival of Divine Command Ethics," in *Philosophy and Phenomenological Research* 50, supplement (fall 1990): 345–65.

8. Thomas Aquinas, *Summa Theologiae* I/II qq. 90–91.

9. Hans Jonas, *The Imperative of Responsibility,* 79.

10. For a recent example of this form of ethics, see Murdoch, *Metaphysics as a Guide to Morals.*

11. Søren Kierkegaard, *Fear and Trembling,* trans. Walter Lowrie (Garden City, N.Y.: Doubleday, 1954). For a further discussion of Kierkegaard, see Schweiker, *Mimetic Reflections.*

12. See John Chandler, "Divine Command Theories and the Appeal to Love," *American Philosophical Quarterly* 22, no. 3 (1985): 231–39.

13. These thinkers admit that not all persons understand the meaning of moral terms in theistic terms; this is a discourse of a particular tradition and community. But since all moral discourse is related to some community and its tradition, advocates of divine command ethics contend that this does not count against the meta-ethical significance of this moral theory.

14. Robert M. Adams, "A Modified Divine Command Ethics," in his *The Virtue of Faith and Other Essays in Philosophical Theology* (New York: Oxford University Press, 1987), 100. Also see Edward Wierenga, "A Defensible Divine Command Theory," *Nous* 17 (1983): 387–407; William E. Mann, "Modality, Morality, and God," *Nous* 23 (1989): 83–99; and Richard J. Mouw, *The God Who Commands* (Notre Dame, Ind.: University of Notre Dame Press, 1990).

15. Robert M. Adams, "Divine Command Metaethics Modified Again," in *The Virtue of Faith,* 128–43. In this essay I am not concerned with modifications in Adams's theory or the differences among recent versions of divine command ethics. My concern is to isolate the central features of this line of reasoning. For a discussion of these issues, see *Divine Command Morality: Historical and Contemporary Readings,* ed. Janine Marie Idziak (New York: Edwin Mellen, 1980).

16. Adams, "A Modified Divine Command Ethics," 108.

17. Ibid., 109.

18. Karl Barth, "Das Problem der Ethik in der Gegenwart" (1922), in Barth, *Vorträge und kleinere Arbeiten (1922–1925),* hg. Holger Finze (Zürich: Theologischer Verlag, 1990), 102.

19. Karl Barth, *Church Dogmatics* II/2, ed. G. W. Bromiley and T. F. Torrance (Edinburgh: T & T Clark, 1957), 674.

20. Karl Barth, *Church Dogmatics* I/1, trans. G. T. Thomson (Edinburgh: T & T Clark, 1936), 426.

21. Barth, *Church Dogmatics* II/2, 606.

22. Ibid., 553.

23. Ibid., 560.

24. Barth's ethics preserves the radical freedom and sovereignty of God, but it specifies the meaning of the divine command in terms of the actual revelation of God. Given this, in his practical ethics, Barth draws on the resources of various disciplines, careful

NOTES TO PAGES 168–176

descriptions of human character and conduct, and also insights from within the various spheres of life constituted by the revelation of God as creator, redeemer, and reconciler in Jesus Christ. The use of other disciplines does not define the meaning of the good or constrict the freedom of God. Put differently, not only must the Christian act in obedience to the divine command, but theology must think about the moral life in obedience to the command of God.

25. In making this argument, Barth defines the goodness of God as good-for-ness. That is, he specifies what moralists call a relational theory of value wherein value is "the good-for-ness of being for being in their reciprocity, their animosity, and their mutual aid." See H. Richard Niebuhr, "The Center of Value," 107.

9. THE SOVEREIGNTY OF GOD'S GOODNESS

1. A version of this chapter originally appeared in *Iris Murdoch and the Search for Human Goodness*, 209–35.

2. See Mackie, *Ethics: Inventing Right and Wrong*.

3. Murdoch, *Metaphysics as a Guide to Morals*, 511–12.

4. Ibid., 428.

5. For a helpful discussion of this point in religious ethics, see Albert R. Jonsen, *Responsibility in Modern Religious Ethics* (Washington, D.C.: Corpus Books, 1968).

6. While different ethical positions might agree on practical matters—say, that war is in principle wrong or that under certain circumstances war is justifiable—they might still differ with respect to what integrates the dimensions of reflection on the moral life. To the extent that ethical positions disagree at this basic level, they represent divergent accounts of how we should live. It remains an open question whether or not this means that these moral outlooks are finally incommensurable. Yet one task of any ethics is to show why in fact a particular idea, symbol, or root metaphor ought to be first in our moral thinking and our actual conduct.

7. Ethics seeks to articulate the meaning and demonstrate the truth of moral convictions, religious or otherwise, for the sake of understanding life and our existence as agents and providing guidance for how we ought to live. An ethics is theological only if human beings are understood to exist most basically in relation to God rather than simply in terms of natural reality, a social totality, or historical existence. See Schweiker, "Hermeneutics, Ethics, and the Theology of Culture." This account of theological ethics is indebted to H. Richard Niebuhr and his conception of "Christian moral philosophy." See his *The Responsible Self*.

8. Murdoch, *Metaphysics as a Guide to Morals*, 188.

9. Ibid., 193.

10. Iris Murdoch, "The Idea of Perfection," in her *The Sovereignty of Good* (London: Routledge, 1991), 16.

11. Erazim Kohák has noted that most "Western thought has been consistently personalistic and specifically *naturalistic*, at least in the generic sense of that term, understanding the human as continuous with and at home in nature." To be sure, there are good reasons to challenge much of traditional Western ethics. The status of being human has too easily been denied some persons, notably women and those in dominated cultures. So, too, the naturalistic tendency of Western thought—that is, the claim that the human good is to be specified in terms of what respects and enhances the

flourishing of life—has been used to delimit the range of human freedom. And this same naturalism and personalism has backed wantonly anthropocentric valuations of the natural world. Still, the picture of the world and ourselves that dominates current Western societies simply cuts against the grain of its own heritage. Ought we not try to eradicate from our view of the world and ourselves a conviction about the primacy of human beings and our relation to the natural world? See Kohák, *The Embers and the Stars*, 7. Also see Lovin, "The Limits of Freedom and the Possibility of Politics."

12. Iris Murdoch, "The Sovereignty of Good over Other Concepts," in *The Sovereignty of Good*, 97.

13. I should note that in this respect my argument represents an Augustinian line of moral and theological reflection. That is, St. Augustine, in *The City of God*, understood that the central problematic of the "earthly city" was the grounding of the political and social order in the "love of ruling." The "city of God," conversely, rejects that foundation of the social and political on principle and affirms the centrality of the love of God. In the terms I am developing, the central issue in ethics and theology is this relation of power and value. This is the case because that relation formulates the most basic principle of human activity and association. Thus, to consider the relation of power and value is, theologically understood, to reflect on the human relation to the divine and what persons and communities hold as sacred.

14. On this point, see Schweiker, *Mimetic Reflections*.

15. Jonas, *Philosophical Essays*, 172.

16. Christians have never thought that Platonists could answer this problem. Given their confidence in mind, Platonists could never really understand St. Paul's insistence on the abyss of the will, the frightful contradiction between mind and inclination that infests human existence. They could never see the fact that the political order is too often, and maybe always, driven by the thirst for power, as theologians from Augustine to Reinhold Niebuhr have insisted. Even human illusions are not simply consoling fantasies; they are idols, icons of the human power to attempt to create unconditional value. Finally, in the eyes of Christian thinkers, Platonists could also never understand the importance of creation—that is, that all temporal natural value, the goodness of being, is dependent on a value-creating power characterized by righteousness, that the Creator acknowledges the goodness of what is finite (God saw that it was good, as we have it in Genesis), and, more radically, that God redeems fallen existence, which is the moral meaning of incarnation.

17. See Taylor, *Sources of the Self*. Also see Schweiker, "The Good and Moral Identity."

18. Iris Murdoch, "On 'God' and 'Good,'" in *The Sovereignty of Good*, 54.

19. Some years ago, Elizabeth Anscombe wrote an important essay in which she insisted that the idea of moral obligation ought to be jettisoned from ethics. This radical move was necessary because in order to make sense of the experience of obligation one needed a moral psychology more subtle than any found in ethics at that time. It also demanded a full recognition of and then escape from the dependence of theories of obligation on Jewish and Christian ideas of God as commander—a dependence, she insisted, that was always present but rarely acknowledged in modern ethics. If I understand Murdoch rightly, her moral philosophy is a complex response to Anscombe's challenge. And by responding to Anscombe, she is also, we might note, responding to our current situation. See G. E. M. Anscombe, "Modern Moral Philosophy," *Philosophy* 33

(1958): 1–19. It is significant that Murdoch dedicates *Metaphysics as a Guide to Morals* to Anscombe.

20. Murdoch's attack on voluntarism runs along several lines. She notes that when ethics focuses on actions and discrete acts of will, one does not need an elaborate moral vocabulary. Good, evil, right and wrong, and just and unjust are action words whereas all of the other evaluative discourse we use to make sense of our world, others, and ourselves seems to fall beyond the scope of moral discourse. This truncates our moral sensibilities. The focus on action words and evaluations of action is consistent with a picture of persons as solitary, substanceless wills who constitute their identity, even their world, in acts of choice. This makes it difficult to speak of the inner life or the continuity of the self over time, and thus of our moral progress, other than through words about individual acts.

21. Murdoch, *Metaphysics as a Guide to Morals*, 265.

22. Murdoch, "The Idea of Perfection," 34.

23. Murdoch, "On 'God' and 'Good,'" 55.

24. Murdoch, *Metaphysics as a Guide to Morals*, 396.

25. Ibid., 406.

26. Ibid., 432.

27. Ibid., 426.

28. Murdoch, "The Idea of Perfection," 30.

29. Value can be defined in naturalistic and relational terms. Value is the fittingness of being in relation to being insofar as this relation respects and enhances the integrity of an existent. The food that we consume is a value to us insofar as it does not thwart our needs, say by poisoning us. Disvalue is what demeans and destroys an existing being. As H. Richard Niebuhr has argued, value is not reducible to subjective evaluations; it is also not simply a property of entities. Value denotes a relation of being to being in terms of what completes or frustrates those involved. Given this account of value, what is morally right is any action or relation that respects and enhances the integrity of natural, personal, and social life. Right and wrong, and also moral duties, are determined and justified with respect to basic values rooted in the needs, capacities, and potentialities of specific kinds of beings, say human beings. Murdoch would seem to agree with some version of this theory of value. She describes herself as a nondogmatic naturalist in ethics. I take this to mean that morality cannot be severed from the question of what enables something to flourish. And it also means that in ethics we are intensely interested in exploring what kind of creatures we are and the world in which we live. For this account of value, see H. Richard Niebuhr, "The Center of Value."

30. By power I mean the capacity to respond to, influence, and shape reality. Power is not simply the capacity to control, coerce, or dominate persons or things. Power is, furthermore, not a thing. Rather, power, from the Latin *potere*, is to be able. It is that which enables things—such as persons, moral values, the world—to come to be and to continue to exist in complexes of interaction. Power can take various forms, both social and natural; it can be exercised legitimately or illegitimately, coercively or noncoercively. Access to power is access to the capacity to bring about states of affairs or outcomes. Freedom is the form of power that is crucial to the individual's moral life, since freedom is the person's capacity to respond to, influence, and shape reality. On this topic, see Joseph Allen, "Power and Political Community," in *The Annual of the Society of Christian Ethics* (Washington, D.C.: Georgetown University Press, 1993), 3–22.

31. Iris Murdoch, *The Fire and the Sun* (Oxford: Clarendon Press, 1977), 4.

32. This is why sin or moral fault for this tradition is not simply a matter of ignorance or error, but the attempt by persons to usurp the divine as the unconditional value-creating power that manifests itself in forms of exploitation and injustice.

33. For a helpful discussion of this point, see Hans Dieter Betz, "Christianity as Religion: Paul's Attempt at Definition in Romans," *Journal of Religion* 71, no. 3 (1991): 315–44.

34. For a fuller treatment of these issues, see Schweiker, *Responsibility and Christian Ethics*.

Index

action, 34, 37, 38–40, 46, 47, 48–53, 82, 88, 140, 144; in Christian discourse, 67, 68; conditions for, 99–100; and freedom, 103; and God, 85, 161–63; and hermeneutics, 78, 80; interpretation as, 112–13, 119, 121–34; and respect, 100–101; responsible, 107, 108–9, 141, 153; and selfhood, 175; and understanding, 76; and value, 4, 60, 61, 151–53, 162, 163, 164–69, 185

Adams, Robert M., 163

agency, 11, 14, 34, 69–70, 78, 80, 86, 113, 176; and conscience, 188, 189; divine, 33–53, 177, 187; and postmodernism, 35, 39–43; and power, 143, 145, 177; and radical interpretation, 91–96, 106, 107, 157; and respect, 99–100; theologically construed, 45–47, 49, 89–90, 109–10, 140, 156, 186–87, 190; and value, 146, 147, 151–53, 173, 184

analysis, 15, 35, 37, 42, 90

Apel, Karl-Otto, 107, 138

Aquinas, Thomas, 82, 159, 161–62

Aristotle, 27, 47, 60, 78, 121, 127, 128

articulation, 15, 35, 37, 42, 90

Augustine, Saint, 74, 79, 80, 96, 184

autonomy, 46, 48, 98, 105–6, 107

Barth, Karl, 80, 158, 165–69

Benhabib, Seyla, 92–93

Biel, Gabriel, 158

Bonhoeffer, Dietrich, 135, 139, 141, 147–53

Cahill, Lisa Sowle, 85

Calvin, John, 74

Christianity, 1, 2, 14, 41, 55, 66, 160–61, 177, 182; and agency, 40, 48, 67; ethically significant features of, 5–8, 24, 73, 96, 174; and hermeneutics, 74, 80; and moral realism, 9, 10, 12, 29, 82, 83, 85, 86, 171–72; and power, 53, 88–90, 138–41, 143, 148–54, 155–57, 168; and radical interpretation, 95, 101, 106–10; and responsibility, 32, 92, 94; and symbol of God, 178, 181, 184, 186, 188

commitment, 13, 36–37, 48, 49, 52, 95, 96, 98; and identity, 6, 88, 108, 109; and moral perception, 34, 68–70

community, 39–40, 47–49, 51–52, 94, 97; and comparison, 114–16, 117, 119, 121, 125–27, 129, 130, 134; and conscience, 189; moral, 52, 77, 93, 108, 110, 113; and moral realism, 84–85; in narrative ethics, 65, 66, 83, 93

conceptualization, 14–16, 77–78, 84, 85, 86, 112, 118, 122

conscience, 15, 27, 56, 71, 84, 92, 107, 188–89, 190. *See also* interpretation, radical

consciousness, 2, 11, 19–20, 73–76, 79–81, 82, 92; of agency, 69–70, 151–52, 176; and God, 85–89, 108, 178–90; of the good, 55, 64, 66

courage, 40

creation, 6, 8, 36, 38, 56, 106, 107, 166, 169, 174, 177, 184, 186, 188, 190

creativity, 85, 110, 186, 187; human, 4,